A Paris
Walking
Guide

Note concerning the English edition

We chose American English for this translation. Readers accustomed to the British and European way of counting floors are advised that we have used the American system throughout this work. Every mention of a "rez-de-chaussée" has systematically been translated as "ground floor" (for the sake of clarity, we have deliberately avoided "first floor"). All the other floors have been raised one level. Thus, any "quatrième étage" in the original work becomes a fifth floor in this edition.

A Paris Walking Guide

20 Charming Strolls

through the Streets, Courtyards, and Gardens of Paris

Photographs
FREDO POPMANN

Translation
DAVID W. COX

PARIGRAMME

TABLE OF CONTENTS

Paris Delights

n September 1993, we published the first three volumes of a collection that would grow to include all twenty of the arrondissements in Paris. These Paris walking guides (*Guides du Promeneur*) were the baby steps of a new publishing house whose sole interest, whose very obsession was circumscribed by the city limits. All Paris; only Paris. Our first books proudly shouted that adventure beckons at every street corner. Our objective, neighborhood by neighborhood, has been to call attention to what ordinarily gets overlooked. Tiny details on an oft-unnoticed façade will delight and fascinate us. Learning which illustrious person haunted a site will thrill us. Seeing beautiful, yet little-known, treasures of Parisian architecture off the beaten track of national tourism will give us warm feelings of satisfaction. Admiration and passion for this city are the ingredients that went into the making of the initial yellow-jacket guidebooks.

The first premise was that we never see – or only poorly see – things that have not been pointed out. How many times have we experienced this? It is only with hindsight that we realize how myopic we were, after discovering an elegant pediment here, a gracious statuette in a niche there, a ceramic composition, etc. They were always there in plain sight, playing their part in the day-to-day Parisian landscape. But, caught up in our thoughts, in the quotidian rush, we too often confine our gaze to our own footsteps.

The second premise in these guidebooks (perhaps we should say their ambition or dream) is to teach the lesson that seeing and learning changes our lives. Enlightened by a historian or architect, we can understand the reason for things; the scholarly background amplifies the soul of a place which might otherwise have remained mute and inert in our eyes. Thanks to a simple explanation, the entire city becomes "inhabited" by its history and its characters. Everything springs to life. One of the great joys for city walkers is stopping in front of an address that hurrying pedestrians will never know. The well-informed walker can take joy in his knowledge. A detour can be savored as a privilege. This is an alternative approach to the city... and perhaps the only way to truly love it.

However, all the considerations above would be useless if we failed to provide the key to this unique urban experience. The best way to discover Paris is on foot. Your greatest sense of mobility will come from being able to rush down steps, sprint across a garden or a courtyard, amble down a one-way street any way you like, stop for as long necessary to observe, soak in, and contemplate whatever you fancy. We might add that the pace of a leisurely stroll is the ideal tempo, allowing the eye to alight on details or engage in more serious contemplation.

Such was the inspiration for Parigramme's founding collection, and for this more compact, single volume containing twenty Paris walks – one per arrondissement. This edition offers a graphic presentation that was lacking in the first collection. Numerous photos illustrate each itinerary; landmarks map it out in a clear and concise manner, so that the user never feels lost, abandoned, or left to wander aimlessly. Readers will be able to enjoy the history and soul of this city in the very best conditions: on foot! The pleasures of strolling through the streets of Paris are endless.

THE EDITOR

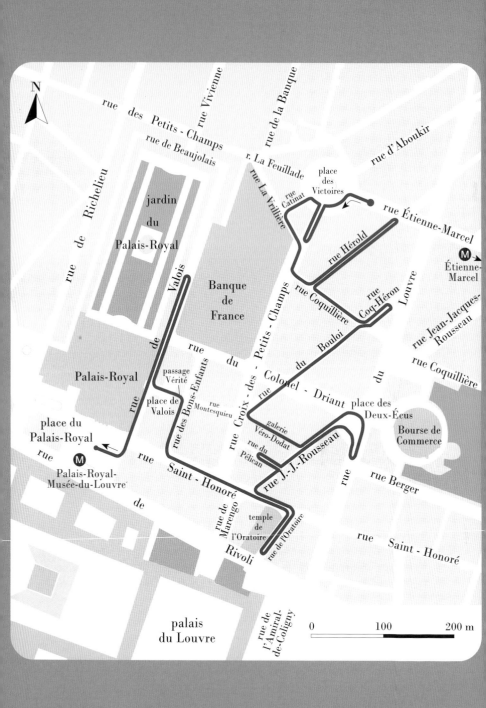

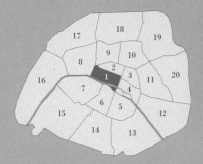

1st

From Place des Victoires to Place du Palais-Royal

▶ Start: Rue Étienne-Marcel,
metro Étienne-Marcel

▶ End: Place du Palais-Royal,
metro Palais-Royal-Musée-
du-Louvre

Place des Victoires

If you wish to discover the Place des Victoires from its most authentic angle, we suggest you enter the Place via **Rue Étienne-Marcel**. This will put the façades of the late 17th-century buildings in the background. The disadvantage to this approach, however, is that the statue of Louis XIV turns its back to us and looks left, toward the Banque de France. Let's walk around the Place by starting with the even-numbered buildings (**from numbers 2 to 12**) on the left, between Rue Croix-des-Petits-Champs and Rue d'Aboukir. An invisible border splits Rue La Feuillade down the middle – 1st arrondissement on the south side and 2nd arrondissement on the north side of the street. The buildings here were constructed between 1686 and 1690 from plans by Jules Hardouin-Mansart. They present a uniform and stately façade: ground floor and entresol placed behind a running arcade decorated with masks; two stories of unequal height braced by Ionic pilasters, and, on the last floor, stone dormer windows alternating semi-circular pediments with segmented arched pediments. The home of the Marquis de La Feuillade once stood at today's **2 and 4**. The façades are historic, but the interior has undergone numerous alterations for business projects. As for the **odd numbers**, they were subjected to significant renovations, ranging from abusively raised ceilings to demolition, as occurred when Rue Croix-des-Petits-Champs and Rue Étienne-Marcel were laid out. These undertakings destroyed the magnificent mansions as well as the harmony of the square's original design. Place des Victoires had been designed to form a closed circle behind the statue and provide a theatrical backdrop for it. When ground was broken on it in 1686 by the Grand Dauphin (heir to the French throne), the diameter of Place Royale was only 29 meters.

Let's admire the **statue** in the center by sculptor François Joseph

◄ Statue of Louis XIV, Place des Victoires

▼ Place des Victoires

A Statue for an Absent King

In 1678, the Duke de La Feuillade, a brilliant soldier, victor of the Battle of Nijmegen and briefly viceroy of Sicily, hoped to gain the favor of Louis XIV, who resided in Versailles. He had a statue erected in the king's honor in Paris.

"Martin Desjardins carved a full-length marble statue of the king in ancient garb. Presented to the king by La Feuillade, this statue is now in the collection in Versailles. In 1682, the duke ordered Desjardins to make a replica in gilded bronze. The king in coronation clothes, crowned by immortality, trampled a three-headed Cerberus symbolizing the vanquished Triple Alliance. The statue stood on a pedestal bordered by four chained slaves and decorated with bas-reliefs illustrating historic episodes in his reign. To provide a worthy setting for the statue, La Feuillade then ordered a royal square laid out [...] In 1792, the statue was removed.. Today, various elements of Desjardins' composition may be found in the Louvre Museum's collections." [Dominique Leborgne, *Le Guide du Promeneur du 2e Arrondissement*] Court rumor had it that La Feuillade had requested a favor in return for the homage. It was said that he asked to be buried in the pedestal. The Duke de Saint-Simon quipped in his memoirs, "We hear that La Feuillade wishes to purchase a vault in the crypt of the Petits-Pères church, and plans to extend it all the way to the center of Place des Victoires so that he can be buried right under the statue of the king."

the royal and military order of Saint Louis. This statue replaced one depicting Desaix, Napoleon's comrade-in-arms who died in the Battle of Marengo. That statue had in turn replaced a wooden pyramid, the Revolution's non-royalist substitute for the original statue (see inset). Legend has it that Napoleon gave the wood from the pyramid to a unit of guards as firewood.

In the 1960s, Place des Victoires was a derelict quarter. The façades were cracked and covered with old billboards. Twenty years later, fashion designers started moving in. World-famous brand names set up shop here, breathing new life into the elegant old buildings. Place des Victoires became fashionable for women who want to shop and to be seen shopping. Unfortunately, while the renovations saved the façades, they did not always respect the interior structures, many of which are still the original walls.

From Rue Croix-des-Petits-Champs to Rue Catinat

Rue Croix-des-Petits-Champs owes its name to the Petits-Champs area, which dates from the early Middle Ages, and to a cross that stood at the junction with Rue du Bouloi. Other equally historic streets like Rue Saint-

Bosio, begun in 1819 under the Restoration and completed in 1822. It shows the king on horseback, dressed as a Roman emperor, and wearing a wig. The rearing horse is balanced on iron bars that bolt the tail to the pedestal, a block of white marble covered with bas-reliefs depicting the crossing of the Rhine River, and

Honoré, Rue Coquillière, and Rue du Bouloi have intersected with it for centuries. According to local lore, Saint Vincent de Paul lived here. By the 19th century, it was lined with hotels to accommodate passengers arriving at the nearby stagecoach station on Rue du Bouloi. In the 20th century, it underwent numerous transformations that left it scarred and damaged.

Number 43 on this street is all the more admirable. It is the sole vestige of a prestigious past: the Hôtel de Jaucourt, also known as de Portalis (from the name of the family that lived there during the First Empire). It was built in 1685, at a time when the area was graced by numerous luxurious manors (or *hôtels* in French) that rivaled the Palais Royal and the Hôtel de Toulouse (the future home to the Banque de France). Formed by two half-moon towers with beautiful balconies, its historic façade is both intriguing and elegant.

Alas, the gracious façade stares back at 1970s glass walls, designed and erected with no consideration for the district's architectural heritage. Standing at **number 39**, on the same side of the street as the Hôtel Portalis, are the buildings erected in 1932 and in 1950, home to the Banque de France. The buildings stretch for one hundred yards up to Rue du Colonel-Driant.

Beneath these buildings, 27 meters deep, is a vast concrete hall. Its roof is supported by 714 pillars 75 centimeters in diameter. It is the bank's gold-reserve vault. Let us return to **Place des Victoires**, and take **Rue Catinat** on the left. Its façades are typical of Paris houses in the time of Molière, at the close of the 17th century.

Looking down the street we see the official entrance to the Banque de France, located on Rue La Vrillière. This is the **Hôtel de Toulouse** (see inset), the prestigious entrance to the institution. An impressive gateway masks an equally impressive façade, dated 1859, copying the luxurious mansion that stood on this site prior to the French Revolution. In 1808, it was a shambles. After serving as the headquarters of the national printing office, it became the head office of the Banque de France, the continually expanding national bank. As a result, the previously picturesque neighboring streets (Rue Baillif and

◄ Hôtel de Jaucourt, also known as Hôtel de Portalis, 43 Rue Croix-des-Petits-Champs

◄ Hôtel de Toulouse, headquarters of the Banque de France, viewed from Rue Catinat

Hôtel de Toulouse

First, it was merely the parapet walk upon the city walls built by King Charles V. Then, around 1634-1640, the Marquis de La Vrillière commissioned a splendid mansion designed by François Mansart. His choice of the foremost architect of the day (whose great-nephew would be Royal Architect Jules Hardouin-Mansart) was more than judicious, for the Marquis de La Vrillière aimed to vie with Cardinal de Richelieu's palace (known today as the Palais-Royal, but then as the Palais-Cardinal). In the 18th century, the luxurious palace became the property the Count of Toulouse, the illegitimate son of Louis XIV and Madame de Montespan. He transformed it and had it decorated in royal style, as did his descendants. At the dawn of the French Revolution, this hôtel was home to his son, the Duke de Penthièvre, whose daughter married the Duke d'Orléans, the future Philippe Égalité. This marriage gave him a grandson, Louis-Philippe. Penthièvre's son Louis-Alexandre de Bourbon, who died at 21 in 1768, was married to Princess

▲ The gilded gallery in the Hôtel de Toulouse
(© Bridgeman Giraudon)

de Lamballe. Her death made history. Because she was Marie-Antoinette's lady-in-waiting and dear friend, her head was paraded on a pike past the queen's prison window. The Duke de Penthièvre was said to have been immensely wealthy and equally generous. He died at the Château de Bizy, near Vernon, protected by his peasants. He owned an exquisite collection of gold and silver dishes which was sold off after the Revolution. Nothing, however, was as scintillating as his palace's Galerie Dorée (gilded gallery). Its sumptuous decor rivaled Versailles' great Hall of Mirrors.

After years of neglect, the Galerie Dorée was restored around 1866 on the orders of Empress Eugénie. The paintings were copied (the originals were taken to the Louvre), and the frescoes and stuccoes were faithfully restored. Today, the gallery is used for assemblies of the Banque de France's executive board. Guided tours are sometimes offered by the Centre des Monuments Nationaux (center of national monuments); call +33 (0)1 4454 9130 for information.

Rue Radziwill) were sacrificed. Rue Radziwill became a dead-end street, locked by a wrought-iron gate open only to bank employees. At numbers 35 and 37, there once stood the magnificent mansion of the Radziwill princes, built around 1780 and razed around 1895 when the Banque de France acquired the property. The curiosity of this mansion was a double staircase on which two persons could simultaneously climb as high as the ninth floor without ever running into each other!

Up and down Rue Coquillière

Let's turn left at **Rue La Vrillière** which has conserved the façades typical of the 17th century (at **numbers 8 and 6**, at the corner of Rue Catinat). Next, let's cross **Rue Croix-des-Petits-Champs** in front of the Hôtel de Portalis so that we stand on the left-hand side of **Rue Coquillière**.

Before we set off down this street, we'll make an incursion into **Rue Hérold**. The odd numbers of this street (**1, 3, 5, 7, 11, and 15**) are old buildings that have no more than two windows per floor. **10** is the presumable birthplace of composer Ferdinand Hérold (1791-1833), after whom the street was named. Demolished in 1893, **17** was where Charlotte Corday was said to have slept when she came to Paris to murder revolutionary Jean-Paul Marat. **Number 20**, which forms the corner with 47 Rue Étienne-Marcel is a lovely building in Louis Quinze style. It has three levels, each with ten windows per floor looking out on Rue Hérold. Each entresol window is ornamented with a mask.

Let's return now to **Rue Coquillière**. It was perhaps named for Pierre Coquillier, a landowner who reputedly laid out part of the street in the 13th century. The city walls built by Philippe Auguste were at number 10. The first numbers along this street (from 1 to 7) stand on the site of the Hôtel de la Reine, a palace which was the property of the Renaissance queen Catherine de Médicis. Coming from Rue Croix-des-Petits-Champs, most of the humble buildings overlooking this street date from the late 18th century and went up on the site of 16th- and 17th-century homes. At **39**, we will see a curious set of paired windows. **37** offers a beautiful gate and an entresol beneath two floors. **35** has a beautiful 18th-century façade with seven windows per floor.

Let's now take a left onto tiny **Rue Coq-Héron**, which runs straight to the city's main post office on Rue du Louvre. At the corner of the latter, at **number 9**, is the lovely Hôtel Ballin, built in 1639 and renovated in the 18th century. Around 1735, it belonged to financier Thoinard Vougy, nicknamed the *Harpagon de la Finance* (the Scrooge of Finance). The site is still dedicated to a treasury, for it has been the headquarters of the Caisse d'Épargne savings bank since 1805. In 1880, its entrance was demolished and moved to be more in line with Rue du Louvre. We can admire the harmony in the proportions of the two floors, the elegant masks ornamenting the windows, and the allegorical

▼ 13 Rue La Vrillière

▲ Hôtel de Ballin,
9 Rue Coq-Héron

entrance to Galerie Véro-Dodat, its starting point on the map. In the early 19th century, Messageries-Générales stagecoaches set out from **22 to 26** for destinations all around France. Today, it is a group of buildings erected in 1890 around a courtyard and fountain. Back in stagecoach days, hotels lined the street (**numbers 3, 5, 13, 16, and 21**, among others).

On your right, as you walk away from Rue Coquillière, numbers **17 to 21** are one large building with seventeen windows on three floors. Until 1631, it was the site of the Saint-Sacrement convent. In the 19th century, the two courtyards were used to park stagecoaches belonging to the company across the street. Then, in the early 20th century, the courtyards and buildings around them were taken over by the national railroad company, SNCF.

We go past the service station and cross **Rue du Colonel-Driant**, at the starting point of **Rue du Bouloi**, where we find the entrance to charming Galerie Véro-Dodat. The manor which once stood at **4 Rue du Bouloi** was notable as the birthplace in 1585 of Armand Jean du Plessis, the future Cardinal de Richelieu. Next door, at **2**, the Hôtel de Dreux d'Aubray became famous in 1670 as the home of the father of the Marquise de Brinvilliers, famous for her passion for poison. For plying her skills on her own father and brother, among other victims, she was publicly tortured to death on Place de Grève in 1679, with the other "demons" in the "affaire des poisons." The name of Mme de Montespan came up in the trial, causing her to fall out of grace with the Sun King.

bas-reliefs over the entrance. We might also appreciate the world-renowned restaurant next door, although folding screens protect patrons from prying eyes.

Let's return to **Rue Coquillière**, but to the opposite side this time, and head down **Rue du Bouloi**. It was laid out in the mid-14th century but changed names many times before its present-day name stuck in the 17th century, when a lawn-bowling court may have been located nearby. Like the parallel Rue Jean-Jacques Rousseau, it was once an important neighborhood thoroughfare, but both streets lost importance and personality when Rue du Louvre and Rue Étienne-Marcel were laid out. The numbers decrease as we move down towards its intersecting point with Rue Croix-des-Petits-Champs, at the

◄► Galerie Véro-Dodat

From Galerie Véro-Dodat to Rue Saint-Honoré

Galerie Véro-Dodat was built in 1826. Note the two ephebes on the façade, typical of neoclassical style, and the impressive copper trim. Two neighborhood butchers, Mr. Véro and Mr. Dodat, bought and demolished the dilapidated mansion that stood on the site, and erected a building in Bourbon Restoration style. It was designed with an elegant covered arcade and had the novelty of being gas-lit. Travelers fresh off the neighboring stagecoaches flocked to see it. By the mid-20th century, however, the gallery had become so run-down, it barely escaped demolition. It was saved in the late 1970s by antique dealers who gave it the refined and nostalgic charm that still enchants strollers today.

As we exit Galerie Véro-Dodat, let's turn left onto **Rue Jean-Jacques-Rousseau**, and go as far as number 22 which looks out onto **Place des Deux Écus**, limited today to two buildings from the late 17th century. The old Rue des Deux Écus was shortened when Rue Berger and Rue du Louvre were carved out. The street was renamed "place" after its entire north side was demolished in 1912. It is a doddering but charming survivor, alone amidst the Haussmann-period buildings on Rue du Louvre, the Bourse de Commerce (the 18th-century wheat and commodities exchange) and the massive 1950s architecture on Rue

The Rousseau Mystery

In 1791, after the triumphant return of the ashes of Jean-Jacques Rousseau to the Pantheon, the National Constituent Assembly renamed this street after the illustrious writer. A sign at 52 asserts that he lived there from 1722 to 1778. This remains to be proven, however. The last years of his life were terribly unstable. His main places of residence were with his aristocratic protectors at the Château d'Ermenonville, outside of Paris. He may have had a permanent address on this street much earlier in his life, perhaps in the 1750s. The only certainty we have is that he frequented Mr. and Mrs. Dupin's literary salon.

outside the Philippe-Auguste fortification walls, and had a bad reputation, being lined with "sin shops." Its present-day name was given in 1806. Not more than three meters wide, lined by rather run-down buildings, it and Galerie Véro-Dodat frame the second block on Rue Croix-des-Petits-Champs.

▶ The apse of the Temple de l'Oratoire, viewed from Rue de Rivoli

du Colonel-Driant... Let's not miss the opportunity to stroll over to **11 Rue du Louvre** and take a glance at the imprint of the Philippe-Auguste fortifications.

We shall return to **Rue Jean-Jacques-Rousseau** toward where the street begins. Do you notice anything odd? Numbers 35 to 51 (once the location of the famous Hôtel de Séguier) were seemingly gobbled up by Rue du Louvre. The street continues on the other side of the Bourse de Commerce and runs to Rue Étienne-Marcel. We will limit our stroll, however, to the first part of the street, where most of the buildings date from the late 18th century and the early 19th century. **Number 20**, turned into a hostel for foreign students, opens onto an interior courtyard off Rue du Louvre. **Number 18** sits on the site of a 17th-century refuge for widows and spinsters over forty. **Numbers 16, 14, and 12** have intriguing façades, with pediments, alternating patterns between the windows and garrets, and an entresol graced by arcs.

Before we go on to Rue Saint-Honoré, let's step into **Rue du Pélican**. It was laid out in the early 14th century,

Around the Temple de l'Oratoire

We'll turn left now and walk to **Rue Saint-Honoré**. Before we set out to explore it, moving toward the Palais-Royal, let's take a few steps to the left to admire **number 145**, a Protestant church (or *temple* to use the French term), misnamed Temple de l'Oratoire. It has a Jesuit-style façade (early 17th century) but the statues and the carved decorations are no longer. The street running beside it is called Rue de l'Oratoire and carries on to Rue de Rivoli. It was built upon the parapet walk of the Philippe-Auguste fortifications. In the late-16th century, a magnificent mansion stood here, the Hôtel de Bouchage, property of Henri de Joyeuse, Count of Bouchage. In 1594, King Henry IV rented it for

A Quirk of History

It is rather paradoxical to see a Protestant church (the culmination of the Reformation) inside the walls of a building designed for a religious order of the Counter-Reformation. An oratory (*oratoire* in French) is place of prayer, a small chapel. In Italy, during the Counter-Reformation, an *oratorio* was a religious musical show with an orchestra, a choir, and narrators. In light of this history, the initial architectural plans for this church contrast sharply with its present assignment. The original design was inspired by Roman Baroque, and was to have statues expressing movement. The interior was opulently decorated with a profusion of paintings, sculptures, and chandeliers. Instead, however, in keeping with Protestant tastes, it is now plain and austere.

Gabrielle d'Estrées, to bring his mistress closer to the Louvre, then the royal castle. The Count of Bouchage's daughter sold the mansion in 1611 to Cardinal Pierre de Bérulle, founder of the Congrégation des Pères de l'Oratoire, similar in spirit to what St. Philippe Neri (its Roman founding father) had established. The community grew. In 1630, the church fathers commissioned Lemercier, the architect of the Louvre's Cour Carrée, to build a vast and beautiful church. Louis XIII granted royal favor to this place of worship. A few years later, the Marquise de Brinvilliers' father and brothers (see Rue du Bouloi) were buried there. Before the Revolution, the Congrégation des Pères de l'Oratoire had a library containing 37,750 volumes, which included 300 manuscripts from Constantinople. It owned neighborhood properties including the convent that contained Rue de l'Oratoire, as well as parts of three streets: Rue du Louvre, Rue Saint-Honoré, and Rue du Coq (now Rue de Marengo). The congregation was disbanded during the Revolution. The convent was closed and the church successively became a Revolutionary clubhouse and a military storehouse. In 1811, Napoleon assigned it to the French Protestant church. Let's take **Rue de l'Oratoire** to look at a memorial behind the temple's apse which we'll see from **109 Rue de Rivoli**. The monument was erected in 1889 in memory of Admiral de Coligny (1519-1572), a Protestant leader slain in front of his own home, located at number 144, during the St. Bartholomew's Day massacre.

Rue Saint-Honoré from Rue de l'Oratoire to the Louvre Antique Dealers

We will now return to **Rue Saint-Honoré**. From **140 to 150**, opposite the Temple, the street is lined with small, late-17th-century buildings with two windows on five levels, maintained

◄ 150 Rue Saint-Honoré

► The Louvre des Antiquaires (antique shops)

and restored to varying degrees. We now stand at the start of Rue Jean-Jacques Rousseau and Rue Croix-des-Petits-Champs. **Rue de Marengo** opens to our left; it used to be called Rue du Coq and ran beside the Hôtel de Bouchage and the Oratoire convent. When it was widened in 1859, this thoroughfare went from 5 to 24 meters in breadth. Its name celebrates Napoleon's victory over the Austrians at Marengo in Italy.

The exit of the Grands Magasins du Louvre, now the **Louvre des Antiquaires** (the Louvre antique dealers' gallery), used to be on this street. The 19th-century department store took up the entire block framed by Place du Palais-Royal and Marengo, Rivoli, and Saint-Honoré streets. In the 17th century, Ragueneau's cabaret and pastry shop stood on this very spot. He went bankrupt from giving credit to poor writers and broke artists who would go drink elsewhere with his money. After that, he found a job as a candle-snuffer with Molière's theater troupe. During the Revolution, milliner Rose Bertin lived on this street; Madame du Barry and Marie-Antoinette were among her customers.

Erected in 1854, the Grands Magasins building was planned as a 700-room luxury hotel. The arcades, fitted out as shops, were entrusted to a certain Mr. Chauchard, a former salesman from the shop called "Au Pauvre Diable" (The Poor Devil's), located on neighboring Rue Montesquieu. Soon, retailers had taken half the building space, forcing the hotel to remove to the other side of the square where it stands to this day. The Grands Magasins opened in 1860. For over a century (up to 1972, to be precise), they represented the height of Parisian chic.

From Place du Palais-Royal, we can continue our stroll through the galleries of the Louvre des Antiquaires, which set up business here in 1978. Today, over 10,000 square meters on three levels are used for permanent exhibitions of veritable treasures and for prestigious events held by about 250 members of the profession.

◄ Ministry of Culture building, on the corner of Rue des Bons-Enfants and Rue Saint-Honoré

Around 1913, the construction of the Grand Magasins' annex on the opposite side of the street swept away the last vestiges of the old Saint-Honoré church, demolished in 1793. Founded in 1209, it had lent its name to the street and spurred the growth of the district. It was rapidly surrounded to the north and west by the Saint-Honoré cloisters with its enclosed cemetery, which was located at the present 10 Rue des Bons-Enfants. The church was enlarged in 1578, when the bakers' guild set up its chapel on the premises and adopted St. Honoré as its patron. While the church no longer exists, the tradition lives on in the name of a famous cake, the creamy "Saint-Honoré." Each year, around May 15 (St. Honoré's day falls on May 16), the bakers on the street celebrate the patron Saint's feast day with a mass at Saint-Roch (at 296 Rue Saint-Honoré) followed by a procession up to Place du Palais-Royal.

From Rue des Bons-Enfants to Place du Palais-Royal

Heading now toward the Palais-Royal, we come to **Rue des Bons-Enfants**. It was shortened in the 1920s by additions to the Banque de France buildings. In 1833, a novelties store opened here called Au Coin de la Rue. It was an innovative concept for the times, the precursor to the modern-day department store. One of the saleswomen, Marie-Louise Jay, later married Ernest Cognacq. The two of them founded La Samaritaine, a major Paris department store.

▲ Rue Montesquieu
◀ Rue de Valois

mental metal grillwork over the façades of very different styles brings unity to the group, without masking any of the façades. Major renovations were carried out at the end of the 1990s, orchestrated by architects Francis Soler and Frédéric Druot, who had to come up with a solution for three buildings from different periods: 1920, 1956 and 1980.

The buildings at **15 and 17**, with their lovely 18th-century façades, frame the entrance to **Place de Valois**; they incorporate a neoclassical arched passage and pediment. **Numbers 3, 4, 5, 6, and 7** on this square also have elegant 18th-century façades listed on the historical register. The ground floor, three upper stories, and attics are identical in design. It is a shame that the façade with no entrance, which is actually the back side of 4 Rue de Valois, was raised and modernized. The square was modified in 1784 when Rue de Valois was laid out. At the same time, the Duke d'Orléans (later Philippe Égalité) opened the Palais-Royal gardens to the public. The square's former name, Place des Fontaines, probably

The **Ministry of Culture** occupies the buildings in the block between Rue des Bons-Enfants, Rue Montesquieu, Rue Croix-des-Petits-Champs, and Rue Saint-Honoré. Orna-

referred to the nearby reservoirs for the Palais-Royal.

Rue de Valois begins at Rue Saint-Honoré and ends at Rue de Beaujolais. The odd numbers are in fact the back sides of the buildings that grace the Palais-Royal garden. Most of the street's even numbers running from Rue du Colonel-Driant to Rue de Beaujolais were swallowed up in the 1920s by the expansion of the offices of the Banque de France.

Let's go into the ever-calm Rue de Valois to admire **number 3**, a townhouse with a wrought-iron balcony and a sculpted pediment. Built in 1766, it is currently owned by the Ministry of Culture. Cutting through the ground floor is Passage des Fontaines, which opens onto the Palais-Royal's main courtyard.

A hotel for academics visiting Paris is located at **number 4** (the architectural harmony with surrounding buildings was broken by renovation). The buildings at **6 and 8 Rue de Valois**, called Hôtel de Mélusine because of the 17th-century frescoes depicting the legendary fairy of medieval tales, have magnificent bal-

▲ 8 Rue de Valois
▲ 6 Rue de Valois

conies - also from the 17th century - supported by splendid carved lions' heads. The residents in the 1670s were the Duke and Duchess de Navailles. The Duchess, one of the queen's ladies-in-waiting, fell out of favor with the Sun King for refusing his overtures. A century later, the mansion was acquired by the Duke d'Orléans for the Marquise de Montesson, his morganatic wife. It was sold off in 1792 by Philippe Égalité's creditors.

You may notice the outline of a bull over the door at **number 8**. From the end of the 18th century up to 1936, this was the address of the restaurant Le Boeuf à la Mode. Its sign changed with the passing fashions and political regimes.

The Orléans chancellery was located at **number 10**, the current-day address of Banque de France annexes and buildings on Rue du Colonel-Driant. The chancellery is often confused with the Hôtel de Mélusine. The first owner was the Regent, Philippe d'Orléans, who loaned the premises first to a cabinet member, Cardinal Dubois, and then to

one of his mistresses, Madame d'Argenton. It was sold off during the Revolution. In 1916, the Banque de France acquired it and had it torn down, despite a commitment to preserving historic sites.

Let's backtrack and continue to **Rue Saint-Honoré**. At the corner of **number 202** is a sign that informs us that this was the address of the Académie Royale de Musique from 1770 to 1781. In fact, it was an opera house built to replace the previous one that had burned down. No lesson was learned. In 1781, the new one also went up in flames, taking the lives of twenty-one people. A group of buildings arranged around a central garden went up on this site. Based on the Duke d'Orléans' Palais-Royal

▶ Conseil d'État, Place du Palais-Royal

▼ 202 Rue Saint-Honoré

development, they, too, have an entresol, an étage noble above, a low-ceilinged attic, and a final, recessed floor with window openings in the mansard roof.

We have now reached **Place du Palais-Royal**. Standing on Rue Saint-Honoré, looking east, we can see the entrance to the Louvre des Antiquaires building. The Napoleon III façade of the Louvre Museum's Richelieu Wing stands to the south. We stand opposite the rear of the Hôtel du Louvre. The imposing building occupying that wing of the Palais-Royal which overlooks the Cour de l'Horloge (the clock courtyard), now houses the Conseil d'État, France's supreme court for administrative justice. It was erected at the end of the 17th century. During the Bourbon Restoration, it was renovated by Fontaine, one of the Louvre's architects, on the orders of the Duke d'Orléans, the future King Louis-Philippe.

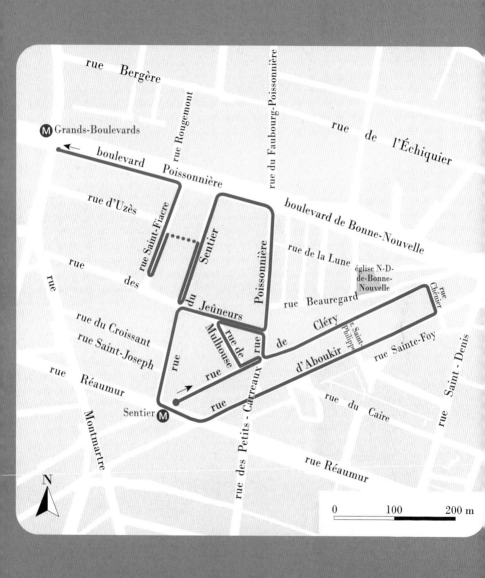

rue Bergère

Ⓜ Grands-Boulevards

rue Rougemont

rue du Faubourg-Poissonnière

rue de l'Échiquier

boulevard Poissonnière

rue d'Uzès

rue Saint-Fiacre

Sentier

du Jeûneurs

rue Poissonnière

boulevard de Bonne-Nouvelle

rue de la Lune

église N-D-
de-Bonne-
Nouvelle

rue

des

rue Beauregard

Cléry

rue Chénier

rue du Croissant

rue Saint-Joseph

rue

rue de Mulhouse

rue

de

r. Saint-
Philippe

d'Aboukir

rue Sainte-Foy

rue Saint - Denis

rue

Réaumur

rue

Sentier Ⓜ

rue des Petits - Carreaux

rue du Caire

Montmartre

rue Réaumur

N

0   100   200 m

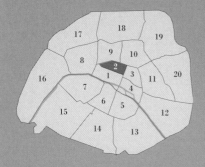

2nd

A Stroll through the Sentier District

▸ Start: **Rue Réaumur, metro Sentier**

▸ Finish: **Boulevard Poissonnière, metro Grands-Boulevards**

We'll start this stroll at the corner of Rue de Cléry and Rue Réaumur (in front of 112), only steps away from Rue d'Aboukir. Rue Réaumur is one of the city's wide 19th-century thoroughfares, designed to plow right through the middle of older, narrower streets like Rue de Cléry and Rue d'Aboukir. The latter two were laid out in an oddly un-Parisian way as a pair of long, parallel streets, connected by a few alleyways.

Let's go back to 1634, when demolition crews brought down a portion of the Charles V fortifications (from Porte Saint-Honoré, at today's 161 Rue Saint-Honoré, to Porte Saint-Denis, at today's 285 Rue Saint-Denis). The rubble from the ramparts and the soil from the leveling of the butte were used to fill in the trench. Rue d'Aboukir was simply built upon the line of rubble, whereas Rue de Cléry was built upon the old path on the slope of the trench. Both streets were sliced when Rue Réaumur was laid out in 1894-1895. Rue de Cléry lost the houses from 16 to 24 on the even side of the street and 11 to 13 on the odd. Rue d'Aboukir lost the houses from 55 to 63 and 62 to 76. Number 1 on Rue du Sentier was also torn down. As a result, Rue Réaumur became an artificial border, intruding upon this homogeneous district with its imposing 19th-century buildings and heavy automobile traffic.

Rue de Cléry, from Rue Réaumur to Rue de Mulhouse

Stepping off **Rue Réaumur**, we'll now head up **Rue de Cléry**. Development occurred in the 17th century and in the early 18th century. Pierre and

Nicolas Delespine, descendants of a dynasty of architects, built several houses on this block around 1735. Similarly, we have evidence of deals negotiated by Victor-Thierry d'Ailly between 1718 and 1720. In the 17th century, playwright Pierre Corneille moved here after leaving the city of Rouen for Paris. After staying with the Duke de Guise, he set up house on Rue Saint-Sauveur near the Hôtel de Bourgogne. In 1674, he and his brother leased a house on Rue de Cléry for an annual rent of nine hundred pounds. It had nine bedrooms (three per floor), an attic, cellars, a kitchen, a drawing room, a study, a courtyard, and a stable. While Corneille had no financial difficulties in the last years of his life, he nevertheless moved to Rue d'Argenteuil sometime between 1681 and 1683. He probably wanted to be closer to the Louvre where the Académie Française met. He faithfully attended every session at the Académie. When he died, his brother was elected to his chair, and Jean Racine read his eulogy.

Let's stop in front of **19**. A plaque informs us that the painter Élisabeth Vigée-Lebrun lived here from 1778 to

▲ Rue de Cléry
(© Gilles Targat)
▼ 19 Rue de Cléry

1789. In 1776, the famous portraitist married Jean-Baptiste Lebrun (1748-1813), a cunning art dealer, collector, critic, and expert. He traveled constantly, buying Italian and Dutch pieces that he would sell to Parisian collectors. In 1778, Lebrun acquired the Hôtel Lubert, a mansion previously in the hands of Robert Poquelin, one of Molière's brothers. It was divided into apartments. Among the tenants were the Marquis de Pezay, the painter Ménageot, and the Lebruns. In her Mémoires d'une Portraitiste (1835) Élisabeth Vigée-Lebrun wrote, "After my wedding, I still resided on Rue de Cléry where Mr. Lebrun had a large, richly appointed apartment. There, he hung his paintings by great artists. As for me, I was reduced to occupying a small antechamber and a bedroom which I had to use as a drawing room." In 1778, she won notoriety by painting the first portrait of Queen Marie-Antoinette from life. Parisian socialites flocked to her parties. The couple's apartment had become too cramped. Lebrun resolved to enlarge it. "I wanted to give my wife a more functional studio, and I needed a suitable gallery for the collection of prized paintings and other fine art objects I had assembled over two decades. The plot of land was uneven, the space was narrow - an illustration of all that can be accomplished by effort and ingenuity." (1811; the Raymond catalogue).

In 1785, Toulouse architect Jean-Arnaud Raymond, a friend of Ménageot who later handled the glazing of the Louvre's Grande Galerie, was commissioned to design the new dwelling. The garden gave way to an elegant home composed of two apartments and a gallery. Lebrun built his art gallery in the courtyard of the Lubert mansion. One hundred and sixty-five auctions were held there, between 1771 and 1813; Lebrun wrote the catalogues himself. His publications brought 17th-century genre artists such as Vermeer to public attention. In 1793, he played a major role in the creation of the Muséum des Arts, showing great skill in the fields of painting conservation and restoration. Lebrun's showroom was requisitioned for wedding ceremonies and baptisms during the Reign of Terror in 1793-1794 which had shut the doors of Notre-Dame-de-Bonne-Nouvelle church. Later, the "oratory on Rue Cléry" served for concerts, then ceased to be used at all. However, by 1789, Mrs. Vigée-Lebrun had been forced into exile, maligned by forged correspondence. She continued her painting career throughout Europe and Russia, and did not return to her mansion until 1802. By then, the entrance had been moved to the Rue du Sentier side.

Let's move on to **34** Rue de Cléry to admire the two medallions over the carriage door. Each male head, in ancient cameo-style profile, is framed by laurel branches intertwined with fluttering ribbons. The center of the façade of **40** is discreetly marked by a crown stone in the arch and a cornice over the first-floor window. The knocker on the carriage door is also

◀ 34 Rue de Cléry

interesting. The building with seven vertical bays at **42** welcomes us with its high carriage door embellished with rococo ornamentation. Next door, **44** has a slender, prow-like corner on Rue des Petits-Carreaux. Its front door is graced by a lovely female face. Its decoration includes a wrought-iron impost with the letters PB in a monogram.

Let's backtrack a little. At **27**, the 17th-century Hôtel Picard was home to Claude Le Blanc (1669-1728), a civil servant who ended his career as Minister of War. From 1765 to 1776, it belonged to Jacques Necker (1732-1804). Madame Necker's salon was famed for welcoming such prominent Enlightenment figures as Buffon, Marmontel, Chamfort, Grimm, and Abbé Raynal. The Neckers' daughter, Louise-Germaine, the future Madame de Staël, was born here in 1766. She grew up in an intellectual circle that included not only writers but politicians allied with her father, appointed finance minister by Louis XVI.

▲ Hôtel Picard at 27 Rue de Cléry

▸ 4 Rue de Mulhouse

From Rue de Mulhouse to Rue de Cléry

Let's cross Rue de Cléry now. On January 24, 1843, the Périer brothers applied for and received permission to create **Rue de Mulhouse**, bordering their property Hôtel Picard. It was they who bore "the cost of the paving stones and the construction of curbed sidewalks in granite." Let's take this street.

The architecture on this street is strikingly homogeneous. All the buildings have four floors atop the ground floor. They all have well-balanced façades incorporating varied decorative elements, inspired primarily by Renaissance design. Foliage, reeds, birds, snakes, and masks enliven the pilasters with their composite capitals at **2**. The façade of **3** emphasizes each floor with cornices decorated with geometric and naturalistic figures. Similarly, the doors and windows at **1 and 5** are set off by carved framework, with the leitmotiv of a rosette in each corner. **Number 4's** doors and windows have carved architraves and impressive cornices. A frieze with foliage embellishes the façade at **6**. On the façade at **8**, a slightly projecting part is bordered by cornices and pilasters with inlays of black lozenges imitating 16th-century Florentine design.

A turn at the next corner will take us onto **Rue des Jeûneurs**. The odd-

▲ 10 Rue des Jeûneurs
▶ Hôtel de Noisy at
2-4 Rue Poissonnière

façade crowned by its broken pediment, we can admire the way the rococo-style decorations escape from the cartouche to form the keystone of the third-floor window. Note the finesse of the grotesques topping the walled-up arches decorating the façade of this floor, as well as the front door (actually located at **number 31 Rue de Cléry**), and the gracious curve of the balconies. The staircase's lovely wrought-iron handrail has been preserved.

numbered buildings from **5 to 1** are nearly identical to the façades seen on Rue de Mulhouse. **Number 10** sits on a very deep lot and its entryway, paved with veritable sidewalks, is also equipped with dual rails for trucking merchandise through the alley. The carriage door framed in a lovely arch graces the center of the 17th-century façade. The staircase has been preserved.

We will now cross over to **Rue Poissonnière** and head up the right side of the street to see interesting wrought iron at **numbers 3 and 8**.

The Hôtel de Noisy at **2 and 4** dates from 1720. While we cannot back up far enough to appreciate this

The 17th-century house at the corner of **1 Rue Poissonnière and 29 Rue de Cléry** has a simple pattern of pilasters. It was once part of the Hôtel Sainte-Catherine. The statue of the saint in the niche at the corner of the building may also be vintage 17th-century. The wheel and the palm tree in the composition belong to traditional iconography of Saint Catherine of Alexandria. Every year since 1926, young unmarried women (*les catherinettes*, in French) have trekked here on November 25 for the feast day of their patron saint. In 1714, Rue de Cléry ended here; it boasted thirtynine houses and fifteen streetlamps.

▶ Statue of St. Catherine
at 29 Rue de Cléry

Rue de Cléry between Rue Poissonnière and Rue Chénier

The next section of the street used to be called "Mouffetard" which comes from the word "mouffette" (or mofettes) for the putrid odors emanating from the city dump then located on Boulevard de Bonne-Nouvelle. Nine streetlamps lit up this block of forty-two houses whose tenants were primarily woodworkers and cabinetmakers.

◄ 39 Rue de Cléry
► 37 Rue de Cléry

Let's take a left onto **Rue de Cléry** toward the Boulevards. Three-storied **number 37** still has its mansard roofs. Its much higher neighbor **39** is graced by an 18th-century balcony that spans the entire façade. From either side of the street, we can see fine wrought-iron work at **41, 48, and 52**.

A giant pair of scissors at **54** attracts our attention. Founded in 1818, the Hamon cutlery shop has been family-owned and operated for six generations. The Hamons were pio-

18th-Century Rue de Cléry: A Furniture Makers' Village

In 1623, Louis XIII granted tax exemptions to woodworkers setting up shop in the Bonne-Nouvelle district. Similarly, cabinetmakers were offered their own special neighborhood in the Faubourg Saint-Antoine. By the 13th century, wealthy dynasties had begun to sprout, thus forming the core of a community which, by the 18th century, had perfected

its skills, talent, and savoir-faire. The woodworkers lived and worked on Rue de Cléry where some sixty workshops prospered. Ten workshops flourished on Rue d'Aboukir, four on Rue Beauregard, and four others on Rue Poissonnière.

This community was composed of freelance workers who were outside the jurisdiction of the Châtelet.

They had the right to ply their trade without a license. Conversely, they had to comply with certain business laws. They were not allowed to stamp their pieces with their own brand. The poorest of the woodworkers had no private clientele and subcontracted for master woodworkers with licenses, authorized to stamp their production.

▲ 54 Rue de Cléry
▼ 97 Rue de Cléry

neers in the cutlery industry and invented a paste for sharpening razors. During the first Universal Exhibition in 1855, they took first prize. They made cast replicas of their medals to include them in the decoration of the façade of their building; among them is the easily recognizable portrait of Napoleon III. The company now specializes in cutting tools for the garment industry. At the turn of the 20th century, the merchants on this street traded in either household linens or in furniture. As we continue along this six-hundred-meter-long street and reach the stretch of **68 to 96** and **65 to 93**, it becomes clear that the old alignment of the street has been protected.

The last house on Rue de Cléry is the narrow and angular **97**, sitting at the corner of Rue Beauregard. A commemorative plaque on the wall reads, "Here lived the poet André Chénier in 1793." The information, however, is incorrect, as it is based on the numbering system from the French Revolution period. Present-day 23 was in fact Chénier's last home. He was arrested in Versailles on January 6,

1794 on charges of having taken the defense of Louis XVI, and was decapitated on Place de la Nation (known at the time as Place du Trône Renversé), then buried in nearby Picpus cemetery.

Rue Saint-Claude was renamed **Rue Chénier** in his honor in 1864. The street's formation at the corner of 92 Rue de Cléry dates back to 1660. It has a slope because it cuts across Rue de Cléry (formerly the old path along the side of the rampart's trench); Rue d'Aboukir (the street's south side was on the ramparts and its north side was on the trench); and Rue Sainte-Foy (the inner wall-walk).

Let's turn right on Rue Chénier to take Rue d'Aboukir. We come upon a four-story house at the corner of the two streets: **132 Rue d'Aboukir** and **3 Rue Chénier**. The façade's horizontal and vertical rows are strongly outlined, and each window and door opening is topped by a cornice set upon carved consoles. Observe the decorative elements on the floors above the street level; scrolls, foliage, and shields come first, then flowers with rosettes; above this, the spaces between the windows are ornamented with female heads.

This was the home that Jacques-Pierre Gisors (1755-1818), descended from a long line of architects, built for himself. During the Convention of 1792, the first democratically-elected government in France, he served as the representative for the Bonne-Nouvelle district. In 1795-1797, he designed the interiors of the Palais-Bourbon for the Conseil des Cinq-Cents (the Council of 500), now the Chambre de Députés at the Assemblée Nationale, the lower house of France's parliament.

Rue d'Aboukir

Let's turn right onto **Rue d'Aboukir**. We will notice 17th-century wrought-ironwork with an indecipherable monogram at **126**. We will also see 18th-century scrolled balcony railings at **135** and **133**. The 18th-century town house at **131**, property of Charles Dupaty, was long a house of ill repute. The mansard roof and the window railings survived a renovation, but the original door was replaced with a modern glass one. Down the street at **123**, future composer Gustave Charpentier - still a conservatory student - rented an apartment with a friend in 1880. Interesting ironwork dating from the 17th century at **121**, and from the 18th century at **114 and 112,** deserves our attention.

Everything at **119** – door, balconies, staircase – dates from the 18th century. The building erected in the same period at **115** on the corner of Rue Saint-Philippe is also unified and harmonious. Notice the grooved molding, the breadth of the arcades along the entresol, the hollowed-out corner niches, and the pleasing pro-

portions of the windows and doors. A female mask graces the keystone over the carriage door, forever conversing with a matching male mask. The staircase is located to the right as you enter. If you look up while on **Rue Saint-Philippe,** you will notice a pitched roof with a pulley overhanging the sidewalk, an architectural element typical of the neighborhood.

102 Rue d'Aboukir offers us a harmonious play of fifteen bays along its façade. It was erected in the 18th century. Wrought iron of varying degrees of sophistication embellishes most of the buildings along this street. Notice the curved wrought iron on **101** and the simpler iron pieces at **111, 96, 87, 85, and 83**.

A Directoire-period building stands at **94**. Notice how its balcony is supported by consoles that are decorated with pinecones and engraved with a monogram of PB or SB. At **87**, a decorative seashell sits over the carriage door. Unlike its neighbors, **88** has a pediment. At **77**, on the corner of Rue d'Aboukir and Rue des Petits-Carreaux, an intricate wrought-iron double gate with an impost might have been the entrance to a mansion which has since been torn down. In 1902, this was the address of a café fitted out in 1812 by Pierre François Léonard Fontaine. **71, 69, and 67** date from the 18th century. They have pre-

◄ 131 Rue d'Aboukir
► 87 Rue d'Aboukir

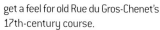

get a feel for old Rue du Gros-Chenet's 17th-century course.

In 1849, this was still Rue du Gros-Chenet. The street's old name is carved in the wall at **9** Rue du Sentier. The two streets merged to become one, running up to Boulevard Poisson-nière. In April 1778, Wolfgang Amadeus Mozart and his mother Anna Maria stayed in a hotel called Les Quatre-Fils Aymon on the old Rue du Gros-Chenet. Around June 15, she began feeling the first symptoms of the disease that would claim her life only weeks later. She died on July 3, probably of typhus. That evening, Mozart wrote a letter to his father telling him

▲ 114 Rue Réaumur
▶ 1 Rue du Sentier
▼ 8 Rue du Sentier

served their stone facades, discreetly marked at each level by wrought-iron window railings.

From Rue du Sentier to Rue des Jeûneurs

Our itinerary puts us back on **Rue Réaumur**, where we will veer right and stroll to the next intersection, to turn right on **Rue du Sentier**. Architect L. Storck, designer of the 1897 building at this corner, **114 Rue Réaumur**, received special permission from the city to exceed regulation roof heights. Across the street, the impressive 1897 building at **1 Rue du Sentier** is a creation of A. Walwein. Neither structure matches the neighborhood's architectural styles. From **7 to 19** we

that "Anna Maria was very ill." In a separate letter, he asked his friend, Father Joseph Bullinger, to brace his family. "Weep with me, my friend. This is the saddest day of my life. I write this at two o'clock in the morning. I must tell you this: my mother, my beloved mother, is no more! The Lord has called her to His bosom. He wanted her back. I see it clearly now. I have submitted to His will. He gave her to me. He took her away [...]." A memorial plaque is visible on the façade of what was once the Lebrun mansion at **8** Rue du Sentier.

Let's walk into the courtyard for a look. The sober street-side façade is rounded out on the inner side, forming a concave hemicycle. The building's noble floor contained the two apartments that the Lebruns lived in (cf. page 27). Oval and round shapes were the height of 18th-century fashion for the main rooms of dwellings. Mr. Lebrun's art gallery took up the entire third floor. It was a spacious room lit by a skylight. Bronze copies of ancient statues were exhibited on the inlaid bookcases. In the garden stood another building: the portrait artist's studio. Its circular façade, carved with niches, fits into the mansion's concave shape. This ingenious layout takes its inspiration from Palladio's designs and can be seen in drawings by Jean-Arnaud Raymond at the Archives Nationales.

Although **13** was fully renovated, its lovely wrought-iron window railings and a handrail were preserved. In 1898, at the corner of Rue du Sentier (**number 15**) and Rue du Croissant, a certain Mr. Carette ordered architect A. Guilbert to build a stone building on a steel structure, and to fit out three

floors of it for workshops. At **10**, a long building made up of ten bays dates from the 18th century. At **12** we will see the outbuildings of the old Necker mansion located on Rue de Cléry. The windows on the "noble floor" are trimmed with cornices matching the main cornice.

We now cross **Rue des Jeûneurs** and turn right. The dilapidated buildings at **numbers 18, 16, and 14** have kept their old balconies. The Selligne print shop located at 14 was one of the rare printers in Paris to operate a steam-powered press. In 1828, Émile de Girardin commissioned the company to print his first journal, Le Voleur. At **11**, a lion's head and a half-man/half-wolf head in poor condition

▲ 13 Rue du Sentier
◀ 15 Rue du Sentier
▼ 11 Rue des Jeûneurs

▸ 44 Rue Poissonnière

blends in with the scrolled ironwork on the consoles. The mask on the outer part of the arch – rather similar to the classic theater mask – appears to have replaced other decorative elements.

Rue Poissonnière and Boulevard Poissonnière

We will retrace some of our steps as we walk to the end of the last block of Rue des Jeûneurs to **Rue Poissonnière**. Up to 1635, it was called "Chemin des Poissonniers" (Fishmongers' Lane) because it was part of the route that fish-carts took to reach the central market at Les Halles.

Let's turn left here and walk north toward the boulevard. At **number 18**, which is the corner of 1 rue Beauregard, is a building designed by Pierre de Vigny around 1737. The 17th-century building-line regulation is most obvious **between 25 and 31**. Aside from the stacked mansard windows, you may also notice several pretty pieces of wrought iron such as the star pattern at **15** and the PCB monogram at **34**. Lyres are the theme at **44**. **33**, formerly Giudicelli's, the famous chocolate-maker, is a 1933 building designed by Leon Schneider. André Joubin designed **38** in 1930.

Historian Charles Lefeuve (1875) describes the neighborhood around **35**, the home of the king's sculptor Jérôme Derbais, in 1700: "A large plot of land along the ramparts, in other words the boulevard, starting from Rue des Poissonniers. This was once a segment of the Vallée-aux-Voleurs (Thieves' Valley), where unsuspecting passersby would get stripped of valuables, and where a different type of vice garnered it the sobriquet of the 'field of women.'" Derbais was commissioned by the Marquis de La Feuillade to complete a pedestal for the statue of Louis XIV which he had planned for Place des Victoires (see page 11). Other marble sculptors set up their studios in this neighborhood, including Misson (father and son) at **37 Rue Poissonnière**. The Derbais and the Dezègre families intermarried and speculated on plots of land in this district.

We now reach **Boulevard Poissonnière**. Its 35-meter width was prescribed by a royal order dated May 4, 1826. **Numbers 1, 3, 5, 7, 9, 17, 23,** and **27** are a neat row of houses separated from the street by ornamental sophora trees. The Rex is the largest movie theater in Paris. The building absorbed old **numbers 1 to 5** (see inset on the next page).

In the 19th century, the Chevreux-Aubertot novelties shop (famous for its "one-price") stood at **7**. It was taken over in 1908 by Léon Gaumont, who opened his first motion-picture theater on the premises. It did business here until 1977. The spacious building at **9** is made up of twelve bays. It replaced the old Hôtel de Rouillé (1728). The carriage door opens **onto 45 Rue du Sentier** and is remarkable for the lattice-work on its door panels and the arrow pattern on the impost (late 18th century).

▾ 45 Rue du Sentier

The Rex, a Temple to the Glory of Cinema

In 1930, wealthy movie producer Jacques Haïk scrapped his initial plan to create a huge concert hall with five thousand seats and instead built a cinema with 3,300 seats.

He took inspiration from American "atmospheric theaters" with interior designs evocative of summer nights. He brought John Eberson, an American specialist in the field, to Paris to team up with architect André Bluysen. The movie palace itself was an attraction. Along the sides were oriental and exotic murals by Maurice Dufrêne featuring Moroccan palaces, ancient colonnades, palm trees, statues, minarets, Spanish haciendas, balconies planted with flowers, and the hunting goddess Diana. Each star in the celestial dome twenty-five meters overhead was set on a cone incrusted with glass beads that reflected and refracted light. Visitors had the illusion of being outdoors. A machine blew clouds across the sky, making the fake night sky come to life and renewing the air in the palace five times an hour. The stage was twenty-four meters wide and eight meters deep. The movie screen was eighteen meters wide and was framed by a gigantic luminous arch in classic Art Déco style. The sloping orchestra pit allowed the audience to watch the fifty musicians who usually played before the show. The cinema offered luxurious and varied services: seats equipped for those with poor hearing, a recording studio, dressing rooms, a nurse's station, a dog kennel, and a nursery.

The cinema was inaugurated on December 8, 1932 with a grandiose program that included Henri Diamant-Berger's movie *Les Trois*

Rue du Sentier and Rue Saint-Fiacre

We will now turn left onto Rue du Sentier and stop for a while at **number 32** in front of the home of Masson de Meslay, an alderman in 1700. The builders of this splendid Louis XIV-style mansion had to comply with a two-meter easement order. Admire the beautiful details of the ornate doorway. It has a cartouche and lion-head consoles. The protruding center section on the courtyard side gives the façade a monumental look. The decorative elements gracing the facades of the two buildings are varied and include rosettes, garlands, ribbons, seashells, laurel leaves, pearls, masks, scrolls, etc. A corridor with a carved ceiling takes us into a second courtyard which contains a similar building.

Stone posts flank the doorway at **28** to protect the entrance from carriage and cart traffic going in and out between the courtyards in the neighborhood. **Number 24**, a five-story townhouse, is decorated with a variety of old iron pieces.

Let's enter **22**. A horseshoe arch includes a wrought-iron impost which accents the base of the staircase. This mansion (**22** and **24**) was home to Charles-Guillaume Le Normant d'Étiolles from 1745 to 1765. After his divorce, he was appointed *fermier général* (city-limit administrator) while his ex-wife (née Jeanne Poisson) was presented to the court under the name of Madame de Pompadour (one of the famous mistresses of Louis XV). Le Normant d'Etiolles consoled himself with dancer Mademoiselle Raime, and later married her. Their oval drawing room had

▲ 32 Rue du Sentier

▲ Le Rex, 1-5 Boulevard Poissonnière

Mousquetaires (The Three Musketeers) as the feature film. Haïk went bankrupt within months. The cinema was operated by Gaumont until it was requisitioned by German military authorities in 1941. After the war, Jean Hellmann bought it. He turned the Rex movie theater in an immensely successful venue. Sometimes, the box office sold as many as 80,000 tickets per week. Crowds thronged the cinema to see movies and variety shows such as trapeze artist Zemganno or music artist Maurice Chevalier. Radio shows were recorded on stage with the likes of Bourvil, Sidney Bechet, and many other greats.

In 1974, the basement dressing rooms were turned into three movie theaters for business reasons. In 1994, a "City of the Eye" stage curtain designed by Edward Allington was hung.

Every year at Christmas, the Rex puts on *La Féerie des Eaux*, a dazzling light and water show. At intermission, the giant screen rises, revealing a fountain designed to spray water twenty meters in the air as twenty-six projectors shine multicolored lights.

Erected on the boulevards, on the very site where cinema began, the Rex remains a testimony to the living golden age of the Seventh Art. About 1,250,000 spectators enter the Rex yearly.

paintings by Fragonard and Boucher. Their collection has long since been broken up. In 1787, this became the address of Harenc de Presles, also famous for his collection of paintings.

Let's continue our stroll up Rue du Sentier toward the boulevard. A lovely three-story townhouse at **33** has less attractive contemporary surroundings. It masks a building in its courtyard which was built at the end of the 17th century and has a secondary façade on 8 Rue Saint-Fiacre. This was the home of Jeanne Poisson in 1741 when she was a young bride. The property is shown on the 1739 Turgot map of Paris. What remains of it are a splendid wrought-iron banister and some early 19th-century paneling. In the middle of the 19th century, the Sentier became the garment district. Old mansions were refitted for business activities. In 1850, at **number 35**, the ground floor, entresol, and next floor were leased out to a "freelance fabric weaver" who had twenty-five looms in operation in the city of Évreux. Similarly, the stables at **39** were turned into a shop, with a sign hung on the carriage doors. The upholsterer Steinbach-Koechlin occupied the entire building at **37**, designed for them by A. Siber. Let's go through the carriage doors into the courtyard and follow the cart rails set in the pavement of the passage. This will take us from this street to the next on our itinerary.

▶ 35 Rue du Sentier

We exit at **12 Rue Saint-Fiacre** and turn left to enjoy a view of **number 8** with its verdant courtyard. This is, in fact, the same building mentioned earlier at 33 Rue du Sentier, now headquarters to the Réunion des Musées Nationaux (the institution which manages all France's national museums).

Boulevard Poissonnière

Strolling up Rue Saint-Fiacre to **Boulevard Poissonnière**, we reach **number 11**, the residence of a certain Augeard, a *fermier général* (city-limit administrator), who was well-known around 1750. In 1929, Paul Farge rebuilt the old Bouillon Duval into the much larger Plaza restaurant with a seating capacity of twelve hundred, and had it painted in shades of blue-green and gold. It became a prestigious variety theater between 1932 and 1956 under the management of Mitty Goldin, who changed its name, say-

ing, "I'll call it ABC. That way, it will always be at the top of the alphabetical listings of Paris shows." Legendary singer Tino Rossi made his Paris début here in 1934, as did the equally legendary Edith Piaf in 1937. The competition from the Olympia concert hall was stiff, and in 1964 manager Léon Ledoux turned the place over to the Boublil brothers. From 1965 to 1981, the Boublils operated the place as a movie theater. After that, it became a restaurant. It is now a retail store.

We continue strolling down the boulevard. The building at **17**, owned by a certain Mr. d'Ailly in the 18th century, is rather unique, with its terrace overlooking the boulevard. In 1787, architect Jacques Cellerier (1742-1814) built the mansion at **19** for Cousin de Méricourt, the States of Burgundy's general cashier. Each floor is outlined by a cornice, while the central portion of the building is discreetly set off by three slightly projecting bays crowned by a triangular

FREDERIC CHOPIN
HABITA CETTE MAISON
1831 - 1832

pediment. According to Paris historian Charles Lefeuve (1875), François-Nicolas Trou, Cellerier's head mason, may have skimmed building materials from the site to build his own house, next door at **21**. There are striking similarities (triangular pediments and the balcony) and noticeable differences (vermiculated stones, curved pediments, masks, etc.). A plaque at **27** immortalizes Frédéric

◄ 8 Rue Saint-Fiacre

► 27 Boulevard Poissonnière
◄ 17 Boulevard Poissonnière

▲ Hôtel de Montholon, 23 Boulevard Poissonnière

Chopin's first stay in Paris in 1831-1832. In a November 18, 1831 missive to his friend Norbert Alphonse Kumelski in Berlin, he wrote, "Up on my sixth floor (I'm staying at 27 Boulevard Poissonnière), you would not believe how pretty my accommodations are. I have a little room with lovely mahogany furniture and a balcony overlooking the boulevards, with a view of Paris stretching from Montmartre to the Panthéon. I can see all the beautiful people. Many envy my fine view, but none the climb."

In 1840, this address became famous for its chocolate factory. Guérin Boutron was one of five chocolate producers in Paris. In 1894, Jandelle turned it into a café-cum-concert hall called Le Parisiana. Édouard Niermans designed a façade with a profusion of flowers, masks, and nude dancing girls. In 1910, Paul Ruez sacrificed this music venue for the latest fashion: motion pictures. His movie theater was a huge success. In 1957, Gaumont converted it to an opulent 1800-seat movie house, the Richelieu, and, after a few decades, split it up into five multiplex theaters before finally selling the premises to a retailer in 1987.

Let's walk back to **number 23** to admire the most beautiful 18th-century mansion on the boulevards. The Hôtel de Montholon was designed in 1775 for Nicolas de Montholon by François Soufflot, a student and relative of the great French architect of the same name. Although the monumental effect of the colossal order on the façade is diminished by the ground floor shops and their signs, the murals in the small and large salons inside, by history painter Jean-Baptiste Robin, were preserved. It was once used as a storehouse by the Aubusson tapestry concern. In 1848, it became the Sallandrouze house. The Hôtel de Montholon has had illustrious owners, notably the Adams. Juliette Lamber's second husband was Edmond Adam. They lived on two floors of this mansion from 1872 to 1886. The Adams were involved in politics and had strong ties to Léon Gambetta. Juliette Adam's salon became a magnet for Republican gatherings. The guests, however, also entertained each other, playing dominoes, bezique, and chess. The actor Coquelin was a frequent guest. After the war of 1870, Juliette Lamber published novels and her recollections of the siege of Paris. She founded *La Nouvelle Revue*, in which she gave young writers like Pierre Loti their chance.

The Hotel de Montholon's terrace offered a splendid view of the boulevard, a panorama immortalized in *Le Boulevard Poissonnière*, a painting by Isidore Dagnan, (1834) hanging in the Carnavalet Museum in Paris. It shows a wide, tree-lined avenue with side paths, lively with shoppers and vendors. The sidewalk cafés and festive ambience attracted crowds of Parisians.

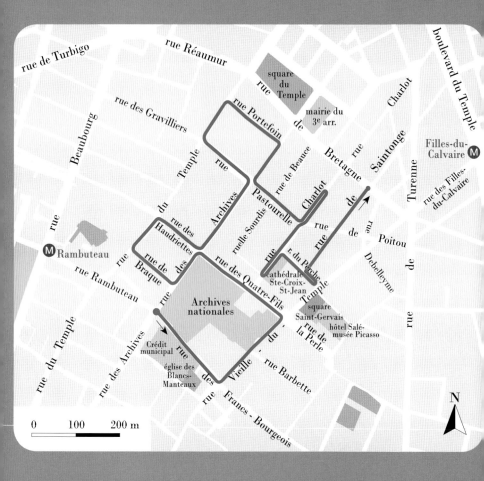

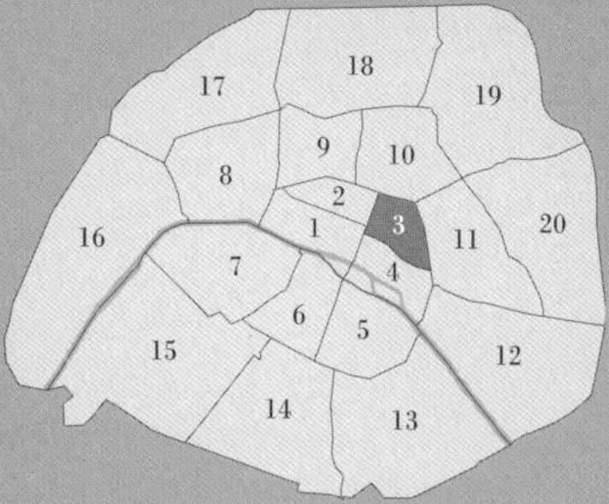
17
18
19
9
10
8
2
3
16
1
11
20
7
4
6
5
15
12
14
13

3rd

Temple Lands

- Start: Rue des Archives, metro Rambuteau
- Finish: Rue de Bretagne, metro Filles-du-Calvaire

The neighborhood we are about to discover arose on lands granted to the Knights Templar, divided into tracts in two different phases. In the late 13th century, the Knights Templar themselves constructed a new town around a north-south thoroughfare, today's Rue des Archives. The rest of the surrounding swamplands (or *Marais* in French), called *couture du Temple* (Temple patches), were sold in 1608-1610 to one man, a certain Michel Pigou, who was a front for a consortium of financiers. King Henri IV wanted the area to be graced by a royal square. It was planned as a semicircular complex, framed by identical buildings with turrets and high slate roofs, and was to be named *Place de France*. The new streets radiating from it would have been named for France's provinces. However, the plan was canceled after François Ravaillac assassinated the king on May 14, 1610. All that remains is a handful of street names honoring provinces, such as Rue de Poitou, Rue de Bretagne, and Rue de Normandie. Curving Rue Debelleyme was a product of the original semicircle plan.

Rue des Francs-Bourgeois

We start this walk at the junction of **Rue Rambuteau, Rue des Francs-Bourgeois**, and **Rue des Archives** on

▲ Hôtel de Soubise, 60 Rue des Francs-Bourgeois

the spot where the Porte du Chaume stood in the 14th century, marking the gateway from Paris into the new town built by the Knights Templar. The intersection is graced by an old fountain that was transformed into an enclosed well in 1705 by architect Jean Beausire. Notice how he dressed it in stone and crowned the roof with a sphere. Let's enter **Rue des Francs-Bourgeois**. This section of the street was called Rue de Paradis until 1867 because of a medieval sign.

Prepare to be impressed by the majesty of the Hôtel de Soubise at **60**. The gateway has a recessed half-moon shape. The design includes Corinthian columns that create a dignified carriage entrance. Let's go in. The courtyard is grandiose. Architect Pierre-Alexis Delamair designed it in 1705-1708 for Prince François de Soubise and his wife Anne Chabot de Rohan. Having just purchased the old Hôtel de Guise (cf. 58 Rue des Archives on page 48), the lord and lady needed it brought up to date. The exteriors was handled splendidly by Delamair, but his client and he had an argument over the interior design, and Delamair had to bow out. Upon the death of François de Soubise, the palace was

◄ Intersection of Rue Rambuteau, Rue des Francs-Bourgeois and Rue des Archives

taken over by his favorite son, Hercule-Mériadec. When he remarried in 1732, taking a 19-year-old beauty named Marie-Sophie de Courcillon as his bride, he commissioned architect Germain Boffrand to create a new décor for the mansion. Boffrand's 1735 creation was hailed as a masterpiece. He demonstrated real genius for decoration, hiring the greatest artists of his time: Boucher, Carle Van Loo, Restout, Lemoine, Natoire, etc. The ensemble was considered to be one of the finest décors in Europe. After the upheaval of the French Revolution, the mansion was returned to the Soubise heirs. They chose to sell it in 1807 to a certain Mr. Chandor, who then made a deal with the State. In 1808, Napoleon ordered that the Palais Soubise be used as a temporary storehouse for the national archives, an arrangement that continues to this day.

As the original entrance for the mansion on Rue des Archives was a tight turn, Delamair decided to place it on the south side of the property. He then seized the opportunity to lay out a spacious main courtyard where a barn once stood. He also convinced the owner's wife that a colonnade

including a walkway would form a pleasing border around the courtyard.

At the far end of the courtyard, the façade of the *corps de logis* or central pavilion is topped by a slate roof trimmed with a balustrade. Delamair cleverly built up a main entrance on what was formerly the side wall of the Hôtel de Guise. He gave it the necessary majesty by adding paired columns to the façade above the ground floor, topped with statues of the Four Seasons. The proper depth was obtained by the addition of a portico with paired columns and a pediment. While it has been stripped of its carved coat of arms, it is unique in Paris for having preserved its reclining statues: *La Gloire* and *La Magnificence des Princes* by sculptor Robert Le Lorrain. In fact, as is the case for the Four Seasons, completed by the same artist with the same fervor, these are also modern copies. Notice that the balconies and window rail-

► The macle – a golden rhombus – an element in the Rohan family's coat of arms

▼ Two of the Four Seasons statues atop a pair of double columns in the main courtyard of the Hôtel de Soubise

ings incorporate the Rohan family's *macle*, a gilded lozenge that was part of the family's coat of arms. It can be found throughout the palace as well as in the Hôtel de Rohan at 87 Rue Vieille-du-Temple. Through the arcade to the left we will see the Cour des Marronniers, which was the main courtyard of the Hôtel de Guise until Delamair relegated it to the rank of secondary courtyard. Higher up is the palace chapel. To the east, on the other side, look through the iron gate and you will see an alleyway. This used to be Ruelle de la Roche. It was swallowed up by the Archives Nationales after 1808. Before the Revolution, neighborhood residents used to take it to reach Rue Vieille-du-Temple.

Let's exit now and head east on the street. As we leave, we have in front of us, across the street at **59**, a vigorous stone façade in neoclassical style dating from 1775. The Archives Nationales owned several nearby mansions which have recently been carefully rehabilitated. They make up a remarkable ensemble. Let's look first at **58 bis**, the Hôtel d'Assy. It was undoubtedly built by architect Pierre Le Muet in 1642-1643

for a financier named Denis Marin de la Chataigneraie. The façade is so sober that the only hint that this was a rich man's mansion is the stone dormers with moldings. Under Louis XVI, the building belonged to Jean-Claude Geoffroy d'Assy, who was guillotined in the Revolution. His descendants sold the residence to the Archives in 1842. Historian Jules Michelet had his office on the second floor. Until 1902, there was a reading hall open to the public on the ground floor. Look closely and you can make out the old arch of a walled-up carriage door.

A powerful façade at **56** has a sturdy balcony supported by consoles decorated with sunflowers. Architect Mansart de Sagonne designed this house in 1752 for Jérôme-Gilbert Claustrier, a public records officer with the Contrôle Général.

The Hôtel de Jaucourt at **54** was acquired after World War II by the Archives Nationales. Built in 1599 for Jean de Ligny, this mansion was renovated in 1684 for Jean Le Camus, then *lieutenant civil* of the Châtelet, one of the highest ranking judicial officers in the kingdom. Robert de Cotte designed a sober doorway in 1687.

◄ Iron gate closing the old Ruelle de la Roche

▼ 59 Rue des Francs-Bourgeois

The house was completely refurbished at the end of the 18th century. During the renovation, workers discovered dormers built in 1599 that had been covered by masonry at a later date. A decision was taken to restore them to their original splendor, but the renovation was disappointingly severe. Beyond this point, the street has no more old homes until we reach Rue Vieille-du-Temple.

Rue Vieille-du-Temple

Overlooking the intersection with Rue Vieille-du-Temple is **Hôtel Hérouet**. German bombing on August 26, 1944 left it in ruins. The shattered structure required extensive renovation. The delicately carved flamboyant Gothic turret is all that remains of the 16th-century house built for Jean Hérouet, treasurer to Louis XII. Let's turn left onto **Rue Vieille-du-Temple**. At **75** we come upon Hôtel de La Tour du Pin, a discreet manor in the Marais, erected in 1724 by architect Villeneuve for Nicolas Bertin, a tax treasurer. The next owners were the Marquis Gouvernet de La Tour du Pin, who gave it its name. It was laid out on a tradi-tional horseshoe plan. The stone structures were built with tasteful sobriety and enhanced only by intricate wrought-iron elements. The next building is a high-rising rental building by the same architect. It hides the courtyard area from the street. It has a stone façade with perfect proportions. It and the neighboring homes, all quite old, form a homogeneous group. Notice the Empire-period shop at **77-79**. Its façade rises to a spacious 17th-century dormer.

We now come to the Hôtel de Rohan at **87**. Its buildings go all the way to Rue des Quatre-Fils. Unfortunately, the entrance is temporarily closed to visitors. Armand Gaston Maximilien de Rohan, fifth son of the princely Soubise family, a bishop and cardinal, commissioned a beautiful residence to be built on the lot that he acquired from his family. It, too, was designed by Delamair in 1705-1708, the same period as the Hôtel de Soubise, but in this case, the architect did not have to dress up an older building. In comparing the two, we notice this one is far more austere. This may be explained by the owner's ecclesiastical position. The straight and narrow façade rises from the back of the courtyard, surrounded by lower buildings. Having later acquired neighboring houses, the cardinal was able to expand the manor's outer bailey and put in huge stables with some

◀ 77-79 Rue Vieille-du-Temple

▶ Hôtel Hérouet

fifty stalls. This marvelous and rather secluded place has a masterpiece by Robert Le Lorrain, carved in 1736-1737: *Les Chevaux du Soleil*, a large bas-relief vibrant with energy. Upon the cardinal's death in 1749, three relatives, also cardinals, succeeded him. The second was Armand de Rohan-Soubise, brother of Field Marshall de Soubise. He had his apartments redecorated by architect Saint-Martin. The third was Louis René Édouard de Rohan who earned fame and scorn for his gullibility in the diamond necklace scandal that shook the monarchy in 1785. The Hôtel de Rohan was seized and pillaged during the Revolution. Like the Hôtel de Soubise, it was sold to the State in 1808. Unfortunately, Napoleon made it his government printing office, which damaged the interiors.

After extensive renovations, the Rohan cardinals' home was assigned to the Archives Nationales in 1938 to house temporary exhibitions. An entrance to one of these will give you a chance to see the grand staircase, a stunning replica built by the Monuments Historiques of the lost original. Three rooms upstairs are still decorated in baroque style. The "Music or Company Room" boasts a mantelpiece mirror ornamented with sculptures of musical instruments, and the cornice is decorated with medallions celebrating military parade music, opera music, drinking songs, and pastoral music. The paintings over the doorways are by Jean-Baptiste Pierre. The second room is the famous Cabinet des Singes paneled with Chinese-style paintings of frolicking monkeys on every side, the work of craftsman Christophe Huet. The third room, on the courtyard side, is the Cabinet des

Fables whose wood panels are decorated with mirthful medallions depicting Aesop's fables. This room was originally part of the Hôtel de Soubise.

Rue des Quatre-Fils

As we walk along Hôtel de Rohan, we will see **Rue des Quatre-Fils** on our left. It was laid out at the end of the 13th century and its name refers to the legend of the four sons of Aymon in the 12th-century epic poem *Renaud de Montauban*. We will head down the street, going by the Rohan stables. At **number 1** we come upon the magnificent annex doorway. The splendid grooved stonework seems to branch out like a living plant. The north side of the street has no more old architecture due to a street-widening program in 1930. CARAN, the

▲ *Les Quatre Fils Aymon* (Aymon's four sons), by Yvan Theimer, on the façade of the CARAN building, 3-11 Rue des Quatre-Fils (© Adagp, Paris 2009)

▼ 1 Rue des Quatre-Fils

▶ The former Hôtel Aymeret, 16 Rue des Quatre-Fils

▲ 20 Rue des Quatre-Fils

▶ 18 Rue des Quatre-Fils

research center of the national archives, occupies **3-11**. Its contemporary architecture – criticized for being too affected – is the work of architect Stanislas Fiszer. The façade is decorated with a relief of the four sons of Aymon by Yvan Theimer (two brothers in the background are barely suggested). The space inside the building is lovely, though not terribly practical. From the lobby of the CARAN building, one has a beautiful view – the only one, in fact – on the gardens and the rear of the Hôtel de Rohan.

At **number 16**, the old Hôtel Aymeret, built in the time of Louis XIII, underwent major structural changes when the street was straightened. Interestingly, its handsome Louis XV doorway was taken apart and moved back. There is also an 18th-century grand staircase. Conversely, neighboring **number 18** lost its doorway but its façades are intact. The slate-sided attic, with its dormers and stone bull's-eye windows, is a fine example of Louis Treize style. This mansion was built around 1634 for the widow of Noël Hureau, and in the reign of Louis XVI it belonged to the Le Rebours family. The next house, **number 20**, also escaped the street-

straightening program. It is a pretty Louis Quinze style, erected between 1730-1735 for Nicolas Le Féron, president of the first chamber of investigation, and his son-in-law René Berger, a municipal tax officer. It is not known who the architect was.

Romain de Sèze, the courageous lawyer who defended Louis XVI, purchased it in 1800. He died here in 1826 (the information on the plaque is somewhat incorrect). The façade is in stone and the door has delicately carved panels. The attic still has two hayloft windows. In the alley to our right is a grand staircase with a gilded wrought-iron handrail. It is encased in woodwork and has two columns. The courtyard is bordered on the right by an older wing. The rest is 19th century. It was in this house that Coline Serreau shot her 1985 film *Trois Hommes et un Couffin (Three Men and a Baby)*. **Number 22** is often mistaken for having been the location of the Marquise de Deffand's salon, but the circle of intellectuals actually met in an outbuilding of the Hôtel Guénégaud (see 60 Rue des Archives, page 50) erected on a small parcel of the mansion's grounds in 1769-1770. The façade was later altered and raised. Opposite, **high walls** close the street. They are the Archives Nationales' warehouses, the work of architect Henri Janniard under Napoleon III. His

design consisted of a single blind wall decorated with Florentine arcades in order to protect archive documents from daylight. Above all, these buildings are functional.

Down Rue des Archives to Rue des Haudriettes

Having reached **Rue des Archives**, we'll turn left and continue walking down the street, to go all the way around the Archives block. Crossing the street will give us an excellent view of **number 58**, the Hôtel de Clisson. Its twin corbelled turrets positioned over a large Gothic arcade (an old entrance to the home) date from the end of the 14th century, a time when Constable Olivier de Clisson (a confidant of King Charles V) chose this location for his home. This is the last vestige of Parisian architecture with defensive elements. The mansion's courtyard sat left of the entrance. Today, it is hidden by a rather dismal warehouse built in 1880. The estate was acquired in 1553 by the powerful Guise family.

They wasted no time in enlarging and embellishing the interior. The chapel was painted by Niccolo dell'Abate. The Guise family was actively involved in the War of Religion and founded the French Catholic League. Their residence served as headquarters for the Catholic party. It was undoubtedly here that the St. Bartholomew's Day massacre was planned in 1572. The mansion's 17th-century history is much more peaceful. It accommodated numerous apartments for friends of the Guises, among whom were the poet Quinault, Pierre Corneille, and the famous collector Roger de Gaignières, who was officially squire of the Duke of Guise. As we saw earlier, the old mansion was purchased in 1700 by the Soubise family (see 60 Rue des Francs-Bourgeois, page 42). Their architect Delamair has often been praised for preserving the two Gothic turrets in a time when this style had gone out of fashion. They seem to stand as symbols of the residence's venerable age.

Our next intersection is **Rue de Braque**, one of the loveliest streets in the Marais district. It was laid out at the end of the 13th century. At that time, it was called Rue des Boucheries-

du-Temple (the Temple butcher shops' street) because of the butchers doing business at present-day **number 12**. The splendid façade at **4-6** holds our attention. This is the Hôtel Le Lièvre

◄ Hôtel de Clisson, 58 Rue des Archives

▶ Carved ram's head in a balcony console at the Hôtel Lièvre de la Grange, 4-6 Rue de Braque

street to **Rue des Haudriettes**, where we will turn right. This lovely name refers to a home for widows. It was founded by Étienne Haudri, thus giving rise to the feminine term "*les haudriettes*," meaning the women taken in by his institution. The first section of the street has a big indentation as the result of demolition that occurred long ago. To cover up the scar, city officials ordered a fashionable mural painting. The rather complex mural before us was completed in 1992 by L. Hours. But prior to the Revolution, this intersection had a very different meaning for Parisians. The Temple gallows, the highest in the city, stood here.

▲ Hôtel de Clisson,
Rue de Braque

► Hôtel de Mailly,
4 Rue des Haudriettes

▼ Hôtel de Chaulnes,
8 Rue de Braque

de La Grange. To be more precise, we should use the plural *hôtels* (mansions), as they are really twin residences designed by architect Victor-Thierry Dailly in 1734. Notice the balcony consoles ornamented with the heads of rams and elderly sages. The high-quality sculpture was the work of Lissy and Bourguignon. On the other side of the street at **5**, you would hardly guess that in the courtyard behind the stern façade is a smaller, overly-restored, half-timbered 17th-century house. With the patch of garden off to the left, it forms a quiet, peaceful ensemble. More classic, however, is the façade of the little Hôtel de Chaulnes at **number 8**. It dates back to the reign of Louis XIV. Notice the lion muzzles decorating the panels of the carriage door.

Once we have reached **Rue du Temple**, a right turn will take us up the

The Hôtel de Mailly (mistakenly called Hôtel de Bondeville) at **4** was renovated in 2004. Given the architectural style, it dates from the turn of the 16th century, and was built either for Jean de Ligny, or for Jean de Creil, a tenant who became the owner in 1605. The famed Maupeou family of parliamentarians acquired it through the marriage of Marguerite de Creil to René de Maupeou. In the 18th century, it belonged to the Mailly family, thus its name today. The doorway, redone in the 17th century, is decorated with a strikingly handsome mask showing Hercules wearing the skin of Nemesis's lion. The attic's six stone dormers are part of the original design, and herald the six we shall see in the courtyard. Originally, the

wings were low, two-story buildings, with a central staircase. This layout was altered in the early 18th century in order to modernize the residence. The restoration of the entire lot was rather harsh, however. At the head of the street, at **number 1**, is a rare example of a neoclassical fountain. It was designed by the architect

Moreau-Desproux in 1767. It has a gorgeous bas-relief water nymph with delicate features carved by sculptor Philippe Mignot.

Back to Rue des Archives

We now stand again at **Rue des Archives** and will turn left to head north. This part of the Templars' new town was close to what they called Rue du Grand-Chantier. Today, the east side is nearly entirely composed of 17th-century homes, which face a huge telephone exchange building on the opposite side of the street. On the corner at **60** is the Hôtel Guénégaud des Brosses, the city's only surviving manor designed by François Mansart (although heavily renovated). It was erected in the years 1652-1655 for financier Jean-François Guénégaud on the site of two medieval homes. In 1704, it was acquired by a *fermier*

général (city-limit administrator) named Jean Romanet who improved the interiors. In 1766, it was sold to Thiroux d'Épersenne, known for his good taste and the collection of Falconet statues he had assembled in the ground floor of his home. Being prudish, however, he draped the nude figures, much to the chagrin of philosopher and encyclopedia-compiler Diderot. The Thiroux family kept the residence until 1895, but by the mid-19th century, businesses and light industry had overrun the premises. The building was soon in deplorable condition. It barely escaped demolition twice. The second attempt was in 1960. It was countered by serious opposition. City Hall was pressured to buy it. The property was soon renovated and refurbished thanks to François Sommer and his wife, whose foundation and Musée de la Chasse et de la Nature (nature and hunting museum) have been located here since 1967.

This small mansion is a masterpiece by Mansart. The lines and proportions are pure and harmonious. Inside, the grand stone staircase is part of the original structure, and is now visible to museum visitors. Standing on Rue des Quatre-Fils, we can admire the garden and the rear façade, also carefully restored.

Number 62 is not as well-known. Here, the Hôtel de Mongelas was recently and masterfully restored to house the annex of the neighboring museum. It was built in 1705, perhaps from plans by Jules Hardouin-Mansart (who should not be confused with his great-uncle François Mansart). In the courtyard to the left is a lovely staircase with an oval shape. The banister has never been replaced. Wasting no time on the 1930s building at **68**,

▲ 70-72 Rue des Archives

let us go directly to the far end of the courtyard to have a look at what remains of the Hôtel de Refuge, built in 1645. The façade is sober and stern.

Next, we come to **70 and 72**, a spacious ensemble composed of two manors built by François de Montescot around 1647. Only **number 70** has a semblance of the original design, but it was also subjected to brutish renovation. **Number 72** was extensively refurbished in the 19th century. It is a good example of the sober, streamlined architecture in stark contrast with the preceding mannerist period, when decoration was intentionally playful and gracious. Do not overlook the two identical doorways. The one at **number 72** was extended up a floor and given a pediment in pure Louis Quinze style with very beautiful woodwork. The carved figures on the door represent the Greek god of medicine Aesculapius on the right and Justice on the left. **Number 70** has preserved its grand staircase, reworked in 1750 while the property was owned by the widow of the treasurer of buildings, Denis Legras. It is simply splendid. **74 and 76** were

built along the same lines as the twin manors. The first was by Gédéon Tallemant, a cousin of memoirist Tallemant des Réaux; the second was by Octavien Le Bys de La Chapelle. Both open onto a yard dating from 1642-1644. The one at **74** was completed by master masons Pierre Grandin and Mathieu Muret. It has kept its sober 18th-century doorway. **Number 76**, however, opens with a stupendous doorway dating from the 1640s. As indicated by the monogram in the frieze of the lintel, this was once the home of Le Bys and his wife Marie Daluymare. At the far end of the courtyard to the left is the corner tower with its own attic, which people used to call the dungeon. It has an exceptionally beautiful staircase with a wrought-iron handrail, then a lovely wooden balustrade on the next flight up.

Around Rue Pastourelle

Let's turn left on **Rue Pastourelle** and go west. This block was laid out in the late 13th century. The entire north side is old. The façades are of modest

▶ 76 Rue des Archives

dimensions. The parcel divisions are medieval. Note, however, that **22** has a small Louis XV façade and **44** has rare Louis XIV window railings.

Once we reach **Rue du Temple**, we will turn right and go up to sleepy **Rue Portefoin**. It, too, was laid out by the Knights Templar. Its pretty rural-sounding name may be from a mangled pronunciation of the name of a wealthy inhabitant in the Middle Ages. A stern, neoclassical house sits at the corner at **19**. A lovely Louis Quatorze manor at **14** still has its original doorway and its picturesque courtyard. At **number 2**, a walled-up arcade was once a doorway into the Hôpital des Enfants-Rouges. This orphanage was founded by King François I and his sister Marguerite de Navarre to take in and raise orphans. The children wore red uniforms, because the color red symbolized charity.

We are now back on **Rue des Archives**, which didn't use to go beyond the hospital buildings. It is a short block up to Rue de Bretagne. When this section of the street was carved out in 1806, irreparable damage to the cityscape occurred. Never-

theless, the Enfants-Rouges survives at least at **85**, a Louis Treize period house that was recently renovated, and at **90**, where as we shall see in the courtyard to our left, stands the apse of the old Saint-Julien chapel. It is easily recognizable with its high and pointed windows (the stained-glass windows were once famous). It wasn't demolished, but it was turned into residential property. A plaque on the rear wall mentions the charity organization which closed in 1772. On the other side of the street at **83** is the small manor where Valentin Conrart, one of the founders of the

Académie Française, died. He was renting it from the Marquis de Breteuil. The estate has suffered much damage, but we can reach the wood and wrought-iron staircase by going round the right side of the courtyard building. Let's go through the same

◄ Rue Portefoin

▼ 90 Rue des Archives
▼ 81-83 Rue des Archives

entrance and the shared cobblestone courtyard to see the lovely Louis Quinze staircase at **81**. Its carved elements remain graceful despite a recent thickening. Next door at **79**, the 1610 façade is crowned by beautiful stone dormers with pediments cutting through the cornice. The architectural term in French for this type of dormer is *lucarne passante*; the ones here are typical of their period. Unfortunately, the esthetics of the courtyard and the ground floor are spoiled by a car dealership.

At **number 78** we come to the impressive Hôtel Amelot de Chaillou,

designed by Pierre Bullet in 1702-1704 for Denis-Jean Amelot de Chaillou, a parliamentarian. In 1722, the mansion was purchased by Marshal de Tallard; in the 19th century, as often happened in this district, it became dilapidated due to commercial use, which finally ended in 1978, when a complete restoration was undertaken. The large mansion is indicated on the street level by a magnificent gate with moldings. The woodwork of the door is quite old, and the

impost has preserved its wooden angels holding a monogrammed medallion. The courtyard sits at the corner of two streets and has but one wing, to our left. The stone façades are typical of Bullet's stern style. The roofline is broken and lit by dormers which were intentionally made in stone rather than the newer and more popular wooden dormers of that time. The mansion has a stairwell decorated with pilasters and niches. It is one of the most elegant in all the Marais, and contemporaries greatly admired it. The façade on the garden is equally interesting, but remains difficult to see (from Rue de Beauce). At ground level, it is decorated with carved medallions and topped by an immense triangular pediment that gives it a definite monumental look.

We shall turn left now to go back to **Rue Pastourelle**, but head east this time. This block was not laid out until 1636. At that time, it was called Rue d'Anjou and ran from Rue Charlot to Rue des Archives. Just after **17**, we come to the entrance to an alleyway called **Ruelle Sourdis**. This L-shaped street used to lead back to Rue Charlot and was private property in the 17th century (see 5 Rue Charlot, page 55).

Its middle portion was blocked off. Flanking the walls are the picturesque "privés" — little towers used as toilets. Straight ahead is the start of **Rue de Beauce** (the former street names are engraved here). Despite major alterations, the memory of Mademoiselle Scudéry and her literary salon is still strong here. This was indeed the home of the famous *précieuse* who dreamt up a map for an imaginary land which she named *Tendre*. Rue de Beauce and Ruelle Sourdis string together like two contiguous back alleys running through the middle of two blocks. They mark the boundaries between the 13th-century tract and that of 1608.

Let's stay on **Rue Pastourelle** to go see **11**. The rear building has a gracious 18th-century staircase.

Rue Charlot

Our next turn is left onto **Rue Charlot**. We will go halfway up the block towards Rue de Bretagne. Until 1851, this part of the street was called Rue de Berry. The façade with the rather flat balcony at **28** is a mansion called Bérancourt. It was built around 1705 for a certain Mr. de La Garde. Immediately to our right through the passage, we will see the lovely Louis Quatorze stairs with a wrought-iron banister. Above all, once in the little paved courtyard, we should take the time to look at the main pavilion with its concave shape. It is a gem of early 18th-century design, in straw-colored stone, and the small-paned windows have been preserved. To the right is the ethereal sweep of the staircase, which has also survived. Looking at the façades along this block, we notice that, while none are excep-

tional, each has an interesting old detail: a window railing here (**29**), a dormer pulley there (**26**).

We are going to backtrack now and continue our stroll in a southerly direction. Beyond the intersection with Rue Pastourelle, Rue Charlot used to be known as Rue d'Orléans-au-Marais. Notice that **15** has a lovely Directoire or Empire style door. Its impost has a palm-frond pattern. Across the street at **12** is the small manor built in 1610 by master mason Jean Notin. It underwent extensive renovation. Admire the carriage door with its neo-Louis-Quinze carved panels. Glance up at the broken roofline where the dormers are trimmed with graceful stone scrollwork. They are

▲ 28 Rue Charlot
▼ 15 Rue Charlot

▶ 12 Rue Charlot

▼ Hôtel Cornuel,
7 Rue Charlot

practically unique among the hôtels in this neighborhood. Let's finish our stroll down this street by popping in at the Cornuel mansion at **7**. Although it underwent significant alterations when the roof was raised in the 19th century, it has preserved its outer wings, which are crowned by powerful stone dormers. It was built in 1614-1616 by Charles Margonne, who then sold it in 1618 to Nicolas de Villantrois. In 1636, it became the property of Claude Cornuel, a successful finan-

cier. A few years ago, the discovery of the mansion's high-quality Louis Treize painted beams and joists caused quite a thrill. Let's go into the small courtyard that replaced the garden to enjoy the ambience. To our left is the façade of **number 5**, where Ruelle Sourdis comes out. It is still lined with bollards and paved with cobbles, sloping slightly to form an old-fashioned central gutter.

From Rue du Perche to Rue de Bretagne

Let's backtrack a little up the even-numbered side of the street, then turn onto **Rue du Perche**, laid out in 1608, like the rest of the neighborhood. The courtyard at **13** is closed by an iron gate. This is the entrance to the former Saint-Jean-Saint-François church, renamed Sainte-Croix in 1970 when it became the city's Armenian cathedral. An unimpressive 1855 façade by Baltard masks the older structure dated 1715. At that time, it was a convent church of the Petits Capucins du Marais, who set up their church here in 1626, but were chased out by revolutionaries in 1791. In the days of the monarchy, the Capucins were volunteer firemen. After the Revolution, it became a parish church. The interior may be viewed when Mass is held. The choir has several good 17th-century paintings, stalls from Saint-Jean-en-Grève (no longer standing) and most notably, around the steps, statues of Saint Francis, to the left, by Germain Pilon (late 16th century), and Saint Denis, to the right, by the Marsy brothers (mid-17th century). They are splendid works of art, highly representative of the *grande manière française* (the grand French manner).

Little remains of the exterior of the old Hôtel du Châtelet at **numbers 7 bis and 9**, wrongly called the Hôtel Scarron. But it does hold an ensemble of four Louis Quatorze painted ceilings. They are perhaps the loveliest in all the Marais and are attributed to Antonio Verrio, an Italian artist.

The name of the mansion at **number 8** is Pomponne de Refuge. It was remodeled for the Count of Walein around 1772, and, more recently, was overly restored, although the carriage door is interesting. The regular stone façade and window railings at **number 5** are those of a lovely rental building erected in the early 18th century.

Let's turn onto the long **Rue de Saintonge**. It is actually three older streets merged into one. We will discover two of them in this walk.

The first was called Rue de Touraine-au-Marais. Because of its proximity with the aristocratic portion of the Marais, it is lined with fine

homes. But, as we shall see, the farther north one goes, the less elegant the buildings are. An austere neoclassical façade awaits us at **4**. The rectangles between the windows are recessed or ornamented with garlands. This was the home of a wealthy notary named Mathis, who had it fixed up by architect Étienne-Louis Boullée, his friend, who also occasionally lent his name to Mathis' business ventures. In the carriageway that leads

to the encumbered courtyard, we shall see two fine Doric columns. We must take a small door to our left to view the staircase. While it is not at all well-known, it is a remarkable piece. It starts with a console that is still Louis Quinze, but the banister already espouses Louis Seize style and appears to roll up and out in a continuous movement.

Neighboring **number 6** is a fine example of unfounded historical guesswork that has since become unshakable truth... A Directoire-era theater was rumored to be behind the poor Louis-Philippe façade. Its alleged originality was such that the historical society zealously protected it. A bit of research revealed that, although the building was not a theater, it is nevertheless an interesting structure, and certainly worthy of conservation. It is an old workshop on three levels, with wooden galleries. It was built in 1830-1832 for a manufacturer of military helmets, a certain Antoine Dida, supplier to the Garde Nationale. The structure can be seen through a few windows. The building is currently empty.

While **number 8** has an austere, unadorned façade, it does have brickwork dormers, a sign of the proprietor's wealth. The mansion belonged to Adrien Bence, a long-forgotten financier, who amassed a huge fortune on the heels of his master, the even wealthier Fouquet. But, unlike Fouquet, Bence managed to hold onto his assets. He had this large residence built in 1660-1661 by Michel Villedo and lived in it until his death, in 1696. The main pavilion is located directly on the street. The secondary pavilions framing the courtyard and garden were occupied by workshops in the 19th century. The left wing's grand

▲ 8 Rue du Perche
▶ 4 Rue de Saintonge

staircase is majestic in its square stairwell. The wrought-iron banister with symmetrical panels is beautiful, and still rather old-fashioned for its time, but the style is masterful and the rise is comfortable. In the wing across the way, a door crowned by an exquisite frieze of pecking birds opens onto a small wooden staircase with squarish balusters. Its origin seems unclear – perhaps it came from elsewhere.

Adrien Bence also owned the neighboring mansion at **10**, which dated from the early 17th century. It was razed after a goldsmith named Gaudin bought it in 1759 and had his brother Pierre, an architect, rebuild the ensemble. It has not changed since. While the street-side façade was designed with simplicity, the panels of the carriage door were richly carved in Louis Quinze style. Farther up the street, **number 15**, also remodeled, was the home of the philosopher-mathematician Blaise Pascal in his younger days. He left it after his father's death in 1651. A tall rental building on the corner of Rue de Poitou at **12** was erected in 1774 for a master baker named Delacroix. The street name is carved into the stones on the corner.

Before we go past **Rue de Poitou**, this is the ideal moment to peek in at the row of old façades, some of which feature charming details, like the thermometer-shaped sign at **38**. We will then continue down the second section of **Rue de Saintonge**, which used to be called Rue de la Marche. A splendid rental building stands at **20**. Its carefully built stone façade with moldings is topped by a triangular pediment with trimmed with carved modillions. Look at how it juts out over the attic level. Entrepreneur and architect Edme-Jacques Blondel built it for himself in 1780. The second floor is accented by a balcony on consoles. It has a cast-iron railing from the early 19th century, which replaced the original stone balusters that probably gave the whole an even sterner appearance.

Number 22 was remodeled at the same time, by the same Mr. Blondel. Let's finish our stroll at **number 24**. At the far end of the courtyard is a small, graceful spiral staircase that time has weathered and given charm. Until just recently, the third floor had a drawing room with Louis Quinze wood paneling. Our stroll comes to its end as we exit onto **Rue de Bretagne**.

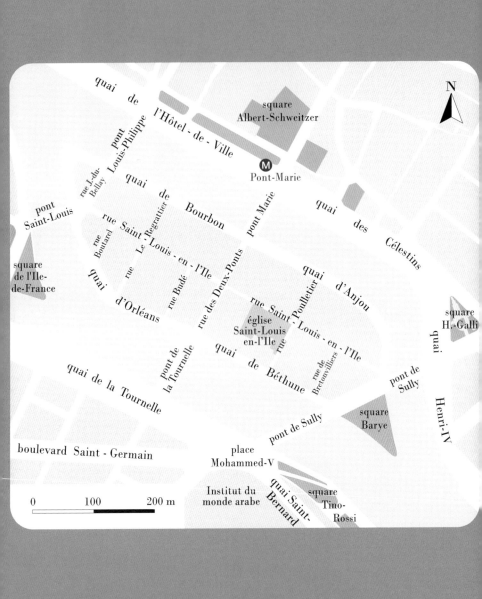

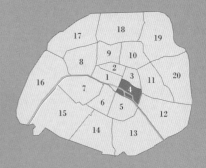

4th

Ile Saint-Louis

▶ Start and finish:
metro Pont-Marie

There is absolutely no place in the world like Ile Saint-Louis. As you cross the Seine River, large shadows may play off the lovely riverside homes with their luminous southern exposures and darker northern faces. Lovers find silence and reverie here; strollers find a wonderland. We shall begin our exploration of the island by walking riverside along the quays; next, we'll move up to the central thoroughfare, Rue Saint-Louis-en-l'Ile. We'll finish by exploring the adjacent streets.

▲ Pont Marie

▶ 1 Quai de Bourbon

Pont Marie

With the exception of **Pont Marie**, all the island's bridges were demolished and rebuilt numerous times. In 1614, Louis XIII laid the first stone of this five-arched bridge, engineered by Christophe Marie. Fifty houses were actually built on the bridge. Each had a ground floor with a shop and kitchen, an entresol, and three single-room upper floors. However, the great flood of 1658 submerged half of Paris, with tragic consequences. The floodwaters took out one of the bridge's piers, two arches, and part of the bridge houses, with some sixty persons and the possessions of a good many others. Communications between the island and the right-bank Saint-Paul quarter were not reestablished until 1659. Thereafter, Parisians realized that every bridge house could be swept away by floodwaters or rammed off its moorings by blocks of river ice. Numerous riverfront houses had a "water door" that opened out onto the Seine River. It was practical for suppliers, allowing them direct access to the service quarters: pantries, kitchens, etc. It was practical, too, for illicit romance, secret liaisons, and escapades.

Quai de Bourbon

We begin our tour on the north side of the island, on **Quai de Bourbon**. In August, when summer's heat is at its height, it's a delicious place for a stroll, with its quiet, old-fashioned charm.

A pleasant restaurant sits at **number 1**. Its iron gate is decorated with curling vines. This address is on the historical register and is a vestige

of an old cabaret called Au Franc Pinot. It was patronized by boatmen. This was also the spot where travelers coming into Paris from Melun would disembark. In 1716, the cabaret was shut down forever when a manuscript copy of Lagrange-Chancel's satirical poems targeting the Duke d'Orléans was discovered on the premises.

Number 9 was built in 1640. Behind its beautiful door is a grand staircase we may be lucky enough to see up close.

Ile Saint-Louis through the ages

It is hard to imagine that this island with its harmonious architecture used to be swampy and uninhabited. Curiously, no real interest was given to the island prior to the year 867 when King Charles the Bald gave it to Aeneas, the bishop of Paris.

It became the property of the Notre-Dame chapter. As a result, the island was called Notre-Dame up through the 18th century. Around the end of the 13th century, however, it was split in half (one part called Notre-Dame and the other the Ile aux Vaches) when a large trench was dug on the lines of present-day Rue Poulletier in order to strengthen the Charles V fortress walls about the city. The grassy islands with reeds and weeping willows were good grazing for cows. City-dwellers might occasionally venture out onto the island for a swim, to dump trash, to cast a line to fish, or to lay out freshly washed sheets to dry in the sun.

A period of construction and urban development was launched under Henri IV, as was a plan to connect the two islands with the right bank. In 1614 Louis XIII commissioned engineer Christophe Marie to fill in the channel between the two islets and build a bridge anchoring the island to the right bank. The construction company was also to work side by side with two land developers by the names of Le Regrattier and Poulletier. Financiers were their first clients. They were followed by high-ranking dignitaries, well-established artists, and Paris's wealthiest people. Lords and ladies took up residence on the waterfront, while artisans opened workshops on the narrow inner streets.

A century later, the island had fallen out of fashion and taken on a sleepy provincial feel. Further decline occurred in the 19th century as developers and wreckers tried to give it a new face. This led to the pointless creation of Rue Jean-du-Bellay in 1862; then came the construction of Pont de Sully in 1874, and the widening of Rue des Deux-Ponts in 1913. After World War II, the island became a prestigious place to live again, attracting painters, actors, singers, politicians, and wealthy lovers of old Paris. An address on the island was a mark of refinement.

▼ Quai d'Orléans

▲ 9 Quai de Bourbon

The Hôtel Le Charron is located at **13-15**. Jean Charron, having profited from his position as treasurer for the wars in Picardy, commissioned Sébastien Bruand to build it in 1637-1640. Since then, it has aged graciously. It changed hands several times around the close of the 17th century. Over the intervening centuries, painters were among its more illustrious residents: Jean-Louis-Ernest Meis-sonnier, Adolphe-Victor Geoffroy-Dechaume and Émile Bernard. The ceilings date from the time of the construction. The entire building is listed on the historical register.

The Hôtel de Jassaud at **19** is a mansion decorated with three sublime pediments. **25** was the home of Léon Blum (1872-1950), a writer, politician, and prime minister of France during the Popular Front in

1936-1937. Novelist Charles-Louis Philippe often came and went through the lovely carriage doors at **31**.

The house at **45** – dubbed the "centaur's house" due to two bas-relief medallions representing Hercules defeating Nessus – was frequented by Apollinaire, Derain, Marie Laurencin, Lucie Delarue-Mardrus, Dorgelès, Giraudoux, Mac Orlan, and Picasso. Residents included writers Charles-Louis Philippe and Drieu La Rochelle. Princess Bibesco, a writer born in Bucharest, died here. The home dates from 1659 and was designed by François Le Vau, the younger brother of the more famous Louis Le Vau.

Our stroll down Quai de Bourbon takes us to the **westernmost point** of the island. There we can take a rest on the prow of this great boat and watch barges plying the waters or immobile fishermen sitting on the banks. Paris seems to rock gently on the lapping river water.

We now reach **Pont Saint-Louis**. This bridge runs from Quai de Bourbon to Ile de la Cité, the neighboring island. From 1634 until the end of the 18th century, only wooden footbridges had ever been built on this spot. The first of the series was called Saint-Landry. City historian Jacques Hillairet related the following anecdote, "On June 5 of the same year [1634], three parish processions were vying to be the first to cross the bridge, bound for Notre-Dame. Shoving and pushing ensued, causing the balustrades and guardrails give way. Believing the bridge was collapsing, many people jumped into the river, while others were crushed to death. About twenty people died and about forty others were seriously injured." Due to this incident, a proclamation was issued forbidding the crossing of wooden bridges by processions anywhere in the kingdom.

In the winter of 1709, breaking ice in the river weakened the bridge. Its successor was painted red and simply named for its color, "*le pont rouge*" (red bridge). It, too, had to be demolished. It was rebuilt four times on the site of the present-day footbridge that connects the two islands.

▲ Medallion bas-relief on the façade of 45 Quai de Bourbon

Quai d'Orléans

Like all the other wharfs on the island, the **Quai d'Orléans** was constructed between 1614 and 1646. Facing south, it is most favored by the rays of the sun. In the early 20th century, residents of the island would often see poet Francis Carco slinking about. "There on the tip of the Ile Saint-Louis, where I had rented a furnished room on Quai d'Orléans, I felt like I was living in a provincial village. Barge trains would float past my windows and wake me early in the morning with their lugubrious mooing, rippling and echoing in the thick smoke billowing from the tugboats, which could suddenly block out the daylight."

▼ 22-32 Quai d'Orléans

Passing by **32**, **30**, **28**, then **22**, we will notice balconies, doorways, and ironwork. But let's take the time to lean on the parapet and admire the flying buttresses of Notre-Dame Cathedral, because this spot provides an exceptional view.

19th-century poet Félix Arvers was born at **12**. His most famous verses are in the sonnet dedicated to Marie Nodier, "*Ma vie a son secret, mon âme a son mystère...*" (My life has a secret; my soul, a mystery...). At the start of the Revolution, Pierre Royer-Collard, later elected to a seat on the Council of Five Hundred, resided here.

The neoclassical mansion at **6** dates from 1655. It first belonged to Antoine Moreau, then secretary to the king. In 1838, it was purchased by Count Ladislas Zamoyski to house the Polish Library, made up of donations from political refugees who had fled to France in 1830, after the first Polish insurrection against Russian rule. Today, the library has over 160,000 volumes, 8,000 engravings, 5,000 geographical maps, a fine collection of old manuscripts, scores by the composer Frédéric Chopin, and Chopin memorabilia. The archives of the three Polish insurrections are also kept here. The library also contains a small museum dedicated to the memory of Polish poet Adam Mickiewicz (who went into exile in Paris after 1832 and taught Slavic languages and literature at the Collège de France, where he was also a librarian). It was set up by his son in 1902.

Before the stone bridges, wooden footbridges with toll booths connected Ile Saint-Louis (formerly known as Ile Notre-Dame) to the left bank. The **Pont de la Tournelle** (1923) is a regrettable replacement of the older bridge built by Christophe Marie, which was embellished with niches and small columns. While the statue of Saint Genevieve, Paris's patron saint, by Paul Landowski shows good intentions, it is of little artistic interest.

Quai de Béthune

Let's continue walking down **Quai de Béthune**. The architect Le Vau designed many houses on this quay with ornate balconies, hence this street's earlier name "Quai aux Balcons," which stuck well into the 18th century. A great many façades remain intact despite the addition of floors to the buildings. Aside from their balconies, these homes often have handsome doorways, and wide staircases with elaborate handrails. Stairwells were often highly decorative, too. From outside on the sidewalks, it is hard to imagine the mansions' splendid inner courtyards and gardens.

The 1913 widening of Rue des Deux-Ponts required demolishing the corner building at 38. Cabaret de L'Ancre stood here; it was popular with people who plied the rivers and canals.

The building at **36** was home to several Nobel Prize winners. Physicist Marie Curie lived here from 1912 to 1934. René Cassin, the 1968 Nobel Peace Prize laureate, lived here from 1946 to 1976. At **32** and **30**, we should heed the architect Le Vau's advice and gaze at the balconies and the beautiful layout of the façades.

The 18th-century façade at **28** is particularly remarkable for its bas-reliefs of mythological figures.

Hôtel Hasselin stood at **24**. It, too, was designed by Le Vau for the king's steward of royal pleasures and ballet. His real name was Louis Cauchon (which happens to be a homophone for the French word for pig, *cochon*). He died of indigestion in 1662 after eating some 294 walnuts, reportedly for a bet. The 1930s demolition of this townhouse, one of the island's most beautiful, may be considered a scandal. The wrecking was ordered by cosmetics magnate Helena Rubinstein. She claimed that her old mansion's foundations were too shaky. The Beaux-Arts architect and administrators are also to blame for this loss. The new building, designed by Louis Süe, kept the magnificent door sculpted by 17th-century master Etienne Le Hongre. French President Georges Pompidou lived here. In 1974, his funeral service was held in the nearby Saint-Louis-en-l'Ile church.

A beautiful door at **22** is topped by a chimera with wings spreading ominously like those of a bird of prey. The mansion at **20** mirrors its neighbor and sister building at **22**; they are two halves of a harmonious 17th-century pair. The staircase has three bas-reliefs depicting the labors of Hercules. The ceiling decoration is attributed to Mignard.

▲ 24 Quai de Béthune

▲ 36 Quai de Béthune
◄◄ 20 and 22 Quai de Béthune

▲ Pont de Sully

While **18** belonged to the Marshall de Richelieu (the cardinal's great-grand-nephew), he never lived in it. The brilliant soldier frequented the royal court. His fine wit and elegance made him a favorite with the ladies and, consequently, won him a few stays in prison cells in the Bastille. The plot originally belonged to Philippe de Coulanges, whose granddaughter was Madame de Sévigné.

The magnificent Hôtel de Bretonvilliers included numbers **14** to **2**. It stood on the triangle formed today by Quai d'Anjou, Rue Saint-Louis-en-l'Ile, and Rue de Bretonvilliers. It fell victim to greedy speculators who had little respect for the past and were quick to demolish.

Before approaching Quai d'Anjou, let's take a look across the parapet. On the other side of the river we can see the famous restaurant Le Tour d'Argent. Looking left, we can see the Arab World Institute.

There are no more bathing beauties going in and out of the old boathouse public baths that once moored at the eastern end of the island. Under the reign of Louis-Philippe in the Second Empire, the Lambert baths' swimming school was a ladies-only institution. Admission cost sixty centimes, bathing suits went for fifty, bathrobes cost twenty-five, and swimming lessons were two francs and fifty centimes.

Alas, the boathouse/bathhouse sank when construction of **Pont de Sully** began. Paris Prefect Haussmann had dreamed of linking Boulevard Saint-Germain with Boulevard Henri-IV. The war of 1870 emptied the State's coffers and postponed the project. But neighborhood residents and wine merchants wanted their bridge. They got it in 1877. During the construction, vestiges of the Philippe-Auguste fortress walls were discovered, as was the mouth of a canal that carried water off the Bièvre River to the Saint-Victor abbey gardens. Located on the eastern tip of Ile Saint-Louis, this iron and stone bridge spans the Seine River twice. The first portion runs from Quai Henri-IV to Quai d'Anjou; the second runs from Quai de Béthune to the point where Quai de la Tournelle turns into Quai Saint-Bernard. The bridge was originally named Pont Saint-Germain, but was later named for Sully, the powerful minister who served King Henri IV, and who, being at the nearby Arsenal, was also a neighbor.

Quai d'Anjou

Of the four riverfront streets that surround the island, **Quai d'Anjou** is the one that has changed the least since it first went up. Located on the north side of the island, it was born from the unification of the Ile aux Vaches and the Ile Notre-Dame, and was named for the brother of Louis XIII, Gaston, the Duke d'Anjou. Its northern exposure gives it an austere and cold aspect that is counterbalanced by the unique architecture of its mansions, most of which were the work of Le Vau.

Practically every shade tree that once lined the street was swept away. A small green enamel plaque set in the stone of the parapet in front of **1 Quai d'Anjou** explains in three words: "CRUE JANVIER 1910." The great flood of January 1910 covered nearly the entire island.

Our attention is immediately directed to the lovely Hôtel Lambert at **1** and its neighbor at **3** that Louis Le Vau added for his personal use by integrating it into the quayside façade and decorating the ensemble with a balcony "running from one building to the other."

Jean-Baptiste Lambert got his wealth from speculation and from "managing public funds." In 1642, he commissioned Le Vau to design a home befitting his fortune. Death put an early end to his dream, however, and his brother Nicolas inherited the property. Le Vau's floor plan laid out the rooms in an innovative way, lining them up in a manner which would inspire the layout of Versailles Palace. His architecture is classical, not academic.

The Hôtel Lambert has preserved its rich interior. While the paintings by Le Sueur were dispersed (only a few medallions remain), Charles Le Brun triumphs in the Galerie d'Hercule with his monumental achievement, heralding his later creations at Vaux-le-Vicomte, the Louvre, and Versailles.

Among the residents who lived in the Lambert mansion were the Marquise du Châtelet who befriended Voltaire. He described his hostess as, "the only woman of her kind, a reader of both Ovid and Euclid with the imag-

ination of the former and the fairness of the latter." In her 1957 novel *Voltaire in Love*, English novelist Nancy Mitford paints the marquise as a libertine, telling a story about how she called a newly-hired valet up to her bedroom, his first day on the job: "While she was giving him orders, she took off her nightdress and stood naked as a marble statue."

Sold off, carved up, turned into a girls' boarding school, then a warehouse for military beds, the property was restored to its original glory after Prince Adam Czartoryski acquired it. Mickiewicz, Chopin, Delacroix, George Sand, and Charles de Montalembert were all frequent guests. Later, Cézanne painted here. We can thank Baron de Rédé, who bought it in 1947, for the preservation of this magnificent testimony to the elegance of the 17th century. French film star Michèle Morgan lived here. Today, the Hôtel Lambert is owned by Guy de Rothschild.

The small Hôtel Marigny at **5**, built in 1640, was home to Rennequin, the inventor of the hydraulic machine that pumped water for the fountains in Versailles. In 1903, writer Charles-Louis Philippe could be found here. A short time later, he moved to 31 Quai de Bourbon.

▲ Plaque at 1 Quai d'Anjou showing the level of the January 1910 flood

▼ Hôtel Lambert, 1 Quai d'Anjou

The house at **7**, owned by the Paris bakers' guild since 1843, used to be an annex of the Hôtel Lambert. In the 19th century, Honoré Daumier (an artist and lithographer) rented a third-floor flat at **9** for seventeen years. He used his studio for entertaining friends such as the painters Bonvin, Corot, Daubigny, Courbet, Millet, Delacroix, the historian Michelet, and the sculptor Geoffroy-Dechaume.

The 17th-century house at **13** was frequented by numerous artists and occupied by the painter Daubigny, one of Corot's friends. Sculptor Geoffroy-Dechaume had a studio here. **Number 15** was one of the richest homes on the island. It was probably built by Le Vau for Nicolas Lambert de Thorigny.

The Hôtel de Lauzun at **17** (see inset), attributed to Louis Le Vau, has sumptuous interiors decorated by Le Sueur and Le Brun. Today, it belongs to the city of Paris. It holds lavish receptions with waiters and lackeys

Hôtel de Lauzun

It seems likely that Le Vau designed Hôtel de Lauzun for a certain Charles Gruÿn, the son of an innkeeper who made a fortune with his cabaret À la Pomme de Pin (literally: the pinecone club) located on Ile de la Cité. It attracted the likes of Racine, Boileau, La Fontaine, Molière, Lully, Mignard, and Chapelle. Gruÿn thought nothing was too good for his interior décor. Elegant paintings and sculptures embellished the rooms. The ceilings and wood panels painted by Le Sueur and Le Brun have been conserved unaltered. Bas-reliefs, gilding, sculptures, and paintings by Mignard and Hubert Robert line the stairwell, the "Italian Room," the drawing rooms, and the music room. Gruÿn wasn't able to enjoy it for long. Colbert found him guilty of embezzlement in 1662 during his tenure as commissary officer for Louis XIV's cavalry.

The property was purchased by the Count de Lauzun, Antonin Nompar de Caumont, whom writer Saint-Simon described as having "the prettiest legs in the world, no letters, but great wit." He bought it after returning from his cell in the Pignerol fortress, where he spent ten years for having planned to marry the Grande Mademoiselle (a first cousin of Louis XIV). He finally did wed her secretly, but their stormy marriage ended after three years. The mansion was sold to the Marquis de Richelieu in 1685. The next owners were the Ogier family, followed by the Pimodan family. In the 19th century, Jérôme Pichon, the famous booklover, opened his home to artistic and literary celebrities. It was already fairly dilapidated by that time. Historian Jacques Hillairet wrote, "Window panes were broken, the stairs were wobbly and loose, the roof had

▲ Hôtel de Lauzun, 17 Quai d'Anjou

numerous patches, and the beautiful gilded and painted paneling had been covered with thick layers of stained and yellowing whitewash." Poet Charles Baudelaire's famed Club des Haschischins met there. Théophile Gautier, Barbey d'Aurevilly, Boissard, Meissonnier, Delacroix, Daumier, and sometimes even Balzac were all members in good standing.

in 17th-century garb, complete with powdered wigs.

Let's continue strolling down Quai d'Anjou, then return to **Quai de Bourbon** as far as **Rue Le Regrattier**, which we'll take to reach **Rue Saint-Louis-en-l'Ile**.

Rue Saint-Louis-en-l'Ile

We now enter the very heart of the island. Rue Saint-Louis-en-l'Ile is the island's business and religious center. Up to its renovation, middle class residents shared the street with shopkeepers. After Sunday Mass, there were lines outside the neighborhood pastry shop and delicatessen. The contractors who lived and worked around the courtyards here are now history. Today, as soon as the weather turns pleasant, the street is invaded by strollers and tourists who dispel any trace of the neighborhood's old village atmosphere.

The corner building at **61** was Les Anysetiers du Roy restaurant. Its sign *"Au Petit Bacchus"* (Little Bacchus's Place) was photographed by Eugène Atget in 1902. The establishment used to be a cabaret that was very likely frequented by jeu-de-paume players. The sign dates from 1665. It is the original sign and even survived a fire. Made of wood, it depicts a baby Bacchus straddling a wine barrel, holding a bottle in his left hand and raising a cluster of grapes to his mouth with his right. The storefront is on the historic register.

Gracing the street at **51** is a lovely 17th-century building. It has an elaborately carved doorway with a faun's head at the top and two sneering chimeras supporting the balcony. The mansion had a large garden that once continued all the way to Quai d'Orléans. In 1840, the State rented it for the archbishop's palace. It was from here that the archbishop of Paris, Monsignor Affre, set off for Place de la Bastille on June 24, 1848. His intention was to intervene between the provisional government's troops and the insurgents, but he was wounded and carried back to his mansion, where he died three days later. A decade later, the State turned this fine home into a police barracks! The garden space was then used to construct a rental building. With the exception of the staircase's handrail, little by little, all the interior décor was stripped and taken away. The facades overlooking the street and the courtyard, however, have remained intact.

The last court-tennis hall in Paris was located at **54**. Of course, it was closed long ago, but the building still has its 17th-century beams. An industrialist stored bakery ovens here for some time. Today, the structure has been turned into a hotel.

Gabriel Le Duc, then Jacques Doucet. The church was consecrated in 1726 under the name Saint-Louis-en-l'Ile. After the campanile was struck by lightning in 1740, a thirty-meter-high steeple with oval openings went up in its place.

This Jesuit-style church is astonishingly luminous. Corinthian pilasters grace the arched rows in the choir, which open onto the ambulatory. The sculptures in the nave are the work of Jean-Baptiste de Champaigne, and date from the 17th century. Playwright Jean Racine had his son baptized in this church, and Le Vau was married here.

Engineer Philippe Lebon, who resided at **12**, changed people's daily lives when he discovered the principles of gas lighting and gas heating, right here, in 1799.

▲ Saint-Louis Church, 21 Rue Saint-Louis-en-l'Ile

▶ 1 Rue Saint-Louis-en-l'Ile

◀ Berthillon ice-cream shop, 31 Rue Saint-Louis-en-l'Ile

Berthillon, the most famous ice-cream maker in Paris, does booming business at number **31**.

The clock at **21** sticks out like a sign, pointing to a church which used to be a small chapel. As it couldn't accommodate the growing neighborhood population for ever, the decision to construct a new church was taken in 1622. Completing the new place of worship took sixty-two years and a series of architects: François Le Vau,

At the end of the street at **1** is the old crossbowmen's residence which was actually a part of the Hôtel de Bretonvilliers. While it has hardly changed much, it did lose a bit of it picturesque flavor when *À l'Estacade*, a café and billiards room, was closed in the early 20th century, much to the chagrin of avid players.

Side Streets

Now follow your fancy, and stroll the side streets. At **4 Rue de Bretonvilliers**, the mansion and the street shared the same name. When Boulevard Henri-IV was laid out and cut a swath through the southeast tip of the island, wreckers had to tear down the beautiful mansion that had once belonged to Claude Le Ragois de Bretonvilliers, the biggest property owner on the island in 1636. All that remains to titillate our imaginations are engravings, floor plans, and paintings. The residence at 6 still has its original wooden staircase.

A few old houses line **Rue Poulletier**. In the 17th century, the Sœurs de la Charité convent was granted the property now located at number **5 bis**. A sign over the doorway announced that this was the girls' school belonging to the Saint-Louis parish sisters of charity. In 1677, **9** was the home of Philippe-Auguste Le Hardy, the Marquis de La Trousse, Mme de Sévigné's first cousin. Note the lovely windows with their wrought-iron railings gracing the façade at **12**. At **20**, a big door in Louis XIV style has two heads of Hercules in a lion skin. The escutcheon with palms has lost its coat of arms. The staircase inside is lovely.

Rue des Deux-Ponts was the first street opened on the island (1614-1620). The 1912-1913 street-widening program made it dull and banal. Old homes were demolished, taking away much of its charm and ambiance. Painter Émile Bernard, who lived in Hôtel Le Charron, did his utmost to prevent the devastation by petitioning the authorities. Although he had collected over a hundred signatures, including those of Rodin and Anatole France, his effort was to no avail. This explains why we see Louis XIII period homes on one side of the street and Third Republic period buildings on the other (from numbers **2** to **14**). At **10**, home to the Halphen foundation, there is a plaque in memory of the 112 residents of the building – including forty children – who were deported in 1942 and who died in Nazi concentration camps.

In the 18th century, one of the residents of this street was the prolific writer, tireless walker, and chronicler of the sights he saw in his travels, Restif de la Bretonne. The realistic descriptions he penned showed no leniency, though he had a penchant

▸ 5-bis Rue Poulletier
◂ 20 Rue Poulletier

▶ Rue des Deux-Ponts
◀ Rue Le Regrattier,
formerly called Rue de
la Femme-sans-Tête

for anecdotes. He was often taunted by passersby and gangs of children for his outlandish appearance. He died a pauper at the age of seventy-one on Rue de la Bûcherie.

Rue Le Regrattier has conserved a provincial ambience with its old houses. The northern block of the street was called Rue de la Femme-sans-Tête from 1680 to 1870 because of the sign that showed a decapitated woman holding a glass in one hand with the written slogan "*Tout est bon*" (everything is good).

Baudelaire bounded up the stairs at number **6** more than once to visit his beloved Jeanne Duval. He had moved her into a small apartment while he lived nearby at 17 Quai d'Anjou in the Hôtel de Pimodan (or Lauzun).

Rue Boutarel got its name from a Rue Saint-Louis dyer, a colonel in the national guard who had set up his workshop here. The creation of **Rue Jean-du-Bellay** in 1867 spelt the demise of the mansions of the west-

ern edge along Quai d'Orléans and Quai Bourbon.

This ends our walking tour. The hubbub of Paris doesn't seem to cross the Seine River, and, while you won't hear the ghost of a tugboat blowing its horn, you can still watch bobbing fishing lines, paddling flotillas of ducklings, and swallows swooping over the water. Standing at the prow, on Quai Bourbon, the maritime odors and the seagulls may set you to dreaming of other travels...

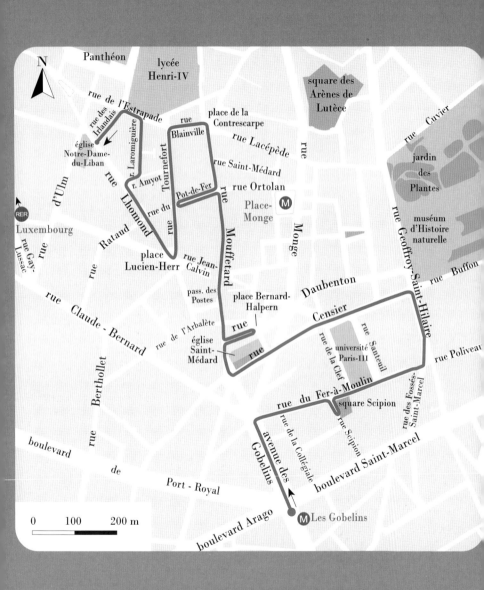

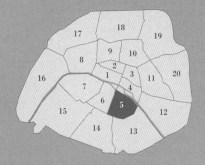

5th

On and Off Rue Mouffetard

▶ Start: Avenue des Gobelins,
metro Les Gobelins

▶ Finish: Rue Lhomond,
RER Luxembourg
or metro Place-Monge

Saint-Marcel and Saint-Médard are two ancient villages that sprang up at different periods on either side of the old bed of the Bièvre River, and then climbed the slopes of the valley around it. The last portions of the Bièvre were covered in the early 20th century. Today's Rue Mouffetard was the first stretch of the northwest-to-southeast Roman highway running from Lutetia (Paris) to Lugdunum (Lyon). Saint-Marcel and Saint-Médard were incorporated into the city in 1724. Prior to that, however, from the late Roman period to the Middle Ages, Parisians considered these villages as their havens of peace, places for the aristocracy to escape the noise and bustle of city life. The older of the two was Saint-Marcel (5th-6th centuries). In the early 9th century, a small hamlet formed around Saint-Médard church, but its first real growth occurred between the 12th and 15th centuries.

The Gobelins Crossroads

The **Gobelins crossroads** straddles the 5th and 13th arrondissements of Paris. It is located at the base of the Italie hill and sits beside the southeast valley of the Bièvre River. Three boulevards laid out by the 19th-century Paris Prefect Haussmann converge here (Arago, Port-Royal, and Saint-Marcel). Avenue des Gobelins was created in 1869 atop the old Rue Mouffetard, which used to go as far as today's Place d'Italie.

From the Early Middle Ages, this crossroads was practically the center of the town growing up around the oratory dedicated to Saint Marcel, the first native-son bishop of Paris, who was buried here in 436. The oratory was destroyed by Viking invaders around 887 and was not replaced by a church building until the early 11th century. The cloister of the new church sat just off today's boulevard Saint-Marcel and just opposite Rue de la Collégiale (numbers 3, 4, 5, and 6) where the church Saint-Martin-du-Cloître went up. It became a parish church in 1220.

In 1753, a gardener discovered fifty very old graves near the church. This was only the beginning. Up through the most recent archeological digs in the mid-1950s, nearly one thousand graves ranging from the 3rd century to the 17th century were uncovered on this site. The Gobelins crossroads and surrounding area turned out to be the home of the city's oldest Christian necropolis. Even before the future Saint Marcel was buried here in the 5th century, the space had been used for cases when Roman officials in Lutetia refused to grant burial rights within the city. The early necropolis then became a Merovingian cemetery, and later, a Carolingian one. Burials continued on this site up to the 17th century.

Down Rue du Fer-à-Moulin

Once past the main intersection, we will walk up **Avenue des Gobelins** with its interesting views of Montagne Sainte-Geneviève and the Pantheon. Past Rue du Petit-Moine, we will turn right onto **Rue du Fer-à-Moulin**. The name of this street in the Middle Ages was Rue Richebourg (literally: rich town) due to the noblemen's country estates lining the Bièvre River.

By the end of the Middle Ages, little remained of their fine mansions.

butcher shop and bakery of the Salpêtrière hospital, built a short walk away from the Saint-Marcel village. The hospital continued to bake its bread here until 1975.

Lovely spruce trees shade the cobblestone courtyard of the old Hôtel Sardini. To our right is the last vestige of this 16th-century residence: a brick and stone wall, the first of its kind in Paris. It has six arches, four of which were later walled up. Medallions with high-relief terracotta figures of warrior women grace the upper stretches of the arcades and give the mansion an Italian Renaissance feel.

Across the street from the mansion is the small **Square Scipion**. At the back of this square is an enamel tile mosaic depicting bakers hard at work, created by Müller and Charpentier (early 20th century). This square was laid out on a portion of the old Sainte-Catherine cemetery, opened in 1783 when the nearby Clamart cemetery reached capacity, and closed in 1824. The Clamart cemetery was bordered by Rue du Fer-à-Moulin and took up the block all the way to Rue des Fossés-Saint-Marcel.

▲ Hôtel Scipion-Sardini, 13 Rue Scipion

The only residence left standing is on the corner of Rue du Fer-à-Moulin, at **13 Rue Scipion**. It was the home of Sire Scipion Sardini. By the 17th century, it was being used as the main

This cemetery was built on the gardens of the old Hôtel des Catins, owned by the lords of Clamart. It began and remained a paupers' cemetery. Unclaimed bodies from the morgue of the Hôtel-Dieu hospital wound up here. The Clamart cemetery was bigger than the Cimetière des Innocents near Les Halles. By the early 19th century, however, the Clamart cemetery was being used less and less. In 1833, an anatomy lecture hall was built upon the common grave grounds. Medical students were rumored to come here to help themselves to human skeletons.

An Italian in the Queen's Court

Scipion Sardini came to Paris from his native Tuscany as a young man around 1535, practically in Catherine de Médicis's baggage. He made a fortune in France. He was given the title Count of Chaumont-sur-Loire, and pursued a brilliant career under Henri III as a collector of taxes imposed on inns and cabarets in the capital. Such a position sparked jealousy and hatred in the hearts of Parisians. They came up with this distich about him, *"Naguère sardine, aujourd'hui grosse baleine ; c'est ainsi que la France engraisse les petits poissons italiens."* (Once a sardine, now a big fat whale; this is how France fattens up little Italian fish.)

Notice the nicely restored old building **at the corner of Rue de la Clef** with its deep terrace-balconies.

Rue du Fer-à-Moulin soon runs into a small intersection where it crosses Rue des Fossés-Saint-Marcel and Rue Geoffroy-Saint-Hilaire. This was where the old Pont Livaux once spanned the Bièvre River. It lent its name to a nearby street, which, a trifle mangled, comes out today as Rue Poliveau.

Rue Geoffroy-Saint-Hilaire

In the Middle Ages, Rue des Fossés-Saint-Marcel ran beside the village's low rampart walls. By the 18th century, it and Rue Geoffroy-Saint-Hilaire were home to the capital's largest horse market. It stretched from one side to the other of today's Boulevard Saint-Marcel and went as far as Boulevard de l'Hôpital. The grand entrance to the horse market still stands at **5 Rue Geoffroy-Saint-Hilaire**, formerly Rue du Marché-aux-Chevaux (Horse-Market Street). It was built in 1760 on the orders of Sartine, a high-ranking police officer. In a chapter of *Les Misérables*, Victor Hugo gives a high-contrast description of the horse market neighborhood. "A person strolling into this area might have thought that this where Paris ended.

It was not, however, a solitary place, as there were passersby. It was not yet the country, as there were houses and streets. It wasn't the city, as there were ruts like those in the highways and grass grew in them. It was not a village, as the houses were too high. What was it then? It was an inhabited place where not a soul dwelt."

Nearby Rue Poliveau inspired two memorable fictional chase scenes. The first one is in Victor Hugo's Les Misérables: fearing Javert is about to find them, Jean Valjean and Cosette flee their hovel at 52 boulevard de l'Hôpital, and race across the Saint-Marcel quarter and beyond. The second famous chase scene is in the

▲ 11 Rue Geoffroy-Saint-Hilaire

◄ Building with deep terrace-balconies on the corner of Rue de la Clef and Rue du Fer-à-Moulin

◄ Entrance to the old horse market, 5 Rue Geoffroy-Saint-Hilaire

1956 movie *La Traversée de Paris*. The characters played by Jean Gabin and Bourvil leave Louis de Funès's black market headquarters for a memorable and action-packed race through the capital.

Rue Censier

Walking northwards along Rue Geoffroy-Saint-Hilaire, we soon cross **Rue Censier**, the continuation of Rue Buffon running towards Rue Monge. It is named not for a great man, but for the fact that it used to be a dead end. The Old French term for that was "*rue sans chief*," which, when pronounced quickly, came out "*rue censier*." In the Middle Ages, it started out at Rue Mouffetard and ran beside a portion of the Orléans palace. This royal estate, encompassing the higher lands of the Saint-Médard quarter and stretching all the way to the Bièvre's left banks, was formerly the property of Isabeau de Bavière, wife of Charles VI. In 1388, the queen sold it to her brother-in-law and lover, Louis, Duke d'Orléans. Dismantled at the end of the 15th century, the palace and grounds (like the neighboring Dormans-Beauvais that had belonged to a long line of bishops) were divided into lots as of 1530. Today, nothing remains of 17th- and 18th-century manors that once stood here. The Censier university restaurant at **3** has an odd, windowless façade tiled with black ceramic. Nearby buildings dating from the 1970s replaced the old buildings at **17** and **19**, which were vestiges of the Santerre family's brewery (one of the members of this family was a hero at the storming of the Bastille).

Past Rue de Santeuil, which was laid out in 1863, there once was a girls' orphanage, at numbers **21 to 25 Rue Censier**. It was founded in 1624 by Antoine Séguier, the uncle of the future Grand Chancelier of France Pierre Séguier. Louis XIV took an interest in the charity, promising to promote any craftsman who married an orphan from this home to the rank of master. The orphanage was shut down by the Revolution. In 1868, the building became a leather market, where tanners operating on the banks of the nearby Bièvre sold their wares. Until the 1950s, thousands of hides were piled up here for trading. They were salted and prepared for leather artisans elsewhere, particularly those in shops upstream.

At the end of the 19th century, photographer Charles Marville provided valuable documentation by photographing much of the old, poverty-stricken Saint-Marcel quarter.

Rue de la Clef runs behind the Censier school of arts and sciences building. The street begins at Rue du Fer-à-Moulin. **Between 12 and 14** of this street, formerly named Rue du Pont-aux-Biches (literally: Doe Bridge Street), a bridge of the same name used to span the Bièvre. A group of houses across the street are the last surviving examples of the type of

◂ Rue de la Clef

architecture in this neighborhood at the end of the 19th century.

Likewise, the two older buildings on the **corner of Rue Censier and Rue de la Clef** are typical of the old housing stock. **Rue Censier** continues past Rue Monge, the new frontier between the villages of Saint Marcel and Saint Médard. It skirts the southern side of Saint-Médard church and finishes its course at the foot of Rue Mouffetard.

Around Saint-Médard Church

At this spot, the Pont-aux-Tripes (now Rue Bazeilles) carried traffic on Rue Mouffetard over the Bièvre River and onwards to the "barrière" at Italie, where the Ancien Régime collected taxes on merchandise entering Paris.

According to the 6th-century chronicler Gregory of Tours, the first **Saint-Médard church** would later be built on this spot, where the apostle Denis, who arrived from Rome in the 3rd century, celebrated the Paris area's first Christian Mass. His flock was a humble group of farmers who were tilling the fertile Bièvre valley slopes. Saint Denis may never have actually entered Paris. Legend tells us he took refuge in the quarries dotting the plateau on the southern side of Montagne Sainte-Geneviève. The capital's first bishopric grew up in the area about the Bièvre River and Saint Marcel was its ninth bishop.

◄ Old house on the corner of Rue de la Clef and Rue Censier

The Saint-Médard Uproar

The events of December 27 and 28 in the year 1561 are often obliquely referred to in French as the "vacarme de Saint-Médard" (the Saint-Médard Uproar).

After the Colloquy of Poissy in 1561, pressed by her advisor Michel de l'Hospital, Queen Catherine de Médicis granted French Protestants the right to worship in a determined number of places. They were given two churches in Paris. One was in the old mansion that had belonged to Simon de Cramault,

the bishop of Reims who became a 15th-century Latin Patriarch of Alexandria. The house had just been leased by a certain Jean Canaye, a master dyer, a son-in-law of the Gobelin family and a staunch Calvinist. He lent it to his fellow Protestants as a place of worship.. On the afternoon of December 27, during the pastor's sermon, the bells of nearby Saint-Médard church began to ring loudly, interrupting the Huguenot service. When they went to complain, an angry

crowd of parishioners chased them out of the church. Armed Protestants came to defend their brothers. Several Catholics died as the church was sacked. The next day, Constable Anne de Montmorency led his troops into the Temple de Patriarches (which today is a gymnasium topped by a housing project). Montmorency set it on fire and hanged a few of the faithful. This violent incident prior to the opening of the Wars of Religion spelled the start of a long period of friction.

▲ Saint-Médard church
▼ Marsh scene decorating the façade of 134 Rue Mouffetard

components of the façade are from varying periods. The large stained-glass window in flamboyant Gothic style dates from the middle of the 15th century. The portico is 18th-century in style. While this church's nave with no transept dates from the late Middle Ages, its choir and its chapels are Renaissance, built some time around 1560. The church was not completed until a century later, and in 1775, the interior was entirely redone. The choir columns were carved and fluted, putting them in line with the style of that time. The apsidal chapels were built and the doorway was altered to give it a Louis XVI style. The church has two 18th-century paintings: *Le Vendeurs Chassés du Temple* (the money changers chased from the Temple) was commissioned from Natoire, although he was more famous for his mythological and love scenes, as well as his décors in the chateau of Versailles. Restout, decorator of the dome at the old Couvent des Génovéfains (today's Lycée Henri IV), contributed *La Multiplication des Pains* (the multiplication of the loaves). He, on the other hand, was known for his paintings with Biblical themes such as *Le Christ Guérissant les Paralytiques* (Christ Healing the Paralytic).

While there is no trace of the first Saint-Médard church, allegedly erected in the 7th century only to be destroyed by a Viking invasion, the town's second church was mentioned in a bull issued in 1163 by Pope Alexander III. It was listed as belonging to lands within the Sainte-Geneviève abbey's fief and was served by canons assigned by the abbey.

The church that we can visit today is, in fact, the third erected on this spot. It was dedicated to Saint Médard, who became bishop of Noyon in 530, then bishop of Tournai, then counselor to the Merovingian kings. Perhaps more than any other church in Paris, Saint-Médard retains its country charm. Its slate bell-tower, adorned with a Gallic rooster in addition to a cross, confers genuine, rustic simplicity.

The structure is indeed composite, taking into account the three periods in which it was built. Even the

The open-air market that spills onto the **esplanade of Saint-Médard** church is probably quite similar to the one that was located here in the Middle Ages - in perfect harmony with the church and its looming entrance. At times, the marketplace looks like a nonstop church bazaar. Merchants call out to each other and joke with shoppers. On the opposite side of the square in front of the church, at **134 Rue Mouffetard**, there is a noteworthy façade. It was designed in 1929 by the Italian painter Eldi Gueri. Between the windows on the entresol level are four admirable painted steel panels of country scenes. Above them, on an ochre background, deer, stags, and boars are depicted beneath a border of exuberant botanical motifs inspired by Italian Renaissance style.

Despite the omnipresent and appetizing layout of food in this market street, we should not forget that this neighborhood was long a center of political unrest. By the 17th century, it had become the last refuge of the wretched, and a veritable tinderbox. For example, during the Revolution, Gracchus Babeuf, whose Club des Égaux was located on Mount Sainte-Geneviève, often recruited partisans here. In 1848, as they did during the bloody week of the Commune in May 1871, the neighborhood residents set up barricades. There are records of one at the corner of Rue de l'Épée-de-Bois, just outside one of the most famous drinking establishments of the area (at number 91), which happened to give its name to this street.

In the late 1800s, anarchist Jean Grave ran his journal Les Temps Nou-

◄ 41 Rue Daubenton
► Walled-up door to the old Saint-Médard cemetery on Rue Daubenton

veaux from number **140**. His friends, the geographers and ideologues Pierre Kropotkine and Élisée Reclus, were on his team of editors. Nadar, Pissarro, and Signac volunteered to illustrate the paper from time to time.

We head back uphill to narrow **Rue Daubenton**, behind the church, and turn right. Formerly called Chemin d'Orléans-Saint-Marcel, it led to the Orléans royal hall. The entrance stood where present-day numbers **19 and 21** are. At **41** is the side door of the church. When it was looted by Protestants on December 27, 1561, this is where they burst in.

We now reach the old Place du Marché-des-Patriarches, now renamed **Place Bernard-Halpern**. On our right is the wall beside Rue Daubenton which has kept a trace of the cemetery door. It was walled up in 1732 after the famous case of the Saint-Médard convulsionaries (a case of collective hysteria over the grave of the Jansenist deacon named Pâris-see inset). The other doorway, also walled up, had been filled in a century earlier, before the commotion started.

Going up
Rue Mouffetard

We shall backtrack now to stroll up **Rue Mouffetard**. The curious name of this street goes back to Roman times. It refers to a small hill, then called *Montus Cetardus*, located on the other side of the Bièvre River. What should have been called *"rue du Mont-Cétard"* actually wound up being mangled and mispronounced as *"rue Mouffetard."* Other linguists, however, suspect that it was derived from the word *"mofettes,"* which refers to foul odors that rose from the banks of the terribly polluted Bièvre.

An old sign on the façade of **122** reads *"À la Bonne Source"* (the good spring). It seems to smile at its neighbor, one of the neighborhood's last great cafés, located at **116**. Over the entrance is a beautiful frieze with clusters of grapes in high relief. Two jovial Bacchus faces act as capitals on each end of the storefront.

By extending Rue de L'Arbalète towards the Marché des Patriarches in the 19th century, city planners demolished **115**, which was the entrance to the residence of Jean de Meulan, archbishop of Paris around 1350. Up to the Renaissance, all the odd-numbered addresses on the street were either noblemen's or clergymen's estates. Some prelates preferred these Bièvre-side estates to those in the Saint-André-des-Arts quarter to the northwest, where they were not granted quite as much land. Here, they had vineyards stretching all the way to the banks of the river. Some of the residents we can name are the bishops of the cities of Senlis, Châlons, and Beauvais. Another illustrious 14th-century resident was Ray-

mond du Temple, an architect of the Louvre in the time of Charles V. Notice that the façade of **103** bears a commemorative plaque of the Prussian siege of Paris in January 1871.

Across the street, an alley cuts through **104**; it is the Passage des Postes (1830). It finishes at Rue Lhomond (formerly named Rue des Postes). Lovers of French comic book literature make pilgrimages here. In *L'Affaire du Collier* (1965), the house to the left of the passage is the very spot chosen by author Edgar P. Jacobs as the location for the underground headquarters of the evil Colonel Olrik, the perennial adversary of Captain Blake from the Intelligence Service and his friend Professor Mortimer, a renowned physicist, heroes of the classic *Blake et Mortimer* series. The south side of Mount Sainte-Geneviève sits on a vast network of abandoned quarries that long served as hideouts and hazing grounds for Latin Quarter students.

The short Rue Jean-Calvin arrives beneath the recent buildings at **numbers 96-100**, just opposite Rue de l'Épée-de-Bois. For many years the space remained empty because a

► Passage des Postes
▼ Old sign on
122 Rue Mouffetard

major urban project was in the pipeline. The plan was to create an expressway connecting Montparnasse and Austerlitz train stations. It would have plowed through several streets in the fifth arrondissement, including Rue de l'Abbé-de-l'Épée, Rue Érasme, and Rue Calvin. A neighborhood-defense committee sprang up to contest the project, which would have shattered the ancient Saint-Médard district. Fortunately, the preservationists triumphed, and the plan was canceled.

A few steps before we reach the long, windowless façade of the Garde Républicaine building at **61**, let's look at **69**, an 18th-century house with two mansard-roofed floors. It was built on the site of the 15th-century Hôtel de Mainville. From 1830 to 1848, it was home to one of the Latin Quarter's most important revolutionary clubs. Vidocq, a famous ex-convict who became an investigating officer, reportedly came here from time to time to eavesdrop on their plots. The singer Fréhel (a prewar Edith Piaf of sorts) used to belt out her realist ballads at the Vieux Chêne in the 1920s. It is still a bar, awaiting its next star.

◄ Garde Républicaine building on 61 Rue Mouffetard

▲ 69 Rue Mouffetard

The military barracks mentioned above first opened in 1821, taking over the estate of the Couvent de la Miséricorde de Jésus, founded in 1652. The convent was entirely devoted to caring for the sick and the indigent. It received financial and moral support from Françoise d'Aubigné, who became the Marquise de Maintenon, the lady who secretly wed Louis XIV.

Opposite the military installation, at **76**, is one of the largest public libraries in the arrondissement. Previously called *La Maison pour Tous*, it was the Mouffetard village cultural center. With the gradual disappearance of most of the street's old pubs, we have seen a repeat of the phenomenon that occurred in the Saint-Séverin neighborhood, where a whole new geography of Mediterranean cuisine has sprung up. Vesuvius pizzerias and Aegean taverns await the patronage of hungry passersby. All this roasting on Rue Mouffetard, however, cannot equal the tremendous output further north on Rue de La Huchette, in the Saint-Séverin area.

From Rue du Pot-de-Fer to Place de la Contrescarpe

Let's turn left onto **Rue du Pot-de-Fer**, for a brief incursion into a street whose name conjures up images of old kitchen utensils. The splendid **fountain** built in 1671 on the corner replaced a medieval well, and was fed by the Arcueil aqueduct. Notice the lovely 18th-century doorway at **7**. This street carries on to the Lhomond neighborhood located just beside the Mouffetard area, and ends after running beside the imposing convent walls of Les Filles de Sainte-Aure on neighboring Rue Tournefort.

Let's return to **Rue Mouffetard**, where we will turn left. Number **38** faces Rue Saint-Médard, a 16th-century street laid out on the grounds of the old estate of Jacques de Pacy, lord of Ablon. In the 1820s, this house on rue Mouffetard was a gathering place for masons from the Creuse region. There was never a shortage of social venues in this popular neighborhood. Let's not overlook the famous ragmen's cabaret at **23**. During the Empire, it attracted a horde of vagabonds and tramps – a crowd that seemed to foretell all the most dire observations of Léon Daudet, the editorialist of the daily newspaper *Action Française* a century later. In his *Paris Vécu* (1910), he penned a scathing description of the poverty in the streets here. "Rue Mouffetard has the degree of filth, sordidness, stench, ancientness, animation, and raw col-

orfulness to make it one of the most remarkable streets of Paris. Tossed together in one coagulated magma one finds rag-pickers, drug dealers, hussies, pimps, muggers, and ageless, reeking, sexless creatures covered in rags of shades of green and yellow... Suddenly, from out of this rotten lot, steps a pretty girl with a short bob and spit curls, an impish face, a Mary Magdalene from the gutters."

Despite appearances, the neighborhood has undergone major changes since the end of the 1960s. Gentrification forced out the old inhabitants as rents skyrocketed, soon after the tramps themselves started deserting the Contrescarpe and the "Mouff'." Today, the stretch of the Mouffetard area between Saint-Médard and the Contrescarpe has become a sort of suavely picturesque set, or background, with artificially-maintained charm. The street was used as for certain outdoor scenes in Éric Rohmer's 1959 film *Le Signe du Lion*, as well as Krzysztof Kieslowski's 1993 film *Three Colors: Blue*.

Place de la Contrescarpe

Our stroll brings us at last to **Place de la Contrescarpe**. The sidewalk cafés always look inviting. This square was created in 1852 when a group of condemned buildings were demolished. In the Middle Ages, it was located in a projecting part of the Porte Bordelles, a gateway into Paris which for centuries had been very animated. In medieval times, it was a noisy transshipping site. Inns and cabarets with good – and bad – reputations opened in the area and did booming business.

▲ 7 Rue du Pot-de-Fer

▶ Formerly the Filles de Sainte-Aure convent on the corner of Rue du Pot-de-Fer and Rue Tournefort

A local named Antoine du Baïf met with his fellow Pléiade poet friends in one such establishment called *La Maison de la Pomme de Pin*. The tavern was mentioned in the Parisian itineraries of Pantagruel and Panurge in the works of Rabelais. The establishment's name was engraved in Gothic letters on the façade of **number 1**, yet the entrance to the old tavern was likely situated on the corner of Rue Mouffetard and present-day Rue Blainville, where, nowadays, the barmen at Requin Chagrin pour draft beers and rum to slake their patrons' thirst.

Looking west, to the other side of the square and Rue Blainville, is a mirthful, 18th-century sign that reads "Au Nègre Joyeux." This old chocolate-shop sign shows a black youth being served a cup of cocoa by a pretty maid.

For thirty years, the Contrescarpe changed little and continued to fit Léo Malet's description with its "touching and provincial air, its Vespasian urinal, its metro-ticket booth, its tree-lined center." Recent rehabilitation gave the square a clean sweep and a ridiculous little fountain, a reduced replica of the one on Place Saint-Médard. Yesteryear's tramps fled the places they helped make picturesque once they became tourist havens.

From Rue Blainville to Place Lucien-Herr

We begin the last portion of our stroll on **Rue Blainville**, formerly named Rue de la Contrescarpe-Saint-Marcel. It was then a lane running on the outer rim of the trenches of the medieval fortress walls built under Charles V.

The **odd-numbered** side of the short street has conserved many of its old low-rising structures with mansard attics. The first workingmen's lending library, located at **9**, was founded in 1862 by typographer Jean-Baptiste Girard. This area located near the ancient convents on Rue Saint-Jacques was also a hotbed of religious fervor. Catherine Théot, also known as the "mother of God," was one of those exalted souls who impassioned laymen. She and her followers met at **11**, on the corner with Rue Tournefort. But tragedy awaited them all. In June 1794, these religious fanatics met their match in the fanatic revolutionaries perpetrating the Reign of Terror. Aside from the "mother of God," the entire group was guillotined; their leader died imprisoned at the Conciergerie.

▲ 1 Place de la Contrescarpe

▶ An old sign on Place de la Contrescarpe

► View of the Panthéon from Rue Blainville

▼ 3 Rue de l'Estrapade

Rue Blainville opens onto a tiny square providing a very pretty view of the Lycée Henri-IV and the Panthéon. To the left is the start of **Rue Tournefort**, which leads us southwards to a different part of the Saint-Médard area. A few yards off this street, you can see **3 Rue de l'Estrapade**, where Diderot lived for several years. The philosopher was arrested in his own home in 1749 after his atheistic *Lettre aux Aveugles* caused a great scandal. He was locked up for a few weeks in the Château de Vincennes, and Rousseau came to visit him. He had begun working on his *Encyclopédie* two years previous to his arrest.

Time seems to have stopped somewhere in the mid-19th century for this provincial village standing between the Saint-Jacques and Mouffetard areas. It sprang up around Rue Lhomond and the **Rue Tournefort**, formerly called Rue Neuve-Sainte-Geneviève. With only a few exceptions, all the housing stock dates from the 18th century and the early 19th. The **odd numbers** of this street are old three-story houses with mansard roofs, such as **25**, once the home of

► 25 Rue Tournefort

young Prosper Mérimée, when his father was a teacher at the Lycée Henri-IV.

The large Couvent des Filles de Sainte-Aure, founded in 1690, stood at **18**. With the substantial support that the convent received in 1753, it bought up all the properties between Rue Tournefort, Rue Pot-de-Fer, and Rue Lhomond (then called Rue des Postes). Far from being an order that excluded the world, the Augustinian community of sisters made helping girls their main mission. However, they were not always successful in keeping them on the righteous path, as witnessed by the fact that despite her long stay in this convent, Jeanne Bécu later became the Comtesse du Barry, the official mistress of Louis XV. The convent was closed during the Revolution. The estate was bought in 1814 by the Benedictine order of Adoration Perpétuelle du Saint-Sacrement. It remained in their possession through the 1960s.

Numbers **19 and 19 ter** belonged to the Filles-Saint-Thomas, a community originally from Toulouse. In 1642, they moved into a part of the Hôtel

du Bel-Air that had gardens extending as far as Rue Mouffetard. Vestiges of it can be seen in the courtyard.

Once past the intersection with Rue du Pot-de-Fer, we enter the part of the street where Balzac, in his 1835 novel *Le Père Goriot*, located the famous Pension Vauquer, where "there is such a steep and treacherous grade descending to Rue de l'Arbalète that horses rarely go up or down it." The topography has not changed since 1820. The old house at **30** is generally considered to be the one that Balzac (the author of *La Comédie Humaine*) described as "embracing a little garden in such a way as to fall at a right angle to the street."

▲ Place Lucien-Herr
➤ 30 Rue Tournefort

the Mouffetard area. The prow-like promontory overlooks the little square where the restaurant Chez Léna et Mimile still proudly stands.

From Rue Lhomond to Rue de l'Estrapade

Setting out onto **Rue Lhomond**, which, on the other side of the intersection, goes down to Rue de l'Arbalète, we will head right and go as far as Rue d'Ulm. Formerly called Rue des Poteries, Rue des Pots, and Rue des Postes, in Roman times and in the Middle Ages, Rue Lhomond was lined with pottery shops. Local potters were taking their clay from the top of Montagne Sainte-Geneviève. In 1867, the street was named for Charles Lhomond (1727-1794), the

Be sure to stop a moment and notice something unusual for Paris: starting from **28 and 30** on Rue Tournefort, there are steps leading up to the buildings' front doors. As mentioned earlier, the street joins up with Rue Lhomond to make the delightful **Place Lucien-Herr**, a little square shaded by purple-blossomed paulownia trees. This particularity was caught by the artful eye of Robert Doisneau, who took many photos of

◄ Rue Lhomond

▶ Saint-Esprit seminary, 28 Rue Lhomond

famous grammar professor at the Collège du Cardinal Lemoine.

The houses from **45 to 41** appear to mirror those we saw earlier on Rue Tournefort. They have that same humble, provincial look with three or four steps leading up to their tiny front porches. In the rear of the courtyard at **45**, you may be lucky enough to spy a modest 18th-century mansion. Across the street from these old houses, the elementary school at **36** was built on the site of the old Collège Rollin, opened in 1826 by the city of Paris on the very site of an educational institution founded by former teachers of the Collège Sainte-Barbe. Historian Michelet taught at this establishment, which took over the Augustinian sisters' convent buildings after the Revolution.

Moving down Rue Lhomond, we soon cross Rue du Pot-de-Fer and **Rue Rataud**. Formerly called Rue des Vignes, Rue Rataud has carried traffic southwards to Rue Claude-Bernard since 1862. All that is left of the iron gate that used to close the street's entrance to Rue Lhomond is a long metal bar with curved rake-like spikes. Names can be deceiving, however. "Rataud" may be pronounced exactly like râteau (rake in English), but it was actually named for the district's mayor in 1870.

Narrow **Rue Lhomond** seems to be crushed by the high eastern façade of the Saint-Esprit seminary, which

has its entrance at **28**. While we cannot visit this impressive building, or its chapel built by Chalgrin, we can admire the majestic façade that is plumb with the street. Atop the towering doorway is a high relief by Duret of a baptizing missionary and an evangelizing missionary.

On another corner of this intersection, at **33**, we can see into the Résidences du Panthéon. This stunning garden once belonged to the Benedictine Convent of Saint-Sacrement, which in 1814 replaced the Sainte-Aure convent. The present-day property, containing a few of the old convent buildings on the east side, dates from the early 1960s. The angled entrance is the spot Victor Hugo chose in his first version of Les Misérables (entitled Les Misères in 1847) for the episode in which Jean Valjean and Cosette scale a convent wall to escape the dastardly Javert and his officers. Past the mansion at **27** the sidewalk widens a bit, and, there, behind three poplar trees, stands a lovely home on the corner of Rue Amyot at number **7**.

The 16th- and 17th-century names of Rue Amyot, Rue Laromigu-

◀ Rue Rataud
▼ 27 Rue Lhomond

ière and Rue des Irlandais might make you regret the simpler and more colorful names in this old medieval quarter where the Philippe-Auguste fortress walls once stood. They were respectively named: Rue du Puits-Qui-Parle (Talking Well Street), Rue des Poules (Hen Street), and Rue du Cheval-Vert (Green Horse Street). Despite the feverish Latin Quarter bustle and the noisy crowds along Rue Mouffetard, this tiny area has somehow managed to retain its tranquility and quaintness through the centuries.

In Roman times, a certain number of villas were built in this area. A small portion of a Roman wall with its decorative elements was uncovered during an archeological dig at **3 Rue Amyot**. It was here in 1614 that the third Protestant cemetery authorized by the 1598 Edict of Nantes was laid out. It was located at **8** on the corner lot of Rue Laromiguière. Some of the members of the big family of Gobelin tapestry makers were buried here. The cemetery was closed in 1685. Around 1830, physicist Gay-Lussac lived at **10**. When they carried him home one evening, his face covered in blood due to an explosion he had accidentally set off in his college laboratory at the École Polytechnique, this is where they brought him. Another tragedy rocked the neighborhood. The day Amadeo Modigliani was buried in the spring of 1920, his young mistress Jeanne Hébuterne (called "Coconut" by her Montparnasse artist friends) jumped out a sixth-floor window at number **5**.

Rue Laromiguière, named after a late 18th-century philosopher, will now take us to **Rue de l'Estrapade** which ends between two old mansions. The one at **7** was home to two writers who died fighting valiantly in the first weeks of World War I: Charles Péguy and Louis Pergaud, the author of La Guerre de Boutons. Filmmaker Alain Resnais shot part of his movie La Guerre est Finie (The War is Over, 1966) at neighboring number **9**. The quaint old sign of a coffee roasting shop still graces the street, but the building has been turned into a pleasant apartment building.

Humanist and pamphleteer Paul-Louis Courier lived in the stylish little house at **11** until 1791. As an enemy of the Revolution, he was forced to flee to his native region of Tours, where he was assassinated in 1825.

Rue des Irlandais

We shall soon turn left onto **Rue des Irlandais**. Its old name, Rue du Cheval-Vert, came from the sign on a local dyer's shop. At the end of the street at **5**, we will enter the Collège des Irlandais de Paris. This Irish establishment, now a cultural center, has stood in the Latin Quarter since the end of the Middle Ages.

The Collège des Irlandais is one of those havens of peace and greenery which are so hard to find in Paris. A Celtic harp, the symbol of Ireland, stands over the threshold, which leads into a vast courtyard shaded by chestnut trees. To the right of the entrance at the end of the outdoors gallery is the door to the college's chapel (18th century). An imposing Virgin Mary and Jesus child watch over the chapel from the rear. On the right-hand side, there are portraits of Saint Patrick, the patron saint of Ireland, and other major figures of the community.

▲ Old sign on Rue de l'Estrapade

Collège des Irlandais

The Collège des Irlandais, established here in 1769, is the last vestige of the group of foreign student colleges that began moving into this quarter. The Irish community had formed in 1578. Under the leadership of Waterford resident John Lee, it took quarters at the Collège de Montaigu at the end of Rue Valette.

In 1677, as several years had passed since the end of the Irish Confederate Wars and the Wars of the Three Kingdoms, the college's membership had grown significantly. Louis XIV, who had just welcomed James II to the court in Saint-Germain, granted them the old Collège des Lombards on Rue de la Montagne-Sainte-Geneviève.

Nearly one hundred years later, the Irish in Paris moved into this great house where they were soon joined by English Catholics from the seminary on 26 Rue des Postes as well as by Scotsmen from the school located on Rue Cardinal-Lemoine. Their building was confiscated in the Revolution, then returned to them in 1805. During the 1870 siege of Paris, it served as a hospital and was very nearly destroyed by Prussian cannon fire. In the spirit of Christian brotherhood, the establishment took in Polish clergy returning from World War II concentration camps. Since then, there have always Polish seminary students here. Karol Wojtyla, who later became Pope John Paul II, stayed several times in the old college.

◄ Collège des Irlandais

Rue des Irlandais enters the top of **Rue Lhomond** right in front of the Curie Institute and the physics laboratories of the École Normale Supérieure, where Alfred Kastler carried out his experiments on optical pumping in the 1950s and 1960s, leading to the development of lasers. These buildings and the neighboring ones at **10 to 26** rue Lhomond were erected between 1925 and 1935 on the site of the École Préparatoire Sainte-Geneviève (founded by Jesuit fathers in 1854). When the Jesuits returned to France after being banished in 1762, they had lost all their centers of learning; their Collège Louis-le-Grand and their seat located on Rue Charlemagne had been turned into great secondary schools. While they were erecting a new church at 33 Rue de Sèvres, the Jesuits were also opening a preparatory school for engineers, better known as the "École de la Rue des Postes" and popularized in all the late 19th-century French literature. The old school's chapel is now used by the Maronite church and called Notre-Dame-du-Liban. Its entrance is on Rue d'Ulm.

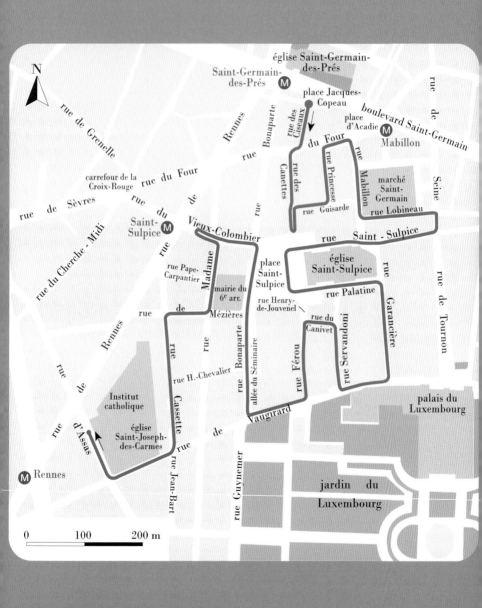

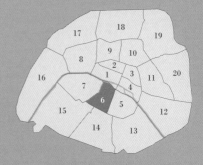

6th

The Saint-Sulpice Area

▶ Start: **Place Jacques-Copeau, metro Saint-Germain-des-Prés or Mabillon**

▶ Finish: **Rue d'Assas, metro Rennes or Saint-Sulpice**

Two ancient Gallo-Roman roads frame the Saint-Sulpice neighborhood. To the north is the ancient Rue du Four, formerly called the Chemin d'Issy et de Sèvres. In the Middle Ages, this was the natural extension of Rue Saint-André-des-Arts and Rue de Buci, beyond the city ramparts. It keeps its name between the present-day Carrefour Mabillon (Place d'Acadie) and Carrefour de la Croix-Rouge where it becomes Rue de Sèvres.

On the south side of the neighborhood, Rue de Vaugirard shares basically the same outline as the old Roman road from Lutetia (Paris) to Dreux (83 km west of Paris). The limit between the Saint-Sulpice and the Notre-Dame-des-Champs neighborhoods has become a bit blurred, however, due to recent urban development.

If you stroll regularly through the 6th arrondissement, you get a sense of how religion is the unifying element and cement of the entire southern part of the Saint-Germain sector. This is especially true from the mid-18th century and the construction of the new Saint-Sulpice church. Through the ages, all the convents and oratories have disappeared. The flame, however, has been taken up by religious

teaching institutions. The sale of religious articles, long a specialty of this part of Paris, has sharply declined. A few shops continue to operate, carrying on the tradition of selling articles that locals long referred to pejoratively as "saint-sulpiceries." Christian bookshops are another noticeable feature of the neighborhood.

From Place Jacques-Copeau to Rue des Canettes

We suggest starting the stroll at **Place Jacques-Copeau**, a quaint square located beside Boulevard Saint-Germain and across from the Abbaye de Saint-Germain-des-Prés where you will find the interesting **statue** of Diderot, sculpted by Jean Gautherin in 1884 for the centennial of the philosopher's death. With his relaxed body and vivacious expression, you might think Diderot was enjoying a witty conversation with someone interested in hearing his dogma-free points of view.

Narrow **Rue des Ciseaux** takes us to **Rue du Four**. Of all the street names that it has carried throughout the centuries (Chaussée du Roi, Rue de la Maladrerie, etc.), its 13th-century name *Vicus Furni* (oven street) has stuck, for the French name is a literal translation. Back then, the neighborhood residents were all required to come bake their bread in the community ovens owned by the abbey that stood at the corner of this street and present-day Rue de Rennes until 1470. As a religious power, the Saint-Germain-des-Prés community also had all the prerogatives of a lord, minus the military might. The bread trade has ended, but

▸ Statue of Denis Diderot on Place Jacques Copeau

it was a happy coincidence when, in 1932, Mr. Poilâne founded his famous gourmet bakery just steps away from Rue du Four at 8 Rue du Cherche-Midi in 1932. The former name of nearby Rue Madame was Rue Gindre (an old French word for baker's boy) and is a reminder of the area's baking history.

Three things greatly changed the aspect of this street: the construction of Boulevard Saint-Germain in 1878, the creation of Rue de Rennes at about the same time, and the widening of Rue du Four in the early 20th century. It has lost its old-fashioned charm as a narrow, bustling street; in its time, it must have had a look and feel similar to Rue de Buci or Rue Saint-André-des-Arts today. A few old façades on Rue du Four remind of us its distant past. But Haussmann-period architecture and, to a greater degree, the moderate-income housing of the 1930s, changed the face of this street which, from the mid-16th century, had to be paved due to the heavy traffic.

Between Rue du Four and Place Saint-Sulpice, there is a labyrinth of tiny, narrow, original streets that make up a veritable enclosure in this neighborhood. It is merely a three-block area, but while strolling through it, you feel as if you can get lost in the centuries-old ambiance. The "reserve" is framed to the north and south by Rue du Four and Rue Saint-Sulpice, respectively, to the east by Rue Mabillon, and to the west by Rue des Canettes. Rue Princesse dead-ends at Rue Guisarde. This old working-class neighborhood remains authentic. It is ancient now. Development began in the 13th century. Rue des Canettes dates back to 1260. Growth occurred in the 15th century in perfect parallel with the success of the

nearby Saint-Germain fair. This and the Saint-André-des-Arts neighborhood are the two 6th-arrondissement areas where the ambience has changed little over the centuries. The main business draws today are the restaurants and wine bars that line the sidewalks.

Liquids have given old **Rue des Canettes** all its color. Its very old name [literally: Ducklings Street] comes from a sign that featured the young aquatic birds. The sign is no longer, but at number **18** there is an early 18th-century bas-relief medallion that keeps the memory alive. It was on this street at **8**, back in 1840, that the "Cénacle des Buveurs d'eau" (The Water-Drinkers' Club) met under the leadership of one Henri Murger, the author of the famous Scènes de la Vie de Bohème. An incident of far greater historical importance, a pre-Revolution plot as murky as the riverbed of the Seine, yet involving a scandalous, scintillating diamond necklace, was hatched by a man who moved to **17** in 1820, many years after he and his wife discredited the French monarchy with the famous diamond necklace affair. That man was the Count de La Motte.

◄ 18 Rue des Canettes
▼ 2 Rue des Canettes

From Rue des Canettes to Rue Mabillon

A café (yet another liquid element) on the corner of Rue des Canettes and **Place Saint-Sulpice** takes up part of the building that replaced the Académie Royale de Manège, which provided an education and boarding to the sons of France's most illustrious families in the 17th and 18th centuries. It was demolished when the square was created.

Like other establishments in the Saint-Germain district, this café could have given itself a pompous name, but in choosing the humble epithet **"Café de la Mairie"** (the café by city hall), it deliberately bucked a bombastic, self-aggrandizing trend in the profession. It was a winning choice. As a sort of antihero in a guild that has had it share of prestige and stars (particularly in this neighborhood of Paris), this establishment is one of the most charming in the area. Its spacious terrace is shaded by plane trees that create a refreshing place to sit on hot summer days. This ordinary café is frequented by ordinary people. Georges Perec, in his *Tentative d'Épuisement d'un Lieu Parisien*, transformed it into a "watchtower" to describe Place Saint-Sulpice during three days of February 1974. Director Christian Vincent paid homage to the site by choosing the upper dining area with its moleskin-upholstered seats for the location of certain scenes in his 1991 movie La Discrète (The Discreet), a fitting description of his own personality.

Rue Guisarde was created in 1620 on the site where the Hôtel de Sancerre and the Hôtel de Roussillon once stood. It leads to Rue Mabillon.

▲ Café de la Mairie, Place Saint-Sulpice

Its name may be derived from the Guise family's name. In the 1580s, during the time of the Catholic League, there were many partisans of the Guise family in this neighborhood.

Nearby **Rue Princesse** was named in honor of Catherine of Lorraine, sister of Henri le Balafré ("Henry the Scarred"), the Duke de Guise whom Henri III had assassinated in 1588 in the Château de Blois. The street has kept its 17th-century charm. The old houses with their narrow façades have high windows that look out onto the street, as if astonished it is no longer an alley. The ambience here is as charming and warm as on Rue des Canettes. In fact, this tiny three-block area off Place Saint-Sulpice is Saint-Germain's equivalent of the Latin Quarter's Rue de la Huchette, in the community around Saint-Séverin church.

During the Reign of Terror, business was booming for pubs on these two streets, which had been renamed Rue des Sans-Culottes and Rue de la Révolution. As at the nearby Café Procope, people gathered here to catch up on the latest news and to solve the world's problems... During the massacres of September 1792, the sinis-

▶ Sunken courtyard on Rue Mabillon

ter Capt. Stanislas-Marie Maillard sent in troops to chase out nonjuring priests, "enemies of the interior."

The first teaching institution in the Saint-Sulpice and Notre-des-Champs area was established in 1688 by Jean-Baptiste de La Salle, who founded the first of his many schools for indigent girls at **12 Rue Princesse**. His commitment to the religious education of the poor had taken shape as the Institute of the Brothers of the Christian Schools in 1680, which now runs schools in 82 countries. A nonprofit branch of the lay organization operated a brandy-making concern in Napa Valley, California from 1882 to 1989.

A stroll down Rue Princesse wouldn't be complete without a bow to Jean-Baptiste Chardin, the 18th-century painter of the family life of the bourgeoisie, depicted as sweet, harmonious, and serenely poetic. He rented a house on the corner of Rue du Four until the death of his first wife in 1735. In 1744, he and his second wife moved into **13**, where they lived until 1757.

▲ Chez Castel, 15 Rue Princesse

▼ Marché Saint-Germain

After the rise and fall of the great basement jazz clubs in the 1950s, Saint-Germain-des-Prés' golden age, came the trend of private clubs. Two of the most prestigious added sparkle to this street. The one at **15** Rue Princesse naturally called itself Le Club Princesse, but regulars referred to it as Chez Castel. Meanwhile, Régine, up on Rue du Four, opened her first exclusive Paris nightclub in an old basement jazz club under Café La Pergola, now a fashion boutique.

At the intersection, a right onto **Rue Mabillon** will take us to an age-old trading center: known in the Middle Ages as the Foire Saint-Germain, it became the Marché Saint-Germain after the Revolution. Across the way from the market is the little Musée du Compagnonnage devoted to its wood craftsmen. A commemorative plaque honors "Tourangeau l'intrépide," the president of the "Duty and Freedom" faction of this historical and influential woodworkers' guild, arrested and deported in 1944 to Mauthausen. At this spot, in a courtyard below, you can see the level of the ground in the Middle Ages.

The Saint-Germain Fair

Since the 12th century, this site has always been a market place. However, in 1486, the abbots of Saint-Germain ordered huge buildings with superb beams to be erected, on a block containing inner aisles lined with shops called loges in French (lodges). Each loge had a ground-floor boutique and bedroom on the floor above. Between fairs, these shops were rented to merchants. To avoid competing with the Lendit Fair in Saint-Denis, the Saint-Germain Fair was always held from February 3 to Palm Sunday. It attracted German and, above all, Italian trade to Paris, after the fairs in Champagne began to decline and the business hub shifted to the big marketplaces in Flanders. The Saint-Germain Fair was a major source of income for the Saint-Germain abbots, who taxed every transaction from merchandise to entertainment and hospitality. This included gambling halls and drinking establishments,

not to mention dancing-bear and tightrope acts. In the 17th century, an Armenian named Pascal opened the city's first establishment serving coffee; the Sicilian Procope learned the art of waiting on tables from him, before embarking on more grandiose ambitions of his own. In the wee hours of March 17, 1762, gusting northerly winds fanned a terrible fire that destroyed the block of wooden market buildings. They were rebuilt in 1763, but the marketplace had lost its soul. It closed down in 1786, well before the Revolution banned fairs. The city of Paris acquired the large lot in 1806. A small part remained a marketplace. It was rebuilt in the years 1813-1818. This space was then greatly reduced around 1900, and finally torn down in the 1970s. The new Espace Saint-Germain is but a tiny portion of the extensive fairgrounds, which, back in the 17th century, ran all the way to the future Rue de Tournon.

Rue Saint-Sulpice

After strolling along the south side of the market down **Rue Lobineau**, we will turn right onto **Rue de Seine** to reach **Rue Saint-Sulpice**. This very old east-west artery connects the Odéon quarter to the Saint-Sulpice quarter, forming the northern border, as it were, of the latter. Beyond the Place Saint-Sulpice and its church, the name of Rue Saint-Sulpice changes to Rue du Vieux-Colombier. This is where 19th-century novelist Alexandre Dumas placed the lodgings for Mr. de Tréville's Royal Musketeers in his classic action novel.) Rue du Vieux-Colombier takes us up to Rue de Rennes, which, since the 1870s, has framed the Saint-Sulpice quarter to the west. Rue de Vaugirard to the south and Rue Garancière to the east sew up this

small neighborhood, with its massive and imposing church.

Suddenly, we are whisked away from this eat-drink-and-be-merry quarter into one of prayer. We move from the fair to faith. Flippant Alfred Jarry, who lived at 20 Rue Cassette in the early 20th century, used to call this quarter "La Grande Chasublerie," a taunt referring to the shops offering liturgical robes and other religious accoutrements in the great church's shadow.

Renamed as a single street in 1851, the various segments of Rue Saint-Sulpice previously had their own respective names. The artery has existed since the founding of the Saint-Germain fair nearly nine hundred years ago.

Let's take a look at the side façade of **21 Rue Saint-Sulpice**, on

▲ Statuette, Rue Saint-Sulpice

▲ Hôtel de Châtillon,
21 Rue Saint-Sulpice

◄ Saint-Sulpice Church
(© Jacques Lebar)

the corner of Rue de Tournon. This old mansion was built for Marguerite de Savoie (1560). In the 17th century it was known as the Hôtel de Plaisance, then the Hôtel de Châtillon. Between 1827 and 1830, while the young Honoré de Balzac was trying to start his career in publishing and printing on Rue Visconti, he lived in an apartment in this mansion. A dedicated coffee-lover even in his youth, he would often head up to Rue Monsieur-le-Prince where, beside the old home of Blaise Pascal, he could purchase the beans for his precious nectar, and candles by the light of which to scribble late into the night, stimulated by the caffeine.

Rue Saint-Sulpice runs along the northern side of the church from Rue Garancière to Place Saint-Sulpice. In the 18th century, the name of this part of the street was Rue des Aveugles (Blind People's Street), because it bordered a tiny cemetery of the same name created in 1664. It was the third parish cemetery. Since the Middle Ages, it had been customary to create parish cemeteries beside their churches. Saint-Sulpice's first graveyard was on its south side. When the church was rebuilt in 1646,

the cemetery grounds were covered by the enlarged building. A second cemetery was then set up at some remove, on Rue de Grenelle in the Faubourg Saint-Germain. The Cimetière des Aveugles located on the church's northern side was surrounded by buildings and was used for over a century (up to 1784). Its entrance, with massive gate posts, was located at about **36** of present-day Rue Saint-Sulpice. Architect Godde, credited for restoring the Saint-Germain-des-Prés church, was inspired by the old gate posts in designing the entrance to the Père-Lachaise Cemetery in 1825.

Saint-Sulpice Church

There was a time when strolling through this neighborhood offered only a narrow view of the imposing façade of the **Saint-Sulpice Church**. Prior to the 19th century, the church did not have its vast esplanade; instead, it overlooked the narrow Rue Férou and the high walls of the Grand Seminary. With the lack of space and the requirement to respect the line of

◄ Saint-Sulpice Church

(over 100 feet). These dimensions are roughly equal to Notre-Dame's. While the impressive and austere façade respects ancient classical lines with its two superimposed porticos, it seems to have been slapped onto the structure. Before becoming the architect of the church in the 18th century, Servandoni had been a theater set designer, and he seems to have applied the same principles to his new job. His plan to make the towers higher was clearly inspired by medieval architecture.

Let's enter. Inside, the staggeringly high nave with its barrel vault is supported by massive arcades. Along the side aisles, the two large fonts, giant seashells, were a gift to 16th-century monarch François I from the Republic of Venice. These royal endowments to the church from Louis XV sit on 18th-century marble pedestals carved by Pigalle.

the street, the church portico had to be placed between the columns.

Actually a hodgepodge of styles (see inset), this church is also one of the largest in Paris. It is one hundred and ten meters long (over 300 feet), fifty-six meters wide (over 150 feet), and its ceiling is thirty-three meters

A Long Story

In 1210, on the site of an older edifice, construction began on a small parish church dedicated to Saint Sulpice. This small church was later renovated and enlarged. But in the 17th century, the population of the Saint-Germain district had grown so much and the quarter had become so fashionable (we scarcely need to remind our readers that it had all the history and color that novelist Alexandre Dumas sought for the homes of his three musketeers and D'Artagnan), that it became imperative to

build a new place of worship. The drive for a new church was spearheaded by the famous Abbot Olier. The decision to build was made in 1646, but actual construction took over a century and exhausted six talented architects. In 1655, the famous Louis Le Vau was commissioned to enlarge the initial plan, judged to be insufficiently opulent. After Le Vau's death, Gittard faithfully carried out his plans, built the choir, the aisles, and part of the transept. A forty-year hiatus (1678-1718) then

intervened, due to a lack of funds. Oppenordt took the project to completion of the nave in 1736.

From 1733 to 1745, Servandoni designed and oversaw the façade. He was succeeded by Maclaurin, whose tower designs differed from those of his predecessor. The reason the two towers are not alike is that Chalgrin, who was commissioned to redesign them, only had the time to complete the north tower in 1788. This history full of vicissitudes explains the church's variety of styles.

▲ *La Lutte de Jacob avec l'ange* (Jacob Wrestling the Angel), painted from 1849 to 1861, Eugène Delacroix, Saint-Sulpice Church (© Clément Guillaume)

Servandoni, then altered in 1774 by Wailly. The ensemble is a fine example of 18th-century decorative art. In a deep niche behind the altar is a delightful Virgin and Baby Jesus surrounded by angels. It was the work of Pigalle as well as Monchy. The chapel walls were appointed with paintings by Van Loo, while the inner surface of the dome offers a beautiful Annunciation by Lemoyne. Bouchardon's delicately carved wooden angels complete the ensemble. Of the nine chapels on the north aisle, we will pause to admire the lovely Louis Quinze wood paneling in the fifth one, devoted to the Sacred Heart. Two lovely chapels with rotundas can be found on the second floors in the north and south towers.

Over the entrance to the church is the great organ case designed by Chalgrin. It is decorated with charming statues by Clodion and elements by Duret. The organ itself, originally built by François-Henri Clicquot, is an 1862 masterpiece by Aristide Cavaillé-Coll. His 6,500-pipe, 101-stop instrument has a reputation as one of France's most impressive symphonic organs.

One of the church's secular curiosities is the meridian traced in 1727. In his 1958 book entitled Les Églises Parisiennes, Amédée Boinet writes, "Pierre Lemonier oversaw the project. He erected a ten-meter-high obelisk in the northern end of the transept and laid out a line of brass to trace the meridian in the church's paving stones, ending at the obelisk. He had a small lens with an 80-foot focus inserted in the southern window of the transept, which had to be laid flat for the operation. Lastly, he positioned a brass plaque, which has

Immediately on the right is the famous Chapelle des Saints-Anges. Eugène Delacroix worked on decorating it from 1849 until he died in 1863. Maurice Barrès greatly admired it during his pilgrimages here. The most famous of the Delacroix frescoes is without a doubt *La Lutte de Jacob avec l'Ange*, the painter's impassioned artistic and spiritual testimonial. It stands opposite *Héliodore Chassé du Temple*. In the ceiling of the dome is *Saint Michel Triomphant de Lucifer* (Saint-Michael's victory over Lucifer).

The other chapels opening onto the south side of the church are less interesting. The only one we might stop to look at is the second, painted in the 19th century by Heim, whose *grisaille* monochromes also ornament the choir of Saint-Germain-des-Prés.

The Chapelle de la Vierge in the middle of the choir was designed by

been preserved, on the floor, to indicate the exact spot where the sun's rays fall on noon of the summer solstice." The calculation, however, was off. In fact, the Paris meridian is slightly to the east in this neighborhood.

For over a century, the church's vast crypt contained the sepultures of privileged parishioners. It has been said that Racine's mistress Marie Champmeslé and Molière's widow Armande Béjart were buried here. Some of the greatest orators of all time preached in the church itself. Sermons by Bossuet, Fénelon, Fléchier, and Massillon filled the pews.

Unlike the Saint-Germain-des-Prés church, Saint-Sulpice was not shut down by the Revolution in 1790. And so, in December of that same year, a very Parisian wedding ceremony was held within these walls. Lucile Duplessis was wed to Camille Desmoulins, her neighbor from the Odéon quarter. All of Paris's top Revolutionary figures attended. Maximilien de Robespierre was the groom's witness. During the Reign of Terror, however, church services were replaced by the Cult of the Supreme Being, and the church was consecrated as a Temple of Reason

Renamed "Temple de la Victoire," Saint-Sulpice hosted a banquet for five hundred guests held on November 5, 1799 (just four days before Napoleon's coup d'état ending the French Revolution) in honor of Generals Moreau and Bonaparte. Moreau had just returned victorious from his campaign in Italy and Bonaparte from his in Egypt. The Directoire held a lavish event and even called for subscriptions to finance the ceremony. Tapestries and the enemies' flags were hung in the nave. The organist for the

▲ Saint-Sulpice's nave (© Bridgeman/Lauros-Giraudon)

event was the youngest in the Couperin dynasty. In reality, though, suspicion was rampant and the plot to overthrow the governing Directoire was ready to be launched.

In the 19th century, Saint-Sulpice returned to its previous existence as a peaceful neighborhood church. The 1808 demolition of the Grand Seminary across the street created a huge empty space and finally enabled the large structure to break out of its confinement. Lastly, the church is one of the stars in the best-selling 2003 novel *The Da Vinci Code*.

Around Place Saint-Sulpice

When **Place Saint-Sulpice** was laid out, it gave the church a much-needed esplanade. As early as 1764, architect Servandoni had drawn up plans for a square similar in design to that of

Place Vendôme, lined with rental buildings which would present uniform façades. The model property is the one still standing on the right angle of this square and Rue des Canettes. While the outcome is not what the architect had planned, the square does have its charm. Its grace is due to combination of tall, leafy plane trees and Visconti's 1844 fountain. The fountain's main figures are statues of the four great bishops who preached at Saint-Sulpice: Fléchier, Massillon, Bossuet, Fénélon.

The grand square was laid out on the site of the old cemetery and the ruins of the demolished 17th-century Grand Seminary. Around 1820, the architect Godde began designing lovely new seminary buildings along a private lane parallel to Rue Bonaparte. Following the passage of the 1905 law regarding the separation of Church and State, the buildings were assigned to the Ministry of Finance.

To continue our stroll, we will have to zigzag through an area framed by Rue Saint-Sulpice and Rue du Vieux-Colombier to the north and Rue de Vaugirard to the south. Aside form Rue Bonaparte, a busy through street leading to Boulevard Saint-Germain and to the Seine River, the rest of the

neighborhood streets (Garancière, Servandoni, Férou, Madame, and Cassette) have a provincial air about them that is unique to this arrondissement. J.-K. Huysmans, in his 1891 novel Là-Bas, described it thus, "On Servandoni, Garancière, and Férou streets, you can breathe in a sort of benign silence and sweet humidity ... It's obsolete and discreet... Not a sound, no crowds, trees all lined up as if belonging on a small-town mall."

Let's start making our way toward Rue Garancière, by turning left on **Rue Palatine** (named for the wife of the Prince of Condé), which borders the south side of the church. Laid out in 1646, when the church was enlarged, this street covers part of the old 13th-century cemetery that once flanked the edifice. The old residence of the Duke de Rochechouart, which once stood at number **5**, was home Louis de Bonald, After the Revolution, he and Joseph de Maistre expounded the theory of the absolute monarchy.

Facing the school of dentistry, we will turn right onto narrow **Rue Garancière**. It was created in the 16th century. You may notice the gentle rise as we move toward Rue de Vaugirard

◄ Fountain designed by Visconti, Place Saint-Sulpice

► 4 Rue Garancière

and the Luxembourg Gardens. Talleyrand was born at **4** on February 2, 1754. He studied at the Grand Seminary down the street, and was neither the first nor the last of its students to scale the wall at night for an assignation with a sweetheart. On the odd-numbered side of the street, most of the buildings are the rear sides of mansions located on Rue de Tournon. Such is the case of **9**, the old Hôtel Concini (a man loyal to Queen Marie de Médicis, assassinated on the orders of young Louis XIII), which later became a Garde Républicaine barracks. At **11**, we see the small Hôtel du Nivernais which was home to historian Thureau Dangin in 1820, then to the economist Frédéric Le Play in 1850. Number **13** is the rear entrance to the Hôtel d'Entragues.

The mansion at **8**, built atop the ruins of the Hôtel Garancière around 1640, is especially interesting. Without a doubt, it is the loveliest building on this street. Unfortunately, the street is not wide enough to allow us a fuller view of the superb pilastered façade, the upper part of which is trimmed with a delicate row of rams' heads. The brickwork on the right side of the façade, in the purest Louis XIII style, suggests the majesty of the original mansion. Renovated in the 19th century, the building served from 1819 to 1849 as the district city hall (for the 11th arrondissement in the numbering system of that time). None of the original architectural elements remain in the courtyard, the centerpiece of a dramatic riches-to-rags story. In 1651, the mansion was inherited by a certain Lord of Sourdéac, an odd character. After his extravagant teen years, the young man became smitten with theater. In

1652, he hosted the premiere of Corneille's opera-tragedy Andromède, before it was staged at the Théâtre du Petit-Bourbon. Corneille was a master of the special theatrical effects of his time, which required incredible machinery. It takes more than will to become a patron of the arts, and Sourdéac was soon bankrupt. He had to sell his mansion in Paris (where Adrienne Lecouvreur later began her career as a tragedian, in 1715), and spent the last years of his life among actor friends, running the box office of the Théâtre Guénégaud on Rue Mazarine.

On hot sunny days, Rue Garancière, like its narrow neighbors, is a haven of cooler, refreshing temperatures. A lovely fountain set in a wall near 10 has been flowing with water to assuage the thirst of passersby since 1715, a thoughtful gesture by the Princess of Palatinate, Elizabeth Charlotte.

◄ 8 Rue Garancière

▼ Fountain commissioned by the Princess of Palatinate, 10 Rue Garancière

◄ Standard meter, Rue de Vaugirard

We've reached **Rue de Vaugirard** by going beneath the recent cement arch connecting the corner buildings. Now, turn right under the arcades, and have a look at a **standard meter** that was placed on the wall by the Convention. The decision was taken to impose the new decimal system nationwide, replacing the Ancien Régime *pied* and *toise*. Several meters in marble were affixed to walls in Paris during the Revolution to serve citizens as a reliable measuring-stick. The one here is the only one remaining in its original location.

We shall now take our first right onto the curving **Rue Servandoni**. Formerly named Ruelle Saint-Sulpice, in 1620 it became known as Rue des Fossoyeurs (literally: Grave-diggers' Street); those who buried the dead at

▲ 14 Rue Servandoni
▼ Rue Férou

the old cemetery lived at **1**. With its row of dwellings dating from the 17th and 18th centuries, this street, named Servandoni in 1806, is the charming twin of neighboring Rue Férou. Number **12** was the first Paris home for Alexandre Dumas' character D'Artagnan.

A commemorative plaque near **15** mentions Condorcet's stay here when he went into hiding after being branded as a Girondist traitor by the Montagnards in the Assembly, soon after the start of the Reign of Terror. The widow of his friend, the sculptor François Vernet, housed him through the fall and winter of 1793, until March 25, 1794. In these more peaceful times, it is a pleasure to stop and admire the old façades here. Some of the buildings on this street have carved doors, such as **14**, with its bas-relief representing an architect unrolling a floor plan. The doorway leads to a narrow courtyard framed by an ivy-covered building. In the 17th and 18th centuries, the street was home to a certain number of religious communities, including a home for abandoned children.

In 1945, a young woman from the provinces took a room in a boarding house on this street. She would become the icon for an entire generation: Juliette Gréco. She met Anne-Marie Cazalis here. They teamed up as a singing duo and were a big hit. Writer William Faulkner resided here during his stays in Paris.

A left on tiny **Rue du Canivet**, with the old Hôtel de Breteuil (1730) at **3**, will take us to **Rue Férou**, where we'll again turn left. This street was carved out of the Férou estate in the 16th century. In 1936, the first block, which once ran along the Grand Seminary,

it is the oldest publisher in Paris. Secondly, it has the longest-running book in print, *Le Tour de France par deux enfants*, by Geneviève Bruno, published in 1877. In *The Three Musketeers*, this address was only steps away from Athos's house, where the first duel with the cardinal's guards took place.

was named for Henry de Jouvenel, a journalist and politician who resided for many years at 6, and who was the writer Colette's second husband and the father of her only child.

The beautiful mansion at **6** was the home of Mademoiselle Luzy, a delightful actress courted by Talleyrand, but who was moved into this address by her "sponsor," a certain Mr. Landry, around 1767. Built by Marie-Joseph Peyre, one of the architects of the Odéon, it is a sign tastes were again turning to classical themes. Two varnished terracotta sphinxes stand guard over the gateway.

Next door, at **8** Rue de Férou, is the small townhouse where Mme de La Fayette lived around 1650 (the main entrance is on 50, Rue de Vaugirard). The publishing company Belin has had its headquarters here since 1777. Belin holds two records. For one,

From Rue Bonaparte to Rue du Vieux-Colombier

A right onto **Rue de Vaugirard** will take us down to **Rue Bonaparte**, which we will now explore. The right-hand (east) side of the street is a pleasant tree-lined lane named Allée du Séminaire, gently sloping down to Place Saint-Sulpice. This mall with its small-town air borders the Grand Seminary as well as the Communauté des Filles de l'Instruction Chrétienne. In the middle of this park-like *allée* is a neoclassical fountain called **Fontaine des Arts et de la Paix**, erected in 1806 on Place du Châtelet, and later moved to this site. Espercieux ornamented it with delicately carved bas-reliefs, representing the arts, farming, trade, and peace.

In the 17th century, a vast complex of buildings went up at **80** Rue Bonaparte, in an area framed by three other streets: Mézières, Cassette, and Honoré-Chevalier. It was for Jesuit novitiates. Unfortunately, one of the city's purest examples of Jesuit architecture was demolished in 1763, when the Jesuits were expelled. The premises became the seat of the Grand Orient de France. This Masonic lodge had a special hall reserved for large gatherings of the Neuf-Sœurs literary circle, which included the intellectual giants of Paris. When Voltaire was initiated as a Freemason on April 7, 1778, a few weeks before his death, this is where the ceremony was held, due to its importance.

The 6th Arrondissement's city hall at **78** Rue Bonaparte dates from 1849. It was built on the site of the old convent of the Bernardines de Sainte-Cécile, which had become the Hôtel de Charost in the 18th century. From 1795 to 1850, the arrondissement had an itinerant city hall; it was successively moved from Rue Mignon (near the Odéon) to Rue du Vieux-Colombier, then to Rue Garancière. In

1860, the arrondissement numbering system changed, and the 11th became the 6th.

Rue du Vieux-Colombier curves northward slightly as it runs west from Place Saint-Sulpice to Carrefour de la Croix-Rouge. It changed names several times from the end of the 13th century to the middle of the 17th, when its present name, which had also been used in 1293, finally stuck. It comes as no surprise that it referred to the old dovecote of the Saint-Germain-des-Prés abbey. The continuation of this street beyond the intersection with Rue de Rennes puts it in the Cherche-Midi quarter.

Like most of the streets in this quarter, by 1650 Rue Vieux-Colombier had welcomed numerous convents and religious institutions. This Saint-Sulpice quarter's temporal realization of the spiritual was mirrored by the Latin Quarter's along Rue Saint-Jacques and past Rue Soufflot. In 1651, upon the request of Anne of Austria, the Augustinian sisters set up their convent at **4 and 6**. The nuns lost their convent during the Revolution and Masonic lodges took over the premises until 1806.

The 1823 fire station at **11** has a lovely façade and a neoclassical pediment that incorporates firefighting emblems. It is located in the buildings for an old parish orphanage named Orphelins de la Mère-de-Dieu, founded in 1680. When it was closed in 1793, the Sœurs de la Charité used it as a shelter before moving to their complex on Rue du Bac.

Rue du Vieux-Colombier has also had its share of famous laymen. The three Le Nain brothers came to Paris in 1629, and kept their art studio here until 1648, when Antoine and Louis

▼ Fire station, 11 Rue du Vieux-Colombier

died. The artists were quite successful, commissioned to paint works for Anne of Austria, the abbey of Saint-Germain-des-Prés, Paris aldermen, and neighborhood convents. Poet and critic Nicolas Boileau also lived on this street from 1661 to 1683, but the exact address is unknown. Among his many guests were Molière, La Fontaine, and a young Racine. They came to read their works and enjoy a good dinner. Once Racine met the lovely Miss Duparc, however, he scarcely kept company with his friends.

◄ 21 Rue Cassette

Rue Madame and Rue Cassette

Let's backtrack to the intersection with **Rue Madame** and take a right. Its various parts were joined into a single street in 1824, when its last two-block segment was carved out, taking it all the way south to intersect with Rue de Vaugirard. Only the part between Rue de Rennes and Rue de Vaugirard actually belongs to the Saint-Sulpice neighborhood. The oldest segment of the street runs from Rue du Vieux-Colombier to Rue de Mézières. Formerly called Rue Gindre, it dates from the 16th century. Its present-day name honors the wife of the Comte de Provence, alias Monsieur, the brother of Louis XVI ("Monsieur" was the title usually given to the king's elder brother). The street cut through several Luxembourg lots that Monsieur owned.

Rather than continuing down Rue Madame's southern blocks, which are a bit impersonal and cold, we can enjoy the more charming **Rue Cassette** in our exploration of the Saint-Sulpice quarter. Previously named Rue Cassel after a nearby mansion,

the street cuts through an area full of 17th- and 18th-century buildings. There are next to no cars here. The street is calm and serene. A large convent was erected in 1659 in the stretch from **12 to 16**. It was built for the Adoration perpétuelle du Saint-Sacrement formerly located at 11 Rue Férou. It was here that late 17th-century figure Madame Guyon chose to withdraw from the world. She was the spiritual leader of a circle of deeply religious aristocrats whom she introduced to quietism, a movement centered on self-abnegation in an effort to silence the mind and soul and reach the ultimate goal: the ecstasy of God's love. She was imprisoned twice in the Bastille for her heterodox religious beliefs. Her enemy was Bossuet, a leader of Gallican orthodoxy, but Fénelon, an equally prominent ecclesiastic, supported her. Between her two terms in prison, she stayed in the convent on Rue Cassette. The mid-1730s property map of Paris, the *Plan Turgot*, shows the extent of the religious institution's lands. They ran all the way to Rue du Cherche-Midi, near the Carmelites' convent. All the houses on the even side of this street **from 18 onwards** were rental properties erected by the Carmelites of the Rue de Vaugirard. Like the Chartreux of the Luxembourg quarter, this community - which also owned houses on Rue du Regard, at the southwestern end of its estate - prospered immensely from its real-estate investments.

The only vestige of the Jesuit novitiate buildings among the odd-numbered houses on Rue Cassette is number **21**. Two doors down at **17**, the Pères Blancs welcomed the founder of the order, Cardinal Lavigerie, archbishop of Algiers, whenever he had to visit Paris. The Dukes de Cossé-Brissac once owned the mansion at **25**.

Before leaving endearing Rue Cassette, heeding the irresistible call of the carillon at Saint-Joseph-des-Carmes church, let's honor the memory of the woman who thrilled gener-

▼ Saint-Joseph-des-Carmes Church

ations of young readers, Sophie Rostopchine, better known as the Comtesse de Ségur. She lived for some time at **29**, a mansion no longer standing. It was also here at the junction of Rue Cassette and Rue de Vaugirard that Alexandre Dumas located the first encounter between D'Artagnan and the three musketeers.

Around Saint-Joseph-des-Carmes Church

Turning right onto **Rue de Vaugirard**, we are immediately greeted by a discreet church at **70**. Saint-Joseph-des-Carmes was the site of one of the French Revolution's bloodiest episodes.

The mendicant order of Discalced Carmelites (Barefoot Carmelites) was a monastic community that formed in Italy, in response to the preaching of Saint John of the Cross, a 16th-century Spanish mystic. In 1611, they received an invitation to come to Paris. In fact, they joined Carmelite sisters who had come from Spain and were following Saint Teresa of Ávila's rules at the Incarnation convent located on Rue Saint-Jacques.

While waiting for the convent on Rue de Vaugirard to be completed, the Discalced Carmelites lodged on Rue Cassette. In 1613, Marie de Médicis laid the first stone of the chapel, which was completed in 1620. Over the years, the Carmelites' territory grew. In 18th-century city maps, the western edge of their property was on Rue du Regard while the northern and eastern edges were on Rue Cassette and Rue du Cherche-Midi. In the large garden, the Carmelites cultivated the herbs they used to make their famous licorice-flavored water sold under the brand name of Eau des Carmes Boyer.

The famous Carmelite white that makes walls look like marble was used on all the convent buildings erected behind the church and those to its left toward Rue d'Assas. Deconsecrated in 1845, the convent, which had been home to a Carmelite community since 1797, was given to the archbishopric for Catholic centers of learning. In 1875, the Institut Catholique took over the buildings and set up its various departments.

Saint-Joseph-des-Carmes is an attractive church built in Jesuit style with a classical pediment. The only departure from austerity is the pair of statues in niches gracing the façade. The church choir is topped by a dome of Italian inspiration. It was the second church in Paris to be built in this style; the first was the Petits-Augustins' convent church on Rue Bonaparte. Behind this dome, a little campanile rises, a highly unusual touch for a Parisian church. This is yet more Italian influence. There is a fine view of the pair of buildings from the top of Rue Cassette.

A doorway on the right opens onto a vestibule with a clerestory, which, in turn, leads to the Carmelite church. After leaving noisy Rue de Vaugirard, we suddenly find ourselves steeped in a world of silence and prayer. As we move toward the high altar, let's look up to the ceiling to admire the beautiful 17th-century fresco by Bertholet Flamaël (a native of Liege). Entitled L'Enlèvement au Ciel du Prophète Elie, it tells the story of the prophet Elijah carried to heaven in a whirlwind. The Carmelites consider Elijah their founding father. On either side of the choir are statues of Saint John of the Cross and Saint Teresa of Ávila. In the transept is a

Massacre at the Carmelite Convent

With its vast garden and the high walls of the mansions surrounding it, the Carmelite convent was indeed isolated from the rest of the quarter and seemed to be sheltered from the fever of the Revolution. In 1789, the popular religious community even gave one of its buildings to be used as a military installation for the Gardes Nationaux. The abolition of religious orders in 1790 had little impact on the community. In April 1792, however, the monks resigned themselves the closing of their church as a place of worship and the dispersion of their large library.

The same year, one day after the fateful fall of the French monarchy, the Carmelites' woes began. On August 11th, 1792, numerous priests who had refused to swear allegiance to the constitution were rounded up and arrested throughout the Saint-Sulpice quarter, where they had been hiding for months. More than fifty of them were imprisoned in squalid conditions at the Carmelite convent. The number grew considerably in the following days. Revolutionary tension gripped the city. Tragedy struck on Sunday, September 2, when a national guard troop led by Citizen Maillard burst into the convent, with cries of "Vive la Nation ! Mort aux réfractaires !" (Long live the nation! Death to the nonjuring!") Therewith, the massacre began. Over the next three days, one hundred and fifteen priests were exterminated in the garden, after a parody of a trial. Only the Carmelites, holed up in their cells, were saved. Powerless, they witnessed the carnage of their brethren. Historian Georges Lenotre, in his Paris Révolutionnaire, gives this wrenching account of those horrible days, "Not a stone has changed at the Carmelite convent. Here is the little doorway where the victims were called forth. Here is the long corridor where they were dragged to their deaths. These are the flagstones they stumbled upon. There are the steps where the massacre began; beneath the branches of the weeping willow, between two yellowed palm trees, were engraved the simple words hic ceciderunt (they fell here). There, at that window, appeared Maillard's pale face shouting to his men, 'Wait! Don't kill them yet, for we must try them!' And there is the dark corridor where the mockery of a trial was held."

▶ *Virgin and Child,*
marble sculpture by
Antonio Raggi, 1662,
Saint-Joseph-des-Carmes
Church
(© Clément Guillaume)

delicate Virgin and Child by Antonio Raggi, inspired by Bernini, sculptor of the magnificent bronze baldachin at Saint Peter's in Rome. The Sacred Heart chapel and the Saint Elijah chapel have some very fine paintings framed by sculptures of angels, the work of Simon Vouet, First Painter to the King in 1627.

The memorial to Monsignor Affre, the archbishop of Paris killed by a gunshot in February 1848, while trying to reason with insurgents in the Saint-Antoine neighborhood, is a reminder of the violent deaths this convent saw. The September 2, 1792 massacre of nonjuring priests has become the symbol of the furor of the French Revolution (see inset).

After this massacre, the last monks were sent away. The convent became a prison. Alexandre de Beauharnais and his wife Joséphine were but two of the illustrious prisoners held here. The former suffered the guillotine while the latter was saved and marched on to a glorious destiny:

empress and first consort of Napoleon. After the Reign of Terror, the premises of the convent were rented to a cabaret owner who turned it into a ballroom. In 1797, Miss de Soyecourt, a Carmelite whose father had been jailed on the Carmelites' premises, bought the buildings to house a community of young nuns.

In 1845 the convent was sold to Dominicans to make room for a teaching institution. Father Lacordaire and Catholic writer Frédéric Ozanam taught there. After a law favoring religious instruction was passed in 1850, the Institut Catholique bought the property and, in 1875, commissioned new buildings to be built on **Rue d'Assas** in a style reminiscent of Flemish neo-Gothic.

Initially a law school, by 1877 the **Institut Catholique** had opened a school of arts, followed by a school of sciences. It then added the School of Oriental Languages. The university has steadily grown. It is now endowed with a business school, ESSEC, which has since moved to Cergy-Pontoise.

Among the flukes of history is the happy coincidence that two fundamental experiments in modern history took place a mere forty years apart in practically the same place. In 1851, at **28** Rue d'Assas, just across from the Institut Catholique, physicist Léon Foucault conducted an experiment proving, with his famous pendulum, the Earth's rotation. A sculpture on the façade on the Rue de Vaugirard side of the building celebrates his accomplishment. In 1890, Édouard Branly, a professor at the Institut Catholique, set up his radio-conduction experiments in the university laboratories. He laid the groundwork for wireless radio transmissions.

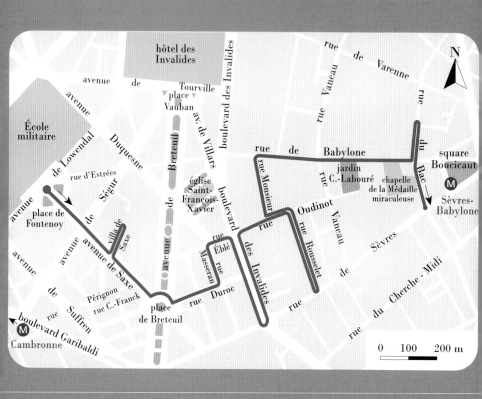

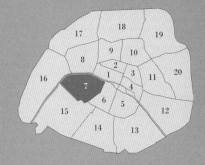

7th

From UNESCO to the Bon Marché

▶ Start: Place de Fontenoy,
  metro Cambronne
▶ Finish: Rue de Sèvres,
  metro Sèvres-Babylone

From Place de Fontenoy to Place de Breteuil

◄ École Militaire and the Eiffel Tower seen from Place de Fontenoy

The semi-circular **Place de Fontenoy** was designed by Jacques Ange Gabriel in 1770. Today, it is surrounded by 20th-century administrative buildings on the corners of Avenue de Lowendal, Rue d'Estrées, and Avenue de Saxe. It stands in front of the magnificent façade of the École Militaire, thus giving a modern frame to the classical architecture of the academy, with its seemingly endless main courtyard and cavalry training grounds. The wings (built by Brongniart, architect and controller of the École Militaire and the Invalides in 1782) and a high wrought-iron gate close the vast courtyard which had originally been designed as the academy's main entrance.

On the corner of Rue d'Estrées and Avenue de Saxe is the **Ministry of Tourism**. The Art Déco building was designed in 1932 by André Ventre. Until 1992 it housed the ministry of the merchant marine, which has been incorporated into today's ministry of the sea. The interior décor befits the

Setting out from Place de Fontenoy, the landscaped backdrop for the grand courtyard façade of the École Militaire, we will explore an area of Paris that was shaped in the 1780s by a large-scale real-estate investment scheme. Architect Alexandre-Théodore Brongniart bought up farmland, divided it into lots, and built mansions, which led to the creation of new streets: Rues Monsieur, Duroc, Masseran, and Éblé. At the same time, broader avenues were laid out to connect the military academy to the Invalides and to Rue de Sèvres. Although the development of the 7th arrondissement dates on the whole from the 18th and 19th centuries, only a few mansions from that period remain, along Rue Masseran, Rue Monsieur, and Rue Oudinot. Their gardens, rarely visible, are off Boulevard des Invalides. We will be strolling a neighborhood which is primarily residential, with many lavish Second Empire mansions, schools, the arrondissement's only open-air market, and religious communities, but also government ministries and the headquarters of an international organization.

◄ Ministry of Tourism at the corner of Rue d'Estrées and Avenue de Saxe

building's original purpose, and includes model boats, lighthouses, buoys, and other nautical motifs.

The enormous United Nations Educational, Scientific and Cultural Organization (UNESCO) building stands at **7** Place de Fontenoy. This is the home of the organization's Secretariat. The main building has a Y shape. Its three incurved sides have over one thousand windows, and stand on piles. Completed in 1958, it is the work of three architects: France's Bernard Zehrfuss, Italy's Luigi Nervi, and the USA's Marcel Breuer. The interior and the gardens, with their scattering of contemporary sculpture are definitely worth the visit. Besides the Japanese garden, there is artwork by Miró, Giacometti, Moore, Picasso, and Bazaine. Reservations are handled by an answering service which may be reached by dialing +33 (0) 145 681 060.

▶ Villa de Saxe

Running straight out the École Militaire's main entrance, **Avenue de Saxe** has carried traffic from Place de Fontenoy to Place de Breteuil since 1780. It was named for the Comte de Saxe, a Marshal of France. He led the armies of Louis XV to victory in the battle of Fontenoy (in present-day Belgium, then occupied by Austria) in 1745. Beginning with Rue Pérignon, only the odd-numbered addresses are in the 7th arrondissement. The luxurious buildings on the even side, dating from 1913-1916, are in the 15th arrondissement.

Since 1912, one of the capital's most important outdoor markets has been held on the median strip twice weekly (on Thursday and Saturday mornings), the famous Marché Saxe-Breteuil. You will find top-quality goods and a friendly ambience.

After crossing Avenue de Ségur, the first street to our left is **Villa de Saxe**. The buildings of the Couvent des Clarisses (in English: the Order of Poor Ladies) at **5** date from 1876. The nuns of this convent are followers of Saint Francis of Assisi and lead a contemplative life. Silence seems to be the rule on this dead-end street.

UNESCO

Established by twenty nations in 1945, UNESCO had 193 Member States and 6 Associate Members at the time of this book's publication. The organization's primary purpose is to organize international intellectual cooperation in order to fulfill the introductory lines in the organization's constitution, "Since wars begin in the minds of men, it is in the minds of men that the defenses of peace must be constructed." Each country can cast one ballot in voting for the development of scientific, cultural, and educational programs. Thus, each of the ex-Soviet republics has one ballot. Financial participation in funding projects is calculated on a sliding scale, based on each nation's gross domestic product. Every two years, the general conference drafts the organization's program and votes on a budget to carry it out. Some of the past projects have included the restoration of the Great Wall of China, of the sanctuaries in Machu Picchu, and of the ancient temples at Abu Simbel in Egypt's Nile Valley.

Leaving this peaceful place, we will return to **Avenue de Saxe**. The Ukrainian Embassy is located in the brick building at **21**. There is a vast garden behind the modern building at **23**.

Just off Place de Breteuil, **Rue César Franck** (15th arrondissement) reminds us that the composer (1822-1890) lived in the 7th arrondissement his entire life, on Rue de Grenelle and Avenue de Villars.

Place de Breteuil was designed in 1782 to provide a magnificent view of the dome of Les Invalides from the intersection of Avenue de Saxe and Avenue de Breteuil. Breteuil is a long tree-lined mall with sweeping, elegant lawns. This perspective was planned by Jules Hardouin-Mansart, who oversaw the layout of the avenue during the construction of the Invalides in 1680. The center of Place de Breteuil is graced by a **monument to Pasteur**, sculpted by Falguière. At the feet of the scientist is the Grim Reaper, stymied by Pasteur's exploits, deprived of victory over a mother and child, a girl, a farmer's oxen, and a shepherd's flock.

From Rue Duroc to Boulevard des Invalides

We will now take **Rue Duroc**, created in 1790. It was named after one of Bonaparte's comrades-in-arms. The emperor made him Duke de Friuli and Grand Marshal of the Tuileries Palace. **Numbers 5, 7, and 9** make up a unit used by the Valentin-Haüy Association, founded in 1889 by Maurice de La Sizeranne, who taught at the school for the blind. The school's main goal is to teach its pupils a trade. Students have access to the largest Braille library in the French-speaking world. The Musée Valentin-Haüy has a collection of prototypes of various devices invented over the past century as aids for teaching the visually-impaired. From time to time, the museum displays artwork by blind artists such as see-and-touch sculpture exhibits. The museum is open Tuesdays and Wednesdays, 2:30-5 pm, except in July and August, and by appointment.

Let's continue to the end of the block and turn left. The gate at **11 Rue Masseran**, on the corner, is always closed. It sits in a long, high wall. Behind that wall is a well-hidden mansion with a garden. Brongniart designed this estate in 1787 for Prince Masserano. In 1805, the prince was

◄ Ukrainian Embassy, 21 Avenue de Saxe

◄ Monument to Pasteur, Place de Breteuil

named Spain's ambassador to France and grand master of ceremonies of the king of Spain, Joseph Bonaparte. The palace and gardens are on the historical register. Étienne de Beaumont lived in this mansion during the Roaring Twenties. He held lavish costume balls, inviting guests like Jean and Valentine Hugo, Jean Cocteau, and Lucien Daudet. The wild goings-on inspired young Raymond Radiguet's novel *Le Bal du Comte d'Orgel*, published after Radiguet's death from typhus at age 20.

At numbers **3 and 5** is a neoclassical mansion (see below), restored in 1994. It is an office building now.

We will turn right onto **Rue Éblé** and walk past **5**. This handsome building was acquired in 1947 by the prestigious Racing Club de France. The building has over six thousand meters of floor space (over 64,000 square feet). It houses the club's headquarters as well as several sports facili-

▶ Statue of Valentin Haüy, founder of the Institute for the Blind, 56 Boulevard des Invalides

▼ 3-5 Rue Masseran

ties, including two swimming pools and a judo gym.

A right turn now onto **Boulevard des Invalides** will allow us to look through the gates and admire the lovely gardens behind the mansion at 3 Rue Masseran mentioned above. The late 18th-century façade is composed of a portico with four Ionic columns, a ground floor with large

arched windows, a second story and an attic floor. However, all we can do is walk along outside the wall hiding the garden. At **56** Boulevard des Invalides is an entrance to the national institute for the blind, founded in 1784 by Valentin Haüy. It is located in impressive buildings with a paved formal courtyard, and was erected in 1838 by Philippon. There is also a garden, behind the buildings. Inside the chapel is an organ by Cavaillé-Coll.

We have now reached "**Carrefour Duroc**," at the intersection with Rue de Sèvres. It marks the southern tip of the 7th arrondissement. In the 18th century, the Boulevard des Invalides (1760) formed the western boundary of the noble Faubourg Saint-Germain.

Rue Oudinot

Let's cross **Boulevard des Invalides** and walk back up the boulevard, on the other side. This is where Les Oiseaux prison was located during the Reign of Terror. It later became a convent, and was finally torn down in 1908.

We will stroll beside the imposing wall of the Ministère de l'Outre-Mer (overseas ministry). Its main entrance is at **27 Rue Oudinot**. At the far end of the courtyard is the main

hall. The ground floor has four simple pilasters with Ionic capitals. Over the second story is a sculpted pediment with military motifs. The lateral façades underwent several alterations. This mansion was originally the Hôtel de Rambouillet de la Sablière. In 1781, it became the property of Count de Montmorin-Saint-Hérem, Minister of Foreign Affairs, executed in 1792. His daughter, Pauline de Beaumont, was the romantic writer Chateaubriand's mistress. Brongniart is credited for the pilasters on the façade. Napoleon rented the mansion for Cardinal Caprara, the Vatican nuncio. After 1847, the premises were occupied by novitiates from the Christian Brothers, founded by Jean-Baptiste de La Salle. They transformed the main hall and added new buildings around it.

In 1910, the property was assigned to the government's Ministry for the Colonies, which became the Overseas Ministry.

The corner lot across the street is occupied by **22** Rue Oudinot and 49 Boulevard des Invalides (note the columns between the ground-floor windows). The arches above the tall, dark green carriage doors are decorated with fox heads surrounded by oak leaves. This was the townhouse that Brongniart built for himself in 1781. Let's go back to the odd-numbered side of this street. Behind the

▲ Ministry of Overseas Territories, 27 Rue Oudinot

◄ 22 Rue Oudinot

► 23 Rue Oudinot

▲ The Saint-Jean-de-Dieu Clinic, 19 Rue Oudinot

◄ Rue Rousselet

Rue Rousselet

The calm and secretive **Rue Rousselet** runs beside the clinic's garden wall. Its name in 1676 was *Chemin des Vachers* (Cowherds' Trail), because it was used to drive cattle to graze on the pastures of the Champ-de-Mars and the Esplanade des Invalides. It was later renamed for Ambroise Rousselet, a high-ranking tax officer, who owned much of the land here in the early 18th century. This street was practically a literary circle of its own at the turn of the 20th century, and is primarily known for the literary giants who lived here: Barbey d'Aurevilly at **25**, from 1859 to 1898, where he wrote *Le Chevalier Des Touches, Les Diaboliques, Histoire Sans Nom, Ce Qui Ne Meurt Pas*, etc. Léon Bloy lived at **22**. Paul-Émile Borduas, a painter from Quebec, lived at **19**. Paul Léautaud lived at **17**.

François Coppée described the quaint charms of his own street in *La Robe Blanche*. "When I came to live in the far-flung corner of the Faubourg Saint-Germain [...], I became fond of the very calm and practically bucolic

carriage door at **23**, there is an entire complex of old houses with little gardens, on either side of a paved lane. It feels like a charming little village from some other era. One of the buildings is the Sainte-Agnès neighborhood community center, offering youth services, workshops, classes, support services, a day-care center, music lessons, etc.

The majestic **Clinique Saint-Jean-de-Dieu** is at numbers **19 and 21**. Founded in 1843 by Paul de Magallon of the Order of the Brothers Hospitallers of St. John of God. It has a large and splendid garden that is a pleasure to stroll through in early summer, when the fragrant roses bloom. Symbolist writer Villiers de l'Isle-Adam died here in 1889 and novelist J.-K. Huysmans was admitted for surgery in 1906. The clinic was built on property that previously belonged to Madame de La Sablière. La Fontaine was her protégé and often stayed in her home. She lobbied for his admission to the Académie Française, where he replaced Colbert on May 2, 1684. Novelist Barbey d'Aurevilly lived across the street at **6**, and **12** was the home of poet François Coppée.

Rue Rousselet at my doorstep. [...] A townhouse from the previous century, located on the corner of Rue Oudinot, has become the hospital of the Brothers of Saint John of God, and the boughs of the trees in their lovely garden droop over the cracking wall that takes up nearly the entire right side of Rue Rousselet. On the other side is a row of rather poor homes where artisans and office clerks lodge. They all enjoy the view of the Brothers' garden. Rue Rousselet is poorly paved, and the luxury of a sidewalk lines the street only intermittently. The old bracket-and-pulley streetlamp is gone, however. [...] Drying laundry hangs out of windows. Chickens peck in the gutter. The whole ambience is more like a distant provincial town, one of those outer suburbs on the way out to the country. It is a place where city turns back into village."

◀ Rue Monsieur

Rue Rousselet is located on the Grande Randonnée trail crossing Paris from east to west, and on weekends, one is likely to encounter hikers.

Rue Monsieur

Let's head back up to **Rue Oudinot**. At 23, we will turn onto **Rue Monsieur**. Its name refers to the creation of the street by "Monsieur," King Louis XVI's brother, who owned a tract of land stretching from Rue de Babylone to Rue Oudinot. The new street was made to provide access to the stables he built in 1779. One year later, architect Brongniart bought the lands for a housing development. In the space of a few years, three magnificent mansions (still standing today) were erected at numbers 20, 12, and 8.

Number **20** is presently home to the Ministère de la Coopération (the ministry of economic and cultural cooperation with former colonies). Across the courtyard, the façade with its large, arched windows is connected to the main entrance by wings off to the side. In 1781, This is the Hôtel de Montesquiou Brongniart built in 1781, across from Monsieur's stables. It was sold in 1853 to the Bénédictines du Saint-Sacrement. The sisters fitted it out with cloisters, a chapter house, and a neo-Gothic church where many major figures of the early 20th century attended Mass: François Coppée, Francis Jammes, Alain-Fournier, Paul Claudel, François Mauriac, Jacques Maritain, and Jean Guitton, who described it in the following terms. "The chapel on Rue Monsieur was - in the middle of Paris - a symbol for the opposite of Paris. Crossing its threshold, one crossed the boundaries of earthly time." The Benedictine sisters remained here until the State bought the property in 1938. Across the street is a plaque informing us that Father Pierre Teilhard de Chardin lived in the house at number **15**.

The famous Hôtel de Bourbon-Condé at **12** has a gated entrance framed by four pilasters with Ionic

▶ 39 Boulevard des Invalides

▼ La Pagode, 57 bis Rue de Babylone

capitals. It, too, was built by Brongniart. He designed it in 1783 for Louise-Adélaïde de Bourbon-Condé. She was a sister of the Duke de Bourbon, an aunt of the Duke d'Enghien, the abbess of Remiremont, and founder of the order of the Bénédictines du Saint-Sacrement (1816). Her remains were transferred to the convent on 20 Rue Monsieur in 1853. Despite the various owners and occupants since the French Revolution, the mansion has preserved its music room decorated with ionic pilasters, Mademoiselle de Bourbon's boudoir, and the magnificent façade on the immense garden (which can be glimpsed from the Boulevard des Invalides).

The white front door flanked by two smaller houses masks the Hôtel

de Jarnac at number **8**, erected between 1784 and 1787 by Étienne-François Legrand and rented by Marie-Charles de Rohan-Chabot, count de Jarnac. Today, it is private property and not open to the public. If you are fortunate enough to be walking by when the gate is open, you may notice its resemblance to a villa designed by Palladio, with a peristyle.

Note that it is possible to get a glimpse of this historical mansion's back façade by going through the building belonging to the Saint-François-Xavier chaplaincy at 39 Boulevard des Invalides to the garden in the rear, adjacent to the grounds of the Hôtel de Jarnac. The garden also reportedly provides privacy for an open-air swimming pool on the property.

Rue de Babylone

Rue Monsieur takes us straight to **Rue de Babylone**, where we will turn right. This street was named for the bishop of Babylon, who donated his houses and lands for a seminary to train missionaries.

The exotic La Pagode cinema at **57 bis** stands on the corner with Rue

Monsieur. The history behind this odd structure begins a bit like a fairy tale. Mr. Morin, the director of the Bon Marché department store, was very much in love with his wife. In 1895, at the height of the trend for Japanese exoticism, he decided to present his wife with a real pagoda for her garden. Allegedly, certain elements in the structure, such as the carved wooden beams, were custom-made by craftsmen in the Empire of the Rising Sun. Petit-Palais architect Alexandre Mar-

cel oversaw the reconstruction with an eye for authenticity in every detail: gilding, varnished tiles, frescoes, dragons, etc.

Mrs. Morin was delighted with the gift. She let her imagination go wild, holding lavish receptions and masquerade balls. Nevertheless, the very year the edifice was completed, she left her husband for his partner's son. The fairy tale had a vaudeville ending.

In 1986, La Pagode, which had been a legendary art-house movie theater since the 1950s, was listed on the historic register. It's a must-see, with its exotic bamboo garden, Japanese maples, and purple and white flowers. The tropical species make it one of the marvels of Paris in the summertime.

Let's continue strolling along Rue de Babylone toward Rue du Bac. Why not stop in for a break at a nice restaurant at **45**, Au Pied de Fouet? It is frequented by regulars and locals who pop in for a quick, inexpensive meal.

After Rue Vaneau on our right, we may go daydream in the shade of the fruit trees in the **Jardin Catherine Labouré**, recently opened on the

◄ Detail of the façade of the Paris Foreign Missions main building, 128 Rue du Bac

grounds of the Hôtel de La Vallière, where the Daughters of Charity grew fruit and vegetables for their convent. Now a public park maintained by the city, the garden welcomes neighborhood children, government workers from nearby ministries, and senior citizens who wish to escape the noise of Rue de Sèvres and Rue du Bac. Its cross-like shape is lined with inviting lawns, shaded by apple, cherry, and pear trees. On the right, a trellis is laden with grape vines, near the hazelnut and raspberry bushes. Schoolchildren can learn about horticulture in the greenhouses.

Behind **36** Rue de Babylone, you can get a hint of the neighboring - and huge – grounds of the Hôtel de Matignon, which houses the prime minister's offices. The Louis Seize style Hôtel de Cassini at **32** has long been given over to government offices, the Direction Générale de l'Administration et de la Fonction Publique having made its home there since 1976.

Rue de Babylone soon runs into **Rue du Bac**, and this is where we shall veer to the left.

Rue du Bac on Either Side of Rue de Babylone

The houses on the corner of Rue de Babylone and Rue du Bac belonged to the first seminary of the Missions Étrangères de Paris (Paris Foreign Missions Society) founded in 1644 at **128 Rue du Bac**. Let's go into the courtyard and explore the chapel which borders it on one side. The chapel doors are framed by two Ionic pilasters and topped by two Corinthian pilasters and a pediment. If it is

between 6:45 am and 6 pm, we can enter the place of worship, built in 1683 by master mason Lepas-Dubuisson on plans drawn up by architect Pierre Lambert for the missionary society. The society itself was founded in 1644 by Father Bernard de Sainte-Thérèse, bishop of Babylon, who wanted a seminary to train eccle-

siastical students for missionary work. Be sure to visit the crypt. The monastic simplicity in the architectural and interior design inspires a prayerful attitude. It is prolonged by a gallery containing the display cabinets of the interesting and moving hall of martyrs, a repository for the souvenirs and relics of missionaries martyred in Vietnam, Korea, Tibet, and Japan in the 19th century. The hall of martyrs and the crypt are open Tuesday to Saturday from 11 am to 6:30 pm, and Sunday from 1-6 pm.

The society has one of the largest private gardens in Paris, lying in front of a magnificent building erected in 1732 to house curiosities brought back by the missionaries: rare plants, a Chinese bell, an oratory, statues, etc. Visits are allowed only during annual national architectural heritage days (*journées du patrimoine*).

Returning to the beginning of the block, let's cross Rue de Babylone to explore the other end of the Rue du Bac. At **136** is a house built in 1737 for the Hôpital des Incurables, which was purchased in 1859 by the Daughters of Charity. In 1812, they had moved into the 1681 Hôtel de Lassay at **140**, after commissioning the architect Damesne to accommodate a convent and chapel for them there. The order was created in 1634 by Louise de Marillac at the instigation of Saint Vincent de Paul. The Virgin is believed to have appeared here five times in

◄ Conran Shop, located in a former Au Bon Marché building, 117 Rue du Bac

► 140 Rue du Bac

July and November 1830, to Catherine Labouré, before she even became a postulate. This belief has made the chapel a special place of devotion, attracting visitors from far beyond the neighborhood.

Let's go through the gate at 140 and take the path lined with convent buildings on our right. On our left is a wall with bas-reliefs relating the life

story of Catherine Labouré. This tiny lane is often crowded with pilgrims who have come to buy one of the famous "miraculous medals" now available in rather prosaic vending machines.

In the chapel, clergy and lay people from all over the world pray to the Virgin. The nave of this sanctuary has a low barrel-vaulted ceiling. The chapel was enlarged in 1843-1845 by the additions of aisles and an apse. In 1930, Alphonse Richardière raised the nave in order to accommodate the growing number of visitors. He made the brackets less intrusive and created a triumphal arch decorated with a fresco illustrating the Virgin's apparition to Catherine. Over the altar, placed against the back wall of the apse, a large white rock bears a Virgin with shooting rays of light (1856), as a reminder that the Daughters of Charity is a Marian order. Beside the choir, to the right, the body of Sister Catherine Labouré (†1876) is displayed behind glass, and to the left is the tomb of Louise de Marillac, whose remains were transferred here in

supervision of architect Alexandre Laplanche; then, from 1872 to 1887, under Louis-Charles Boileau, who hired Gustave Eiffel to design an iron framework for the building. In 1923, another building was erected across the street. The entrance was placed on the corner of Rue de Sèvres and Rue du Bac and included three wide glass walls set between columns with a projecting awning. Most of the original interior décor is now gone, but the first store has preserved its skylights and its wrought iron balustrades.

The light metal structures supporting the skylights allowed designers to open wide, adjustable spaces (hallmarks of 20th-century open floor-space design). At the same time, the stairs and the opulent decorations were distinctively 19th-century. The Bon Marché was an architectural success for two reasons: its combined use of iron and stone for a commercial building, and its novel overhead lighting, which flooded aisles and counters. The hearts of the shoppers from the newly affluent bourgeoisie were immediately won over. This is the store that inspired Émile Zola's Au Bonheur des Dames. Mr. Boucicaut was also an innovator in the field of sales and distribution techniques, introducing the price tag on merchandise, setting up a profusion of aisles, and announcing a return and exchange policy. Store employees were entitled to certain social benefits, as well as perks like evening classes to learn history, music, or a new language. Upon her death, Mrs. Boucicaut willed the store to her employees.

The Bon Marché Department Store: A Model

The impressive façades date from the last third of the 19th century and the early years of the 20th century.

Aristide Boucicaut's first partner was Videau. In 1852, they operated a hosiery shop called Au Bon Marché. Later, as the sole owner of the business, he had the store rebuilt in two phases: first, from 1869 to 1872, under the

1920. Visitors are awed by the realism of these bodies.

Across the street from **136** Rue du Bac, on the façade of the department store, one can still make out the engraving reading simply "Magasin Aristide Boucicaut," known far and wide as the Bon Marché (see inset).

It stands not only on the site of the old Hospice des Petites Maisons, which provided care for sick children, the poor, the crippled, the insane, and those with venereal diseases, but also covers two cemeteries closed in the 18th century: that of the hospice, and a parish cemetery of Saint-Sulpice.

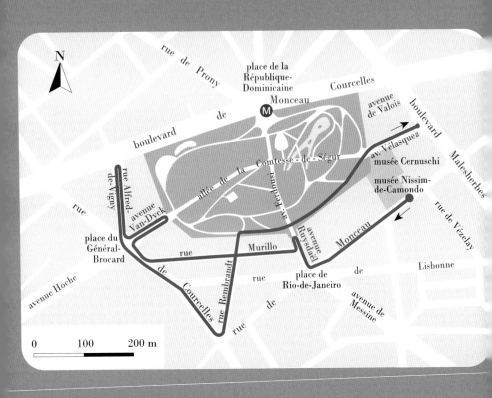

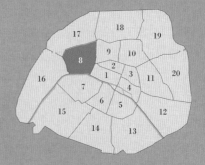

8th

The Parc Monceau Neighborhood

▶ Start: **Boulevard de Courcelles, metro Monceau**
▶ Finish: **Avenue Velasquez, metro Monceau**

Since the first decades of the 18th century, wealthy Parisians had been keeping their paramours in "little houses" in the still bucolic Faubourg Saint-Honoré. Lords and financiers vied to see whose folly could be the most lavish. The Duke de Chartres, future Duke d'Orléans, better known by his post-Revolutionary name, Philippe Égalité, acquired a long lease in the Monceau village (1769) on land belonging to Louis-Marie Colignon, an architect. The contract stipulated that Colignon would design formal gardens and a villa.

By way of introduction, before we set out on our neighborhood stroll, let's wander through **Parc Monceau**. We'll take the entrance located on Boulevard de Courcelles, graced by lovely rotunda.

The Folly of Louis Philippe, Duke de Chartres

The main building was square, with doorways at each of its four corners, opening onto garden paths. Immediately after it was completed, in 1773, the Duke de Chartres turned his attention to landscaping. He wanted something larger and more in line with the tastes of the day. The famous portrait painter Louis Carrogis, also known as Carmontelle, was hired to draw up plans. Instead of the natural-looking gardens then fashionable (the jardin à l'anglaise), Carmontelle wanted the grounds to represent "all times and all places." The estate was completed in 1780. The initial lodge and grounds had become elements in a much larger whole. Carmontelle's illustrated written record of his endeavor was published in 1779. The entryways at the corners of the lodge were extended, giving it an X-shaped floor plan. Unlike Bagatelle, which was built in less costly materials, the Duke de Chartres' folly incorporated marble, breccia, and bronze work. The estate grounds featured quaint farms, a cabaret, an Italian vineyard, French country houses, watermills, windmills, a minaret, Turkish and Tatar tents, fake ruins of a temple to dedicated Mars, and a naumachia – that is, a pool in which naval battles could be reenacted. The colonnade ornamenting the Duke's allegedly came from the funerary chapel called la

rotonde des Valois, a part of the Saint-Denis basilica demolished in the 18th century. There was also a white marble temple and an outbuilding called the salle des marronniers (the chestnut hall). One of the niches in this hall was graced by a delightful copy of Barberini's Faun, executed by Edme Bouchardon, now in the Louvre. Other curiosities included a Chinese ring game, an Egyptian tomb, and the bathing beauties' pool, for which Houdon carved a woman in white marble being bathed by a black slave girl, made of lead. The marble figure has survived, and although the lead one did not, there are bronze replicas of her bust. A splendid one is on display at the nearby Musée Nissim de Camondo.

In 1780, Thomas Blaikie, a famous Scottish gardener, was hired by the Duke de Chartres, and made alterations to Carmontelle's concept.

The Fermiers-Généraux wall that ringed Paris was built in the 1780s. Few of the toll buildings designed by Ledoux survived; the one at Parc Monceau is one of the few that did. The city wall halted the westward expansion of the duke's estate and kept it within

the Paris city limits. Despite the encroachment, the estate continued to grow and be embellished. Blaikie added a winter garden with a hypogeum (underground room) connected to the main hall by greenhouses, and more exotic tree species were planted on the grounds.

All work was halted when Philippe Égalité was executed on November 6, 1793.

The Jardin de Monceau became national property. It was rented out by organizers of large events and festivals, and was the site for the first parachute jump in history by Jacques Garnerin in 1797. The estate quickly became dilapidated. The hall was torn down around 1806. In 1811, the grounds became an imperial domain. A new hall was designed by the architect Bénard on the site of the original. After the Restoration, the park returned to the Orléans family. It was 1819 and the duke, the future Louis-Philippe I, gave the estate serious attention, by hiring the Alsatian poet and gardener Schoëne.

In 1830, wishing to keep the property in the family, the king bequeathed his part to his children, while his sister Adélaïde

bequeathed hers to them in 1847. In 1852, the State contested their inheritance from Louis-Philippe. In any case, his possessions had already been confiscated by the future Napoleon III, then prince and president. In 1860, the decision to finish construction of Boulevard Malesherbes resulted in the loss to Louis-Philippe's descendants of the portion of the estate that had remained theirs, inherited from their Aunt Adélaïde. The city acquired the 45-acre estate (18 hectares), which then stretched from today's Rue de Courcelles to Rue Monceau. Soon, over half had been sold to banker Émile Pereire for development. The rest (about 20 acres, or 8 hectares) remained city property. Adolphe Alphand, head of the Paris parks department, was put in charge of making it a public promenade.

◄ The naumachia in Parc Monceau

A City Park since the Second Empire

Napoleon III held opening ceremonies for both Parc Monceau and Boulevard Malesherbes on August 13, 1861. By that time, all that remained of the Folie de Chartres was the naumachia, the pyramid, and fragments of the temple to Mars. King Louis-Philippe (Égalité's son) had had the little round marble temple removed to the Île du Pont at his favorite estate, in nearby Neuilly. It was moved again in 1930 to the southern tip of the Ile de la Jatte.

A higher and more ornate dome was put on the observatory, or rotunda, designed by Ledoux for the Fermiers-Généraux (city-limit administrators). The park had been re-landscaped to look natural (the jardin à l'anglaise), and now had two main paths. The one running east-west was called Boulevard de Monceau (now Allée de la Comtesse-de-Ségur); the north-south promenade, Avenue de la Rotonde (now Avenue Ferdousi). Magnificent gates in Louis Quinze style, designed by Davioud and forged by Ducros, closed these walkways. Winding paths, a bridge, a manmade grotto, and various exotic plants now graced this public park where music, dance, and theater performances were no longer allowed.

Émile Pereire, the investor developing the neighborhood around the new park, had three short exit avenues (Van-Dyck, Ruysdaël, and Velasquez) and three side streets (Murillo, Rembrandt, and Alfred-de-Vigny) laid out. The names indicate

▲ Pyramid in Parc Monceau

◄ The gates of Parc Monceau

Second-Empire fondness for 17th-century Dutch and Spanish artists. In the early 20th century, monuments celebrating literary figures and musicians were added to the park. Among the statues now in Parc Monceau, you may see Raoul-Charles Verlet's statue of Guy de Maupassant, unveiled in 1897 in the presence of Émile Zola; Antonin Mercier's statue of Charles Gounod; and Falguière's 1902 monument to operatic composer Ambroise Thomas. The sculpture depicting Frédéric Chopin at his piano, in the company of allegories of Night and Harmony, is a 1906 work by Jacques Froment-Meurice, a man born into a dynasty of goldsmiths. Russian artist Léopold Bernstamm created another monument (1904) celebrating a now-forgotten playwright, Édouard Pailleron. Bronzes such as Charles Valton's

Wounded Lioness (1889), however, like many others around Paris, were melted down by the Vichy government to make weapons for the Germans. Parc Monceau and its immediate vicinity have inspired artists and writers such as Claude Monet; Émile Zola, who took photographs and used the mansions beside the park as settings for his novel La Curée, as did a later author, Philippe Hériat, for his La Famille Boussardel; and Guy de Maupassant, whose novel Fort Comme la Mort takes place here. The park continues to inspire French and foreign artists: Carzou, Yves Brayer, Kojiro Akagi, and the remarkable comic-strip artist Jacques Tardi.

▼ Statuary celebrating (left to right): Guy de Maupassant, Charles Gounod, and Édouard Pailleron

Rue de Monceau

Leaving the park either through the east-side exit on Avenue Velasquez or the southern one on Avenue Ruysdaël, we shall begin the neighborhood walk on **Rue de Monceau**. As far back as the 17th century, this street ran alongside the lands acquired by the Duke de Chartres, connecting what were then two villages, Le Roule and Monceau.

Our first stop is in front of **63**, the Hôtel Moïse de Camondo, now the Musée Nissim-de-Camondo, one of the most splendid mansions that we will see in tract developed by Émile Pereire. In 1935, when he bequeathed the estate and its collections to the Union Centrale des Arts Décoratifs, Count Moïse de Camondo named the institution for his son Nissim, killed in an air battle in 1917. During World War II, the Vichy government did nothing to rescue the Camondo family from being deported and murdered at Auschwitz. A plaque at the entrance to the mansion relates the family's tragic fate.

Aside from the museum's exceptionally rich collections, the building offers elegant, tasteful, Louis Seize façades, and houses decors and art

▲ Musée Nissim-de-Camondo, 63 Rue de Monceau

objects that were for the most part made in Paris in the second half of the 18th century. Some pieces once belonged to estates in the 8th arrondissement. A tour of the museum will give us a good idea of what a mansion in the Faubourg Saint-Honoré must have been like in the days of the Bourets, the Beaujons, and the Andlaus. Moïse de Camondo's mansion differs significantly from the estates of other 19th-century art collectors like the Rothschilds, the Ganays, or the Jacquemart-Andrés in that Camondo shunned the stylistic eclecticism then popular. The collection is a perfect expression of his personal tastes.

▲ 52 Rue de Monceau

Originally from Spain, the Camondos settled in Venice, moved on to Turkey, and then finally came to France during the Second Empire. In 1866, when it was decided to divide the Duke d'Orléans' estate into lots, Abraham de Camondo and his brother Nissim, both bankers, commissioned two mansions to be built side by side on Rue de Monceau at numbers 61 and 63. Although the mansion that Destors designed for Abraham de Camondo has survived, it has lost its interior décor. The owner had eclectic tastes, and bequeathed his collections to the Louvre and the Musée Guimet.

Nissim's son, Moïse, wanted a home that would match his collection of decorative art from the second half of the 18th century. In 1911, he had his father's mansion razed, and hired René Sergent to draw up plans for a new home. Long a junior partner in Ernest Sanson's firm, Sergent had restored and built a number of chateaux and townhouses in France and the United States. For the Hôtel Camondo, he opted for sobriety. Viewed from the courtyard, the façade is concave. On the garden side, a central rotunda separates it from two V-shaped wings. The décor is strict and inspired by Jacques Ange Gabriel and other great architects from the 1770s and 1780s. Grooved stonework is the only façade ornamentation on the ground floor, although the courtyard façade has colossal Corinthian pilasters framing the windows of the upper floor. On the garden side, more colossal Corinthian columns enhance the central rotunda. The only decorative element on the wings is an austere molding on windows of the two upper floors. A powerful cornice topped by a balustrade crowns the entire edifice.

Next door at **61** is the mansion built by Abraham de Camondo, also a financier. Destors, who had trained with Charles Garnier, drafted the plans. Completed in 1874, the main hall of the mansion looks out onto a garden adjacent to Parc Monceau, on one side, and a courtyard separated from an outer bailey by arcades, on the other. The rich Renaissance-style decoration is the work of a sculptor named Schoenerwerk. In 1892, the mansion was purchased by Gaston Menier, scion of the Menier chocolate fortune. His family owned other splendid homes in the neighborhood.

Although this dwelling was slated for demolition in the 1970s, it now belongs to an American bank, Morgan Stanley. While the lovely awning has survived, the marble staircase was replaced by a banal, imitation-luxury entryway. The large stained-glass window depicting Abraham de Camondo receiving the floor plans for the mansion from his architect is now stored at the Musée d'Orsay.

Édouard Pailleron died at **55** in 1899. There is a marble monument honoring the playwright in Parc Monceau. The neo-Gothic mansion at **52** belonged to Mrs. de La Ville Le Roux in the early 20th century.

A mansion designed by Langlais for Adolphe de Rothschild stands at **45-49**. It once housed sumptuous collections.

From Avenue Ruysdaël to Avenue Van-Dyck

After passing number 41, let's turn right and stroll down **Avenue Ruysdaël**. The curious townhouse standing at **4** was built by J.-A. Pellechet for Gaston Menier, mentioned above in

◄ 3 Avenue Ruysdaël
► 4 Avenue Ruysdaël

our discussion of Abraham de Camondo's mansion. The caduceus adorning the shield recently added to the polychrome brick-and-stone façade is a tip that behind the arched doorway is the headquarters of the national pharmaceutical association.

Our review of architectural history continues, as we move on to the lovely neoclassical mansion at **3**, now

the headquarters of the Rolex company. In 1910, however, it was the home of the Marquise of Villahermosa.

Another mansion, more a mixture of styles, with its polychrome marble cartouches, belonged to Mr. Crosnier, a financier who committed suicide. It stands on the corner at **1 Rue Murillo**, the next street on our itinerary.

On our right is a series of matching townhouses around a courtyard separated from the street by an iron fence, with a small pavilion in the center. Soprano Lucienne Bréval once lived in numbers **4-6**. **8** was designed by Tronquois. **16** is also part of the set. Their rear windows look out onto Parc Monceau.

The building at **2** was designed by P. Boeswillwald, an important architect known for his restorations

of old monuments, very much in the Viollet-Le-Duc tradition.

Number **9** stands at the corner of Rue Rembrandt. Architect Gustave Clausse began erecting this interesting building in 1870. He planned the ground and second floors made of stone for his own use. He rented out the upper floors built in brick. All the windows on the second floor are semicircular arches decorated with polychrome ceramics. The arched bay windows on the corner of the building are flanked by two narrower windows, in what is known as Serlian style. The drawing room on this floor was designed for concerts and chamber music. Albert Gérard adorned the ceiling with paintings of musician-angels carrying scrolls bearing the names of great composers: Mozart, Beethoven, Weber.

The mansion of a certain Mrs. Viollier at **10** was erected in 1878 by H. A. Destailleur. The third-floor gable wall of **12** is decorated with a relief which may be a copy of an Italian Renaissance masterpiece in Florence's Duomo.

The top floor of a brick and stone building erected in 1870 by J. Bourdais at **19** has painted ceramic portraits of Raphaël, Michelangelo, Murillo, and Rubens.

Architect E. Morin planned the mansion located at **26**. Its neo-Greek décor is original. According to Rochegude, it was the property of the Duchess d'Uzès. One of its residents was the Duke de Brissac.

The **brick building** across the street with the staircase in the turret might belong to the complex comprised of a rental building and a mansion built in 1881 by N. F. Escalier on a lot which also has entrances at 64-66 Rue de Courcelles and 68 Rue de

Lisbonne. The façade on the Rue de Courcelles is decorated with a beautiful frieze of foliage patterns. This structure replaced the mansion owned by the Count Guyot d'Arlincourt, erected in 1879 by Crouslé.

Let's turn right onto **Rue de Courcelles** and go up to **Place du Général-Brocard**, named for the commander of the World War One flying-ace squadron Les Cigognes. To our right, we'll find the remarkable iron gates of **Avenue Van-Dyck**. Going in, it is interesting to note number **6**, the mansion that belonged to Joseph Reinach. A legislator who ardently defended Alfred Dreyfus, he helped found the League of Human Rights. Designed

▲ 9 Rue Murillo

▲ 19 Rue Murillo
◄ 6 Avenue Van-Dyck

▲ 5 Avenue Van-Dyck
▶ 8 Rue Alfred-de-Vigny
▼ 58 Rue de Courcelles

This is yet another of the Menier family's estates. It was built for Émile-Justin Menier's son Henri, and designed by Henri Parent, the same architect who had done 5 Avenue Van-Dyck for the family. While the street-side façade and entrance are Gothic, the courtyard façades were inspired by the Franco-Flemish Renaissance. Admire the half-timbered outbuildings, similar to those at 4 Avenue Ruysdaël. The main staircase was sculpted in Flemish Baroque. This building is currently the home of the Conservatoire International de Musique de Paris.

by the architect A. Normand with references to the Italian Renaissance, this building is currently used by the École Active Bilingue.

Across the street at **5**, H. Parent built a mansion for Émile-Justin Menier. The building's main portion is perpendicular to the avenue and overlooks the park. There is also one wing angling out along the courtyard. Dalou likely helped decorate this highly ornate ensemble credited to Lefebvre, a sculptor and ornamentalist. Completed in 1874, the structures on the property included stables and a winter drawing-room made more pleasant by a hothouse. The Hôtel Menier narrowly escaped demolition in 1969. In 1972, it was listed on the historical register, and restoration was completed in 1980.

Émile Pereire, the developer of the Parc Monceau area, built his own mansion at **10**. The sober neoclassical façade has a high arched front door opening onto a courtyard, which is fenced off from the street. The property is currently used by the Simone and Cino Del Duca Foundation, now administered by the Institut de France.

Let's go back down the block to the square and turn left on **Rue de Courcelles**, running southwards toward the Faubourg Saint-Honoré. The odd-numbered side of the block between Avenue Hoche and Rue de Monceau presents little interest, being entirely occupied chiefly by a barracks erected on land belonging to the Hospice Beaujon. On the even-numbered side, opera singer Lucienne Bréval (1869-1935) lived at number

Rue Alfred-de-Vigny and Rue de Courcelles

Let's retrace our steps and go back out the big gates. We will turn right onto **Rue Alfred-de-Vigny**. The sidewalk on our right is lined with townhouses that have direct views on Parc Monceau. Although Hôtel de La Béraudière no longer stands at **4**, its near neighbor at **8** is worth visiting.

58. An equally famous singer, albeit of the Moulin Rouge variety, Yvette Guilbert (1867-1944), lived next door at **56**, in 1902.

You can't miss **48**, at the corner of Rue Rembrandt, so unusual is its pagoda-like architecture. The five-story, red ochre house with its curved roofline and varnished roof tiles dates from 1926. It was commissioned from architect Fernand Bloch by C. T. Loo, a Chinese art dealer. The headquarters of C. T. Loo & Co. is still located in this "pagoda." The decorative elements in the cornice moldings,

pilasters, framework, and window railings are uniformly repeated. A little gate and front yard separate it from the street.

Let's skip the block of Rue Monceau between Rue Rembrandt and Avenue Ruysdaël, where the Hôtel Furtado-Heine-Murat stood at number 28. Built by F. Convents in 1856, it was demolished in 1961. US President Woodrow Wilson was a guest in this mansion from December 14, 1918 to February 14, 1919. Wrecking crews also demolished the elegant townhouses at 31, home of Madeleine Lemaire, a socialite and painter, and

32, which was the birthplace in 1799 of Oscar I of Sweden, son of Marshal Bernadotte, to make way for the hideously ugly headquarters of France's power utility.

From Rue Rembrandt to Avenue Velasquez

At this point, we'll pass the "pagoda" and head up **Rue Rembrandt**, which has several interesting estates. The gabled Renaissance-style townhouse at **1** has high, coffered, painted ceilings, and once belonged to Mr. Ziegler. Take a look at **4**, which was the home of the architect himself, A. G. Guérinot, and later, that of Dr. A. Millard. Number **6** is called the Hôtel de Billy.

Rue Rembrandt runs straight into **Parc Monceau**, discussed above.

◄ 1 Rue Rembrandt
➤ 48 Rue de Courcelles
▼ 6-8 Rue Rembrandt

You might wish to walk around it to admire the rear façades of the mansions overlooking the lovely trees and monuments of the park before continuing to **Avenue Velasquez**. Art seems to be everywhere along this street: in its name and in the homes lining it.

▶ Musée Cernuschi,
7 Avenue Velasquez

Hippolyte-Alfred Chauchard (1821-1909), founder of the Grands Magasins du Louvre in 1855 (see page 19, 1st arrondissement walk), was also a great art collector and philanthropist. His vast collection of 19th-century paintings included famous pieces such as Millet's Angélus, pieces from the Barbizon school, and works by Meissonnier. They were part of his 1906 endowment to the Louvre. He lived at **5**.

Next door at **7**, a wealthy financier originally from Milan named Enrico Cernuschi (1821-1896) befriended Garibaldi and the heroes of the Risorgimento. He commissioned Bouwens van der Boijen to build him a fine mansion. In 1871, Cernuschi went to China and Japan via America. He returned in 1873 with artwork of all sorts. His friends included Philippe Burty, the Goncourt brothers, and Théodore Duret, who advised him. After visiting the Universal Exhibition of 1867, Cernuschi developed a passion for Oriental art. The centerpiece of his collection was a large 18th-century bronze Buddha from Banryûji temple in Meguro (now a district of Tokyo). Upon his death in 1896, he bequeathed his mansion and his collections to the city of Paris, ordering the city to turn it into a museum, which opened shortly thereafter, in 1898. The first curator, Henri d'Ardenne de Tizac, focused on acquisitions from much earlier periods, barely represented in Cernuschi's collections. In 1920, he acquired "the tigress," a bronze vase from the 12th-century BC Shang dynasty. His successor René Grousset and architect Pierre Fournier adapted the museum to display these acquisitions.

By participating in archeological digs in Indochina, the museum

enriched its collections and, in 1937, presented a major exhibition of ancient Chinese bronzes. Since then, the museum has continued to grow. In 1956, it acquired a rare 8th-century scroll by painter Han Kan, entitled *Chevaux et Palefreniers* (horses and grooms). The society of friends of the museum has helped with major acquisitions. Temporary exhibitions and demonstrations of contemporary Oriental artists at work provide visitors with an introduction to the beauty of art from the Far East. This City of Paris museum (free admission to permanent collections) underwent an overhaul in 2005. Its Oriental garden was also renovated. The museum doubled its usable space and streamlined the traffic flow, yet preserved the mansion's charms as an original private home.

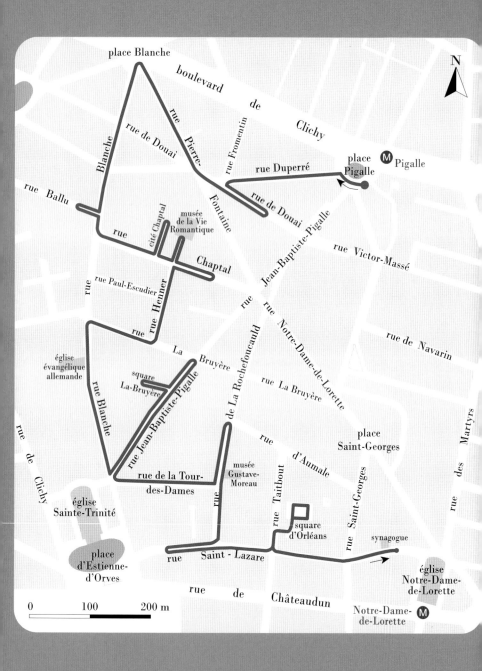

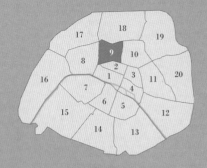

9th

Nouvelle Athènes

▶ Start: **Place Pigalle,
metro Pigalle**
▶ Finish: **Rue Saint-Lazare,
metro Notre-Dame-
de-Lorette**

Beginning in 1819-1820, Jean Joseph de La Peyrière, head of the Seine's tax collection agency, and architect Auguste Constantin began selling lots from the old Hôtel de Valentinois. The property had belonged to Honoré de Grimaldi, Prince of Monaco. It was situated between Rue Saint-Lazare, Rue de la Rochefoucauld and Rue de la Tour-des-Dames. Their program was, "to build private homes according to the needs of the various fortunes, [...] to arrange them around each other so as always to have a considerable mass of air, [...] to gather insofar as possible selected buyers who have made names for themselves in the fields of literature, sciences, or arms, and lastly, to introduce them to our young and talented architects by holding a competition." (Thiollet, *Choix de maisons et édifices publics de Paris*, 1838) The new neighborhood immediately attracted musicians, painters, writers, and actors who sought greenery and quiet in a location that was nevertheless convenient to Montmartre and the Grands Boulevards.

The development and vicinity were called "Nouvelle Athènes" – a name "chosen by the public" – due to its neoclassical architectural style and the type of residents drawn to the project. A veritable "republic of arts and letters" was in the making. Multi-talented Dureau de La Malle, also a resident of this neighborhood, lodging at 11 Rue de La Rochefoucauld, wrote in his October 18, 1823 column in *Le Journal des Débats*, "The name may sound rather lofty, but for two years, it has been commonly used by the public to designate the portion of the faubourg between Rue des Mar-tyrs, Rue Saint-Lazare, and Rue de La Rochefoucauld. This neighborhood is connecting nicely with the quarter bordered on its west side by Rue Blanche, on the south by Rue Saint-Lazare, and on the east by Rue de La Rochefoucauld, crossed by rue de la Tour-des-Dames."

Place Pigalle

Let's begin on **Place Pigalle**. The world-famous half-moon was laid out in 1826 on the site of the Barrière de Montmartre, the toll station at the city limits wall, torn down in 1862. Its *p'tit jet d'eau* (little spray of water) shooting from a fountain was made famous in a song by Georges Ulmer, as were its *p'tites femmes* in another, sung by Serge Lama. The ever-bustling Place

Nouvelle Athènes

"This new quarter, with its pure, healthful air, fresh water brought in from the Canal de l'Ourcq, delightful southern exposure (and Montmartre hill protects it to the north), slight elevation, and the lovely view we enjoy, [...] located so close to the centers of business and leisure activities, and yet removed from the noise and crowds, seems to offer a solitary yet lively haven of peace. It quickly attracted poets, artists, scientists, world travelers, warriors, and statesmen, in search of a sanctuary wherein to meditate, of a refuge from the duplicitous ambitions of illusion and glory.

"Numerous gardens planted with fragrant trees purify the atmosphere here; blackbirds and nightingales add their trills to the stanzas being recited or composed. When evening comes and all is calm on this hill of knowledge, the roar of carriage traffic in Paris sounds to our ears no louder than the distant rumble of a great waterfall."

Dureau de La Malle, *Journal des Débats*, October 18, 1823.

Pigalle, a bastion of *gai Paris*, attracts fans of strip-tease shows and bars ranging from seedy to trendy.

The artists' studio at **5** is a survivor: in the early 19th century, it was one of many low-rising buildings lining the plaza, housing famous literary cafés and cabarets. The Cupidon, a bar at **7**, replaced Le Rat Mort, which may have owed its repulsive name to the fact that a dead rat was once found on the floor. However, others believe it may have been due to the stench of the place, which purportedly prompted a

newcomer to exclaim, "It smells like a dead rat in here!" This Mecca for Bohemians and the opposition press was frequented by Gambetta, Degas, Jules Vallès, Édouard Manet, Gustave Courbet, and François Coppée. It was here that Rimbaud stabbed Verlaine in the leg several times with a knife.

By 1870, Impressionists had started gathering at La Nouvelle Athènes café that used to stand at number **9**. Monet, Degas, Forain, and Pissarro could be seen chatting with the likes of Verlaine, Maupassant, Zola, Jean Richepin, and Mallarmé. Édouard Manet painted this café several times. It is the setting for his painting entitled *L'Absinthe* and for his pastel *Femmes à la Terrasse d'un Café*.

Crossing **Rue Jean-Baptiste-Pigalle**, we shall see over the doorway at **77** a circular pediment containing a large bull's-eye window framed by half-caryatids. In 1907, this was the location of the Théâtre de la Folie-Pigalle. At **11 Place Pigalle**, the Folie's Pigalle nightclub has replaced the artist studios used by Puvis de Chavannes (or *pubis de cheval* as Toulouse-Lautrec nicknamed him, making a pun), Jean-Jacques Henner, and Eugène Isabey. Hiring models was a snap; they merely had to step outside. The *marché aux modèles* was regularly held on Place Pigalle. Thus, as the story goes, Suzanne Valadon

gave up her career as an acrobat to become one of Puvis de Chavannes' models for his painting *Le Bois Sacré*.

On the corner of Rue Duperré, the Omnibus-Café takes up the ground floor of number **13**, a building erected by H. Vielard in 1879. The chimeras were carved by François Crozier. Up to the end of the 1960s, it was a hang-out for out-of-work musicians, hoping to get hired by a band leader. Its name recalls the famous horse-drawn bus line that ran from Place Pigalle to the Halle aux Vins (a line frequently abbreviated as "Pigalle-aux-Vins"). In 1900, it ran from Montmartre to Montparnasse, connecting Paris' two great literary and artistic centers. That bus line was in fact the precursor of the capital's first north-south metro line, line 4, completed in 1910, ten years after the first line was opened.

Rue Duperré and Rue de Douai

Let's now turn left onto **Rue Duperré**. A fine artists' studio at **9** stands across from the lovely twin doors at **12-14**, elegantly topped by a bas-relief and ornamented with masks over the windows.

Number **16**, formerly a shop, is Notre-Dame-des-Grâces, an Orthodox Catholic church under the Romanian patriarchate.

Number **24**, a former city school of applied arts founded by Élisa Lemonnier, was turned into a vocational school specialized in sales and trade.

Number **34**, Café Carmen, is in a polygonal corner building with as many addresses as it has sides: 22 Rue de Douai, 26 Rue Pierre-Fontaine, and 1 Rue Fromentin. In 1867, it

became home to three generations of the brilliant Jewish-Protestant Halévy family, living in three different apartments. Léon Halévy (member of the Institut de France and brother of the composer Fromental Halévy) and his wife Alexandrine, daughter of Hippolyte Lebas, the architect of Notre-Dame-de-Lorette, lived in one. Meanwhile, their son Ludovic, who, with Henri Meilhac, wrote libretti for light operas by Offenbach, Delibes, and Bizet, lived in another with his wife and their two sons, Élie and Daniel, who grew up to be a historian and an essayist, respectively. Then there was Fromental's grown daughter, Geneviève, who

▲ 13 Place Pigalle

▼ 12-13 Rue Duperré

had married one of her father's students, Georges Bizet. Their son Jacques and his cousin Daniel studied with Marcel Proust at the Lycée Condorcet. After Georges Bizet's death on June 3, 1875 at the age of 37, Geneviève stayed at this address until 1886, when she wed the lawyer Émile Straus. Marcel Proust modeled the Duchesse de Guermantes after Geneviève Straus and her famous salon of intellectuals and socialites from the Boulevard Haussmann quarter. In his book *Pays Parisiens*, Daniel Halévy recalls his neighborhood, "Certainly, in 1867, not

▼ 34 Rue Duperré

Café Carmen

▲ The Moulin Rouge seen from Place Blanche

a farm was left in Montmartre, but there was still open space with grass and trees... Artists, a few people of station, had taken residence here and formed a busy and pleasant little republic, a mere fifteen minutes from the boulevards. Friends drew us there, the Gounods, Degas, Fromentin, whom my father liked very much." Despite their friendship, once Degas had joined the anti-Dreyfus camp in 1898, he broke off with the Halévy family.

Let's take a quick look at the left side of **Rue de Douai** to get a glimpse of **15**, called the "maison Milon," built by Viollet-le-Duc in 1860-1861 for an entrepreneur. The particularity of this generally sober house is its balcony consoles carved with plant motifs.

From Rue Pierre-Fontaine to Rue Blanche

Once back in front of Café Carmen, we shall turn right onto **Rue Pierre-Fontaine**. The Villa Fontaine stands at **34**. Its old carved gate at **36** has been preserved. It opens onto a lovely house in July Monarchy décor – i.e., 1830-1848. Number **42** is the Art Déco style Comédie de Paris, a theater built in 1930 by architect Georges-Henri Pingusson. Past it is a courtyard building where André Breton set up house in 1922 on the fourth floor, the one with a tall window. He moved in with his collections of Hopi Kachina dolls, and paintings by Picasso, Braque, de Chirico, and Seurat. His collections were auctioned off in April 2003 in 4,100 lots. However, one can still lay eyes on the studio wall, which was donated to the Pompidou Center. After the famous Café Certa in Passage de l'Opéra was closed, Breton transferred his surrealist group's meetings to Le Cyrano, a bar located at **52**, close to his home. (The bar is now a Monoprix store.)

37, the Académie Julian, was a hotbed of Impressionist and Fauvist painters. In 1870, it became the first school of painting to admit women, but it placed them in separate studios, located nearby at 5 Rue Fromentin.

45 has a plaque commemorating Villiers de l'Isle-Adam's stay in 1888-1889. When he left, it was to go die in a clinic on Rue Oudinot.

The silhouette of the Moulin-Rouge dominates **Place Blanche**. Rue Blanche widened here at the old Porte-Blanche, the toll house for the Fermiers Généraux (city limits) wall. Some historians believe that this – rather than the Barrière Rochechouart – was the location for the "Trou aux Suisses" (the Swiss hole), the spot where the bodies of three hundred of the eight hundred Swiss Guards slain in the August 10, 1792 massacre at the Tuileries were dumped into a disused quarry.

The barrier and **Rue Blanche** got their name from the white dust floating off the wagons hauling gypsum from the Montmartre quarries. As you may already have guessed, gypsum is the base for the famous plaster of Paris. It was heated in ovens beside the Seine, fueled by timber floated down the river. Quarry operations began in the 13th century, and the earliest record of a road to the Paris quarries dates from 1398 and describes today's Rue Blanche.

As we stroll down **Rue Blanche**, we'll take a look at the odd decoration

at **73**, on the corner of Rue Douai. The names of the months of the year are engraved in Latin running across the building's twelve bays within the trim between the entresol and the floor above it. If we look higher, we will see the signs of the zodiac carved in twelve medallions. The façade has a profusion of floral elements as well as balconies with rosette balustrades carved in stone.

A little further down at **78**, we come upon what appears to be a 15th-century house. In fact, it is pure Renaissance revival, built by Théodore

Ballu, architect of La Trinité church. This was his home and he died here in 1885.

To our right is **Rue Ballu** with its refined villa at **5**, erected by J. Brevet in 1868. It is home to the society of playwrights and music composers. At **6**, in the Théâtre des Pantins, Alfred Jarry's play *Ubu Roi* premiered with marionettes on January 20, 1898.

Rue Chaptal

Doubling back to **Rue Blanche**, we'll stroll a few yards down and turn left on **Rue Chaptal**.

Take a look at **24**, a 1900 building by Henri Petit. The side bays are crowned by large rams' heads. At the far end of the narrow Cité Chaptal, at **20 bis**, you will find Théâtre 347. As you might expect, it has three hundred and forty-seven seats. As the International Visual Theatre, its productions are performed in sign language. The theater used to house one of the biggest attractions during the Belle Époque: the Grand-Guignol. From 1897 to 1962, it made faithful audiences roar with laughter... and shriek

▸ 73 Rue Blanche
◂ Cité Chaptal

▲ Musée de la Vie Romantique, 16 Rue Chaptal

Let's go through the gate at **16** and to the end of the passage to discover a garden that, quite fortunately, has been preserved. This is the Musée de la Vie Romantique, opened in 1982 under the name of Musée Renan-Scheffer. Ary Scheffer, one of the leading painters of the Romantic period, lived here from 1830 to his death in 1858. The house was built in 1830 by Wormser shortly after Rue Chaptal was laid out in 1825, by developers Delessert and Ladvocat, on lands belonging to the family of the chemist Jean-Antoine Chaptal. Born in 1795 in Dordrecht, Holland, Ary Scheffer came from a long line of artists. His father, his mother Cornélia Lamme, his brother Henry, and Henry's daughter Cornélia Scheffer were all painters. He moved to Paris in 1811 and in 1825 was hired by the Duke d'Orléans (later Louis-Philippe I) to instruct his children in art. After his patron's ascension to the throne, Scheffer executed numerous portraits of the king and royal family, and was commissioned to create paintings for the Versailles museum of history. Scheffer added two studios to Rue Chaptal, one for his brother Henry, and one for himself, where he painted, gave lessons to his students, and entertained artistic and literary giants such as Chopin, George Sand, Liszt, Pauline Viardot, Rossini, and Dickens. It was here that Ernest Renan was introduced to the woman he would marry, Ary's niece, Cornélia Scheffer.

10 was built in 1937 for the Société des Artistes, Compositeurs et Éditeurs de Musique (SACEM). Look up at the sculpted figures on the cornice: a mortal harp player and violinist are accompanied by angels, also playing instruments.

with terror. "This theater is not recommended for nervous or impressionable women," kindly warned the *Guide des Plaisirs à Paris*. Agonizing suspense, terrifying torture, and squirting hemoglobin guaranteed a good fright.

Starting in 1868, Paul Verlaine became a regular in Nina de Villard's literary salon at **17** Rue Chaptal. The publisher Alphonse Lemerre had printed his *Poèmes Saturniens* in 1866. Extravagant Nina, the muse of the Parnassian poets, often posed for Manet. She had dumped her alcoholic husband, journalist Hector de Callias, and loved giving boisterous parties where bohemian artists and political firebrands mingled with literary giants like Jules Vallès, Villiers de l'Isle-Adam, poet Charles Cros, and Anatole France.

In 1875, Vincent van Gogh held a job for some time with Goupil, a publishing firm, which had a gallery located at **9**. A plaque informs us that Greek composer Iannis Xenakis lived here from 1970 to 2001.

From Rue Henner to Rue Jean-Baptiste-Pigalle

Rue Henner is opposite the lane leading to the Musée de la Vie Romantique. This street was named for another painter, Jean-Jacques Henner. He died in 1905 at 41 Rue La Bruyère, the

next street down. **9** Rue Henner was the Parisian residence of poet Guillaume Apollinaire after his 1901-1902 stay in Rhineland, where he fell in love with a young English governess, Annie Playden. She inspired his masterpiece, *La Chanson du Mal-aimé*. While still unknown, he wrote for various literary reviews and, in 1904, became friends with Pablo Picasso and Max Jacob. He moved closer to them, taking a place in Montmartre in April 1907.

And here, we will turn right onto **Rue La Bruyère**, walking down the block to Rue Blanche. This area was once part of the old Folie-Boursault estate, a country home with magnificent gardens belonging to actor Jean-François Boursault (1752-1842). It opened onto numbers 44-50 Rue Blanche. The Boursault development was launched in 1837 and gave birth in 1840 to Rue Henner, initially named Rue Léonie after the developer's daughter. This portion of Rue La Bruyère was initially named Rue Boursault. The Alliance Israélite Universelle, founded in 1860, moved its library to **45** in 1937. With over 100,000 volumes, it is Europe's largest library for Judaica and Hebrew studies.

Hector Berlioz remarried and moved into **53** after the death of his first wife, Harriet Smithson, from whom he was separated.

◄ 9 Rue Chaptal
► 9 Rue Henner

◄ Rue Henner

▲ 15 Rue Blanche

▲ 25 Rue Blanche

► Fire station,
22-28 Rue Blanche

◄ 21 Rue Blanche

We return again to **Rue Blanche**. Let's continue to walk down it. The German Evangelical Church stands at **25**. This neo-Romanesque church was built in 1911 by German architect Mohrmann. Carved over the doorway are a phoenix and a pelican, symbols of resurrection and charity.

The curvaceous building at **21** is a fine example of Art Nouveau design. Formerly the École Nationale des Arts et Techniques du Spectacle, it was built by Charles Girault (architect of the Petit-Palais) in 1901 for the Paul de Choudens music publishing firm. Next door at **19** is the seat of the civil engineers' guild. Two dates were engraved on the façade: 1848, for the creation of the guild, then located on

Rue Buffault, and 1896, the year this building was erected by Ferdinand Delmas.

The old Hôtel O'Donnell at **17** is set back a bit from the street. In 1891, the Nouveau Théâtre had just gone up at **15**, behind the old Pôle Nord roller-skating rink on Rue de Clichy. It was where Lugné-Poe staged his experimental Théâtre de l'Œuvre symbolist manifestos. Réjane, one of the star actresses, managed to buy the establishment in 1906. She gave it her name, enlarged and renovated it to its present-day shape, and brought its seating capacity up to 1,250. Paul Bessine was the architect. When Léon Volterra bought it in 1918, he renamed it Théâtre de Paris. In 1958, Elvire Popesco and Hubert de Mallet endowed it with an 350-seat annex. Now called Le Petit Théâtre de Paris, it began as the Théâtre Moderne.

The fire station at **22-28** was rebuilt in 1902 on the site of the 18th-century Folie-Roncières. It boasted a vineyard in its courtyard. The annual grape harvest produced about twenty bottles of wine.

Let's begin heading up **Rue Jean-Baptiste-Pigalle** to our left. In 1803, after a long series of other names, Rue Royale (1772), Rue de la République (1795), Rue de l'An-VIII (1800), it was named after the illustrious sculptor who had resided at number **1**, Jean-Baptiste Pigalle (1714-1785). In 1783, the bailiff of Montmartre sentenced him to pay a fine of three hundred pounds for having allowed mud and filth to accumulate at his doorstep. By the end of the 18th century, it had been home to numerous artists and actors, such as the tragedian Miss Raucourt, Miss Ruggieri from the Comédie-Italienne, and her sister, Marie-Catherine, whose stage name was Miss Colombe. She was the mistress of Jean-André Vassal who, in 1790, had had the mansion at **19-21** erected. It was designed by architect François-Nicolas Trou, who had adopted the pseudonym Henry. Two years earlier, the same architect built a home for Jean-André Vassal's brother, tax official Vassal de Saint-Hubert, on the triangle formed by the junction of Rue Blanche and Rue Pigalle.

Square La Bruyère, at **19**, was created in 1894. On October 15, 1839, novelist George Sand moved into **16**, taking possession of two buildings on large grounds. She and her daughter Solange lived in one of the dwellings. The other was originally meant for her son Maurice, whom she intended to turn into an artist. He took painting lessons from Delacroix for eight years. In 1841, however, composer Frédéric Chopin moved into the home, and they struck up a love affair that would last nine years. She described him thus: "He is a musician, nothing else but a musician. His thoughts can only be translated by music. He is infinitely

witty, refined, and impish, but... he gets locked into the narrowest, most conventional modes." (*Impressions et Souvenirs*, 1873).

The Henry Lemoine music publishing house, founded in 1772, took possession of its brand new premises at **17** in 1850.

Let's stop at **28**. High up on the seventh floor, the Nabi (post-Impressionist) painters Édouard Vuillard, Pierre Bonnard, and Maurice Denis shared a studio. Now, let's backtrack as far as the lower portion of Rue Jean-Baptiste-Pigalle.

◄ 17 Rue Jean-Baptiste-Pigalle

Rue de la Tour-des-Dames

We now come to **Rue de la Tour-des-Dames**. A left here brings us right to the heart of La Nouvelle Athènes.

Let's go beyond the city electric power station built after 1910 at **14-18**

◄ 14-18 Rue de la Tour-des-Dames

TALMA
NE A PARIS
LE 15 JANVIER 1763
EST MORT
DANS CETTE MAISON
LE 19 OCTOBRE 1826

▲ 9 Rue de la
Tour-des-Dames
▶ 4 Rue de la
Tour-des-Dames

on the lot previously owned by Les Voitures Camille. Its prior owner was a horse-changing post. Records dating from 1316 and 1323 mention a path going to a mill called *le Moulin de Dames* which belonged to the Montmartre abbey. As it followed the long stretch of Rue de La Rochefoucauld, at one point it had a bend providing access to the mill that was located at present-day **4**, formerly a mansion belonging to Count Étienne de Cambacérès, then de Clary. Although abandoned before 1717, the mill remained standing (though its blades had been removed) until 1822, the probable date of the construction of the de Clary residence by architect Clouet. Notice the Greek border frieze

along the second floor. The sunroom was a later addition.

The house at **2** was begun by architect Biet for the Prince de Wurtemberg, but only completed in 1823 for Baillot, a peer of France. It then belonged to Madame de Lestapis.

The row of smaller townhouses on the **right side** of the street is altogether typical of the way the neighborhood looked in the 1830s. Property lines stretched all the way south

to Rue Saint-Lazare, with back lanes leading up to the dwellings. Parts of one of these lanes have survived at 56 Rue Saint-Lazare (see below). Three prestigious members of the Théâtre-Français settled into quarters here, prompting Dureau de La Malle to suggest the street be named Lekain after the famous 18th-century actor.

In 1820, following his separation from Julie Carreau, with whom he had been living on Rue de la Victoire (then called Rue Chantereine), Talma, Napoleon's favorite actor, commissioned Charles Lelong to build him the big mansion at **9,** where he died six years later. Delacroix decorated the ground-floor dining room early in his career, while the actor was upstairs in the mirrored room where he stored his costumes and rehearsed. The garden-side façade is visible from the rear of the courtyard of the office building located at **11**, the CLEISS.

Painter Horace Vernet commissioned architect Haudebourg to design **5**, then purchased **7**, designed by Auguste Constantin.

The elegant concave façade on **3** was also the work of Auguste Constantin. He built it in 1820 for the speculator Jean de La Peyrière. It was purchased in 1822 by Miss Duchesnois, the stage name of Catherine-Joséphine Raffin, a tragedian who had acted opposite Talma. She owed her triumph over her great rival, Miss George, in part to him. Illness forced her to retire from the stage in 1829. In 1833, she gave a farewell performance, creating barely a ripple. The following year, she had to sell the mansion to provide her daughter with a dowry, and moved into 19 Rue de La Rochefoucauld, where she died penniless on January 8, 1835. Talma had drawn others to his street, such as his friend, Miss Mars. She was adored by Parisian audiences who, like Stendhal in 1804, found her "divine, sublime, charming, perfect." In 1824, at the age of 45, she bought **1**, the residence of Marshal Gouvion de Saint-Cyr, built in 1820 on plans drawn up by Louis Visconti. In 1826, she commissioned him to make a few alterations to the property. Several drawing rooms were laid out about a vast billiards room that had a skylight. The neo-Pompeian décor in the grand entryway can still be admired inside the present-day branch office of the Crédit Mutuel bank. In this house, on October 19, 1827, Miss Mars' jewels were stolen by François-Jean-Scipion l'Africain Mulon and Constance Richard, his wife and accomplice, the actress's maid. The heist was the talk of Paris. In 1838, a former domestic attempted a second jewel theft. The culprit was found hiding in a broom closet near Miss Mars' bathroom. He had hidden a huge knife under the cushions of an armchair. The actress decided to move away.

Rue de La Rochefoucauld and Rue Saint-Lazare

Turning right onto **Rue de La Rochefoucauld**, we come upon a gate at **7** (open on weekdays), through which we can admire the lovely neo-Palladian garden-side façade of Miss Mars' residence, crowned with Greek-style vases, as well as part of the Duchesnois mansion. What this property is lacking, however, is the depth provided by yesteryear's large grounds that went as far as Rue Saint-Lazare.

After this glimpse of splendor, we will cross Rue de La Rochefoucauld and stroll up a bit farther. In 1790, the street was named for Catherine de La Rochefoucauld-Coursage, the abbess of Montmartre from 1737 to 1760.

Note the carved medallion of a ship's anchor and telescope at number **12**, a remnant of the old Compagnie des Aciéries de la Marine (navy steelworks company). It moved into these premises in 1914. The building now belongs to the ESMOD, a school of fashion design.

The Musée National Gustave-Moreau at **14** was the family home of the master of Symbolism. In a rare move, the painter himself chose in 1895 to turn his house into a museum, where his work would be displayed in one gallery and his personal belongings in another. He jealously kept his parents' old second-floor apartment and their furniture. Mixing in the furniture of his beloved Alexandrine Dureux, he turned it into his own *musée sentimental*. He had Albert Lafon re-work the façade and build two large exhibition halls on the

◄ Gustave-Moreau Museum, 14 Rue de La Rochefoucauld

▲ 56 Rue Saint-Lazare
► 58 Rue Saint-Lazare

19 belonged to Joséphine de Forget, Delacroix's mistress. She lived here with her mother, Mrs. de la Valette, heroine and victim in her husband's prison break. The former aide-de-camp to Napoleon had been sentenced to death in 1815, and was languishing in jail. His wife came to visit and swapped clothes with him, enabling him to walk out past the guards while she took his place in the cell. But she went mad in prison.

Let's go back down to **Rue Saint-Lazare**. We will begin by turning right and walking through the gateway at **56** which opens onto a driveway laid out under the Directoire and still paved with cobblestones. It was a back lane leading to the mansions on Rue de la Tour-des-Dames, providing access to Rue Saint-Lazare. As we walk up the alley, we can see some of these home's garden-side façades.

upper floors, connected by a fabulous spiral staircase, to display his own works. In his will dated September 17, 1897, he bequeathed his home to the State with the provision that "the nature of the whole not be disturbed." The secretive and visionary painter died on April 18, 1898 and the museum was inaugurated in 1903. Its first curator was Moreau's former student, Georges Rouault.

Playwright, cartoonist, and actor Henri Monnier moved into **21** in 1835 and the painter Millet lived at **17** in 1867. His *Angélus* was sold in Sedelmeyer's art gallery. The art dealer's old mansion can still be seen through the gate behind the modern building at **6**.

Moving on to **58**, we will discover a stunning façade in Tuscan Doric style. In 1974, it was painted in blue, pink, and white for a British advertising firm. The un-Parisian color scheme couldn't last forever; it has since been re-painted in muter tones of gray, pink, and ochre. It was built around 1830 for the son-in-law of Horace Vernet, painter Paul Delaroche, who moved into it that same year. The entryway is also painted and has a stucco coffered ceiling.

Square d'Orléans

◄ Square d'Orléans
off 80 Rue Taitbout

Let's backtrack on this block of Rue Saint-Lazare to the intersection with **Rue Taitbout** , where we'll turn left. At number **80,** behind a gate decorated with finials, we'll find a passage leading to **Square d'Orléans**, open to the public Monday to Friday. With the coffered vault overhead, let's turn left through a second passage, where a plaque on the front of **9** informs us that Chopin stayed there. Cité d'Orléans was purchased in 1822 by the shrewd Miss Mars for 250,000 francs. Seven years later, she sold it for twice that price by English architect Edward Cresy, who, in the years 1830-1842, turned it into a London square. In 1855, the garden area in the center was graced by a splendid fountain and magnolia trees. The square's four buildings have partially exposed English basements. Front steps lead up to the raised first floor. The most interesting façade is at **6**. The second and third floors are framed behind a portico of colossal Ionic pillars. Until 1854, the square's only exit was out 36 Rue Saint-Lazare.

Alexandre Dumas, the elder, was one of the first residents at **2**. In his memoirs, he tells how he threw together a grand costume bal for Mardi Gras 1833. In just three days, his apartment had been completely redecorated for the occasion by his friends Eugène Delacroix, Célestin Nanteuil, Decamp, Barye, the Johanot brothers, Louis Boulanger, etc. "I invited nearly every artist in Paris. Some 700 guests showed up, for a long night of revelry. At nine o'clock in the morning, music still swirling in our heads, we bounded out onto Rue des Trois-Frères [Rue Taitbout] for a last galli-vant. When the front of our procession had reached the boulevard, the tail was still wiggling in the courtyard of the square."

Around 1840, some of the residents here included Pauline and Louis Viardot, the famous cantatrice and the theater director, the ballerina Marie Taglioni, musicians Charles Alkan and Friedrich Kalkbrenner, the writer Marmontel. In 1842, George Sand left Rue Pigalle and moved to a second-floor apartment at **5**, to be closer to her friends, the Viardots. Her son Maurice had a studio over her apartment. Her daughter Solange had a room next door. Chopin took up small quarters, a two-room flat, at **9**. Charlotte Mariani, George Sand's dearest friend, lived at **7**. "Our generous and active Mariani set up family life for us. We only had to walk across the large courtyard with its plants and sand, always very neat, to gather either at her place, my place, or at Chopin's, whenever he felt like playing for us. It worked out well for everyone concerned. Like all such systems, it was economical. When I felt like company, I went to Mrs. Mariani's; I could have close friends over in the more intimate setting of my own home, and yet I could retire and return to my work when I saw fit. Chopin was delighted to have a fine, isolated drawing room for composing or daydreaming. But he loved socializing and only used his sanctuary to give lessons. It was in Nohant that he created and wrote." (George Sand, **Histoire de ma Vie**, 1856).

The novelist mothered the composer when he became ill with tuberculosis. Because of the children, and due to problems connected with the musician's illness, Sand and Chopin broke up in 1847. She left Square d'Orléans, but he stayed on for a few more months, no longer composing.

Back onto Rue Saint-Lazare

▲ 24 Rue Saint-Lazare
▼ Rue Saint-Lazare

We will head back to **Rue Saint-Lazare** now. Its gentle bends along the slopes of the Butte Montmartre are quite unlike its rectilinear sister street running parallel to it to the south, Rue de Châteaudun. At 27 (notice the head

of a man in Renaissance garb) and at **29**, we can catch of glimpse of the courtyard buildings with their neo-Renaissance garden-side façades overlooking 32 and 34 Rue de Châteaudun. Notice the handsome Restoration-period doorway at **24**. The house was built in 1823 on old Rue du Désert, named for a certain Jean Désert.

Going beyond the intersection with Rue Saint-Georges, let's look at numbers **16-18** with dual arched double doorways rising two floors, the ground floor and the entresol. These were the gates to Les Jardins Ruggieri. The leisure park was created in 1765 by the Ruggieri brothers, famous for their firework displays, the first in Paris. During the Directoire, the gardens were renamed Les Bosquets d'Idalie and had "truly frightening" attraction call the "Le Saut du Niagara" (the Niagara drop). The promotional flyer went on to reassure prospective customers that "the police would never have authorized it if it actually endangered citizens' lives." Nevertheless, they had to shut down in 1819. Number 16 on this street now houses a Sephardic synagogue.

Let's not overlook **10**, Detaille, a little perfume shop founded in 1905 by the Countess de Presle, a sister-in-law of painter Édouard Detaille and creator of a skin moisturizer called Le Baume Automobile, originally designed for women drivers worried about the wind drying their skin in their open automobiles. The shop has preserved its original interior décor. Here between La Trinité and Notre-Dame-de-Lorette churches, having reached the southern edge of the old Nouvelle Athènes quarter, we end our stroll.

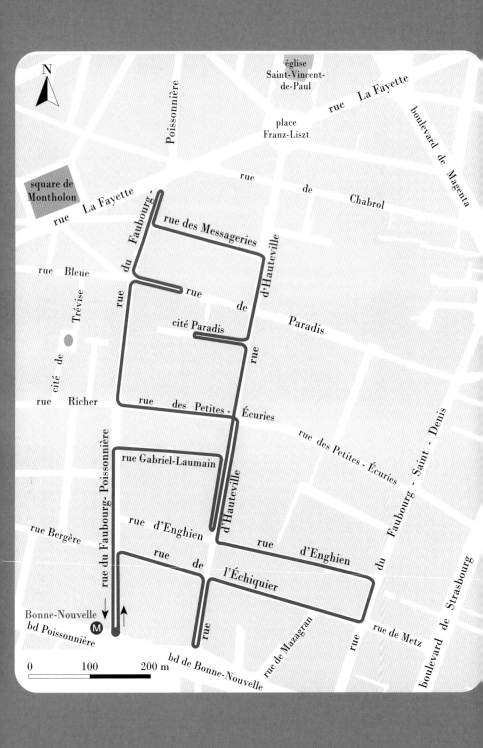

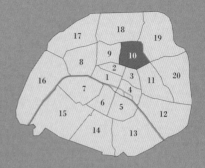

10th

Faubourg
Poissonnière

▶ Start and finish: **Boulevard de Bonne-Nouvelle, metro Bonne-Nouvelle**

H ere we stand on Paris's old city limits, marked by the ring of boulevards built atop the 14th-century Charles V ramparts. As Rue Poissonnière continues northwards, it becomes Rue du "Faubourg Poissonnière" (*faubourg* meaning "outside the city limits"). It was named for the old itinerary that fishmongers took to bring their goods from the ports on the North Sea to the Halles marketplace in Paris. Surrounded by marshland dotted with vegetable patches and orchards, the long road ran through monastery lands farmed by the Filles-Dieu (a congregation of Hospitaller sisters). Portions of their property had already been sold off by the end of the reign of Louis XV. Fine homes were erected on the lots, creating an elegant neighborhood. In the development of the new quarter, two men's names will go down in history: Claude-Martin Goupy and Benoît de Sainte-Paulle. They are to be credited for the construction of many of the magnificent mansions that have partially survived or left a contour. This neighborhood was in its heyday between 1770 and 1850. Its decline was due in part to the creation of Rue de Rivoli, as well as, at a later date, the arrival of the department stores, which lured customers away from its businesses. The quarter never quite recovered from this stroke of bad luck. Even today, it somehow manages to continue being a sleepy backwater, despite the lunch-hour crowds in the streets. But let's forget for a moment the rumble of today's traffic and the blaring horns. Let's forget the drab old façades, the cracked roughcast exteriors, and let's push through the darkened carriage doors

▲ 8 Rue du Faubourg-Poissonnière

and go back in time to discover – quite unexpectedly – one of these charming little homes that the passage of time has thankfully spared.

From Rue du Faubourg-Poissonnière to Rue de l'Échiquier

Our walking tour begins at the corner of **Boulevard de Bonne-Nouvelle** and **Rue du Faubourg-Poissonnière**, which is the modern-day border between the 9th and 10th arrondissements. Let's head north on Faubourg-Poissonnière.

It's worth a stop at **2** to go into the courtyard. At the far end, to the left, we will see a projecting building in Louis Quinze style. The great tragedian Rachel Félix (1821-1858), generally known by her first name alone, is said to have lived here when she was beginning her career at the nearby Théâtre du Gymnase. Notice the tall windows on the second floor, with their balconies trimmed with elaborate wrought-iron curlicues. This courtyard is now part of a private high school, the Lycée Edgar Poe.

As we exit, let's stay on the sidewalk on the right-hand side to view number **6** up close. This was once the home of the Viscount Évariste de Parny de Forges (1753-1814), the author of *Poésies Érotiques*. You'll note the rail in the pavement at the threshold, of which there are still more traces next door at **8**. In the 19th century, after de Parny de Forges had passed on, this became an industrious neighborhood. Rear courtyard workshops were commonplace, and carts on rails were used to haul raw materials in.

A handsome office building stands at **10**. It was the first designed by Auguste Perret, who went on to be one of the founding fathers of modern architecture. The five-story building features large windows, three to a floor, framed by four sturdy pillars running up to the top floor. Their capitals repeat the pattern decorating the entrance. Before it was built, this was the site of the Alcazar d'Hiver, a Moorish-themed concert café, all the rage in the Second Empire. A singer named Théréza attracted crowds, fans of her sentimental songs of romance. The building was demolished in 1896.

Let's turn right and take **Rue de l'Échiquier**. Baron Louis, Minister of Finance when the monarchy was restored in 1814, had a lovely townhouse built at **43**, still standing today. Its garden ran as far as the old Bonne-Nouvelle Cemetery, which is now the location of the Théâtre du Gymnase. Notice the door and its medallions. Beside this fine home, to the left, is an alley that dead-ends, but will allow us a view of the courtyard façade, the identical twin of the street-side façade.

The interior of nearby **39** was laid out according to a floor plan popular at the time, with the three center bays allotted to the living-room area. The bays to the sides corresponded to the master bedroom and the dining room.

On the other side of the street, **36 and 38** preserve the memory of Henri IV's old hunting lodge. A few vestiges of the royal lodge were discovered during renovation at 36 (old courtyard paving stones and a few columns). The king donated his lodge to the nearby Filles-Dieu convent. During the Revolution, the lot and several other convent assets were sold off. The buyer was a certain Joseph Thomas Wenzel, a florist, who built what would later be known as the "Pavillon de l'Échiquier." You can still make out the structure's rhythmical arcades. Designed as a café-cum-dance hall, the Pavillon was a fashionable watering-hole during the Directoire and the Consulate (1795-

► Hôtel du baron Louis, 43 Rue de l'Échiquier (© Gilles Targat)

1804). Beginning in 1850, the complex of buildings was taken over by a luxury hotel called the Grand Hôtel du Pavillon. Some of its beautiful 1900s rooms have survived at number 38. In the early 1980s, the hotel was split in two, giving birth to two distinct travel hotels.

Once we reach **Rue d'Hauteville**, we'll turn right for a quick trip down the block to the courtyard at **1**. The old house we'll find at the rear was built at the end of the 18th century for a certain Armand Jean Thouroux de Bertinval. The façade will perhaps interest us less than the staircase in the vestibule.

Let's go back to **Rue de l'Échiquier** and resume our neighborhood walk. A bit further up, at **10**, is the old Concert Parisien, which moved into the premises in 1867. The popular singer Yvette Guilbert (1867-1944), one of Toulouse-Lautrec's favorite subjects, appeared here, and this is also where famed playwright Georges Feydeau kicked off his career as a writer of comedy. In 1910, the Concert Parisien was bought by Mayol, a singer from Marseille, who promptly named the place after himself. Screen actors like Raimu and Fernandel played here. In the 1930s, the Concert Parisien was known for its revue of scantily clad girls. Ticket sales soared. The establishment went into decline and closed in 1979. The old burlesque theater's front door has changed little. In the arched pediment above it, two terracotta cupids still fly on either side of the oculus, holding up the garland.

As we continue along our way, we can enjoy the view of the lovely **Théâtre Antoine** at the very end of the street, looking back at us from where it stands on Boulevard de Strasbourg.

◄ Rue du Faubourg-Saint-Denis

From Rue du Faubourg-Saint-Denis to Rue des Petites-Écuries

Having reached **Rue du Faubourg-Saint-Denis**, we shall turn left and take **Rue d'Enghien**. This street's name pays homage to the Duke d'Enghien, shot in the trenches of the Château de Vincennes by an execution squad in 1804 on the orders of Bonaparte. Number **18** used to be the headquarters of the Petit Parisien, founded in 1876. It was the epitome of the popular city daily, printing a mil-

▼ 18 Rue d'Enghien

lion and a half copies at its peak. A double-P monogram still decorates the façade. The building rises with six high, arched glass bays. It was renovated from top to bottom, and is now partially residential.

Next door, **16** was also once *Petit Parisien* offices. Notice the capitals with their lion heads, topped by the double-P logo. The arcatures formed by two rows of blue and red ceramic and the presence of short, slender iron columns connecting the bays between the third and fourth floors, enhanced by the mosaics on a golden background, give the façade a much more solemn air than its neighbor's. The *Petit Parisien* vanished in the aftermath of World War II because of its collaboration with the Germans. Its successor, *Le Parisien Libéré* (now

▸ Hôtel Botterel-Quintin, 44 Rue des Petites-Écuries

known as *Le Parisien*), operated from the same premises, before moving to larger quarters in the suburbs.

A lovely Louis-Philippe building at **27** with its three central bays is similar in many ways to the architecture of the Baron Louis mansion we looked at earlier on Rue de l'Échiquier. Right across the street, the façade at **26**, although from the same period, has a profusion of pilasters, half columns, and window friezes.

Let's turn right and go two blocks up **Rue d'Hauteville** to Rue des Petites-Écuries, admiring, as we go, the fine view of Saint-Vincent-de-Paul church in the distance. In terms of elevation, we now stand in the district's lowest spot. The Grand Égout (main sewer) used to run along **Rue des Petites-Écuries**. Let's take a left onto this street. This part of the street was built up in the 1780s, but today, little remains of that period of development.

Behind the imposing façade at number **44** is the Hôtel Botterel-Quintin, now an office building. Construction began in 1780 by architect Pérard de Montreuil for the governor

of Bourgogne, Charles-André de La Corée. Usufruct of the property was later granted to a lieutenant of the Gardes Françaises, Count René Christin Jérôme de Botterel-Quintin, a Breton of minor nobility.

The count not only finished the construction, he enlarged and embellished the building. Most of the original decorative elements have now vanished, except in the staircase and a few lovely ground-floor rooms. The vestiges include the antechamber overlooking the garden, the wainscoting in the drawing room, and, especially, the oval dining room in the wing to the right, with its twelve Doric half-columns interspersed with painted panels, and its ceiling fresco with mythological figures. As they are private property, they cannot ordinarily be visited. The front door is locked, but the garden-side façade is visible from the courtyard at 46, next door. What we see here is a three-story townhouse with rather sober architecture. The spiraling frieze along the attic level and the pinecone-shaped consoles beneath the second-floor windows are the only embellishments. The doorstep is framed by a peristyle with two Tuscan columns.

The lovely little townhouse at **46** is from the same period, and was also designed by Pérard de Montreuil.

At **48,** one's eye is attracted by two early-20th-century cast-iron atlantes. The figure on the left is Mercury, the god of trade, with a caduceus and a winged helmet. One the right is Abundance, with the attributes of Demeter, the goddess of harvests and the Earth, pointing at a ram. This "praise for labor" was commissioned by Charles Prévet & Co., a firm whose name is still engraved over the main entrance.

Rue du Faubourg-Poissonnière and Rue de Paradis

The row of townhouses on the right side of this part of **Rue du Faubourg-Poissonnière** are some of the most remarkable in the neighborhood. The transfer of the property of the Prieuré des Filles-Dieu, primarily into the hands of the entrepreneur Claude-Martin Goupy, began in the 1770s. The records show that he invested in several lots in the swampy area called *le Paradis*, which he then sold off.

◄ 48 Rue des Petites-Écuries

◄ Rue du Faubourg-Poissonnière

► Hôtel Cardon,
50 Rue du Faubourg-
Poissonnière

▼ Hôtel Titon,
58 Rue du Faubourg-
Poissonnière

One of the buyers was Nicolas Vincent Cardon, a sculptor and the director of the Académie de Saint-Luc. In 1773, he had a home built by Goupy at **50** on this street. It became known as the Hôtel Cardon. The courtyard façade alone has survived, and it is quite damaged.

Another buyer, Pierre Hyacinthe Deleuze, the decorating painter of the Académie de Saint-Luc, chose **52** as his home, also designed by Goupy in the same period.

A bit further on, a plaque at **56** informs us that this was the last home of the painter Corot, who had a studio a short walk away on Rue de Paradis. The façade is old and dates from the First Empire. This three-story structure also includes an entresol sandwiched in a series of three arcades in grooved masonry. In the far end of the courtyard, a Louis-Philippe period building is known to have been the home of art collector Alexandre-Charles Sauvageot. His passion for Renaissance art was such that his apartment soon became a veritable little museum, where jewelry, paintings, statuettes, and ceramics made up his collections. He bequeathed it all to the State, and the works of art were transferred to the Louvre. The original townhouse only had two upper floors; the "noble" floor's design included with high windows framed by pilasters with Corinthian capitals.

Let's stop for a while at the Hôtel Titon, located at **58**. We enter through a large 18th-century carriage door, which contrasts strikingly with the rest of the façade, renovated in the late 19th century. Niches in the passage walls hold superb stone vases with ribbed fluting, sculpted by master decorator Jean-Charles Delafosse. At the far end of the courtyard, the

recently renovated mansion is a fine example of pre-Revolutionary architecture. The structure was elevated in the Second Empire with a skillful pastiche, using the same honey-colored stone. Note the elegance of the frieze of foliage beneath the entablature, and the pediments alternating with garland motifs over the windows. In the center, a perron unifies the three center doors. The courtyard façade curves gently in the area around the double doors to the passage, and the walls are ornamented with niches holding small statues of mythological figures and Greek and Roman philosophers. Constructed in 1776, the mansion was purchased by Jean-Baptiste-Maximilien Titon, an advisor in Parliament, a patron of the arts, an art collector, and an architecture enthusiast. He left his name and imprint on the dwelling.

Last in this series is the Hôtel de Goys, another masterpiece by architect Jean-Charles Delafosse. It is visible from the courtyard of number **60**, next door. As with the Hôtel Titon, pediments alternate with bas-reliefs (olive leaves, in this case) over the windows.

Now we'll continue walking up to **Rue de Paradis**, turn right, and enter at **47**. Immediately to the right, there's a small courtyard. This point provides a fine view of the back of the Hôtel de Goys. Though it is not nearly as fancy, it echoes the façade we just saw. Notice that here, above the windows, there are oak-leaf ornaments rather than olive leaves. A lovely perron flanked by two lions facing each other leads into a garden. In a corner to the left, we can just make out the back of the Hôtel Titon.

To get a clearer idea of what the quarter was like at the end of the 18th century, we must imagine these fine buildings surrounded by sumptuous, sweeping grounds, most of which went as far as Rue d'Hauteville.

Let's resume our stroll on Rue de Paradis heading the other way, towards **Rue du Faubourg-Poissonnière**. This is where the Nouvelle-France village began. Founded in the 17th century, it was inhabited by people of modest means, and its name probably came from a dance hall called Le Canada-Français. We are immediately struck by the architectural difference from this point on. No more fancy mansions, no more bourgeois homes: these are small houses with narrow windows and doors and no-frills façades. The architecture is clearly for a lower class.

The wrought iron gate on a restaurant located at **80** used to close a wine dealer's shop. You can tell it was a wine shop, because of the grape leaves, fruit, and Bacchus head,

▼ Restaurant door, 80 Rue du Faubourg-Poissonnière

▲ Garde Républicaine installation in the Nouvelle-France district, 82 Rue du Faubourg-Poissonnière

the doorway to the right, standing against the gable of the house next door. It informs us that "Hoche [who went on to become a great general] was a sergeant here." Today, the barracks house Garde Républicaine soldiers and their families.

From Rue des Messageries to Rue d'Hauteville

Let's walk a short distance down Rue du Faubourg-Poissonnière and turn left onto **Rue des Messageries**. It was built on the old Messageries Royales yard (royal mail coach service). At the end of the street, we come to a little square of sorts. In fact, Rue des Messageries started out as a narrow lane that had a sharp bend here before running south to Rue de Paradis. Stagecoaches heading in and out of the yard needed a wide turning space. This was it. This southern section of the lane became part of Rue d'Hauteville when it was extended northwards around 1826.

We will turn right now to take **Rue d'Hauteville** again. In 1772, there was much hesitation over the naming of this new street. It was originally to be called Rue de La Michodière, for Jean-Baptiste de La Michodière, Count of Hauteville in Champagne, provost of the merchants, because it crossed his property. However, a street in the Bourse quarter had just been given this name. A new name had to be found quickly, and yet it still had to honor the count: Hauteville! Thus, our dear count is one of the rare historical figures to have two Paris streets perpetuating his memory.

Rue d'Hauteville was hardly developed at all prior to 1800, but by

all a promise to passersby that good drink could be had here. Fences have been used to secure wine shops since the 18th century.

A little further up, we will come upon the **Nouvelle-France** military barracks. The austere architectural style sets it apart. It was rebuilt in 1936 on the site of the Gardes-Françaises' old barracks, erected in 1773 by Goupy as part of a city-wide program to house the garrison. The Gardes-Françaises regiment had been created for Charles IX in 1593, "to serve as the king's guard in the courtyards and exteriors of the Louvre, to follow his majesty in his travels, and to participate in warfare." For a long time, the Gardes-Françaises were housed with locals in the suburbs of Paris. But it eventually became apparent that there was a real need to set up barracks for the corps, which was continually growing. Numerous projects were submitted, but shelved due to a lack of funds. The reign of Louis XV finally brought the project to fruition.

Nothing remains of the old structure, except the trophy of arms over

the First Empire, it had stolen some of the glory of the Faubourg-Poissonnière. A few splendid mansions were built along this street, usually on the east side, because the west side was part of the estates bordering the Faubourg-Poissonnière. The smallish Hôtel Bourrienne at **58** is one of the best-preserved specimens and is certainly worth visiting (see inset).

Having become fashionable, Rue d'Hauteville attracted numerous officers and top-ranking civil servants of the Empire. Another little mansion, built somewhat later and less lavishly, was erected at the far end of the courtyard at **54**.

Let's cross the street and angle slightly to our right to locate the entrance to the **Cité Paradis**. This private lane was built beginning in 1893, laid out on the Hôtel Titon's old grounds. The back of the mansion is partially visible.

Having resumed our stroll down **Rue d'Hauteville**, let's peek into the courtyard of **53**, immediately to our right. Since 1988, the second courtyard has been filled by a glass and brick building that houses a city day-

Hôtel Bourrienne - A Small Mansion

In 1787, Goupy sold the lot in the "Le Paradis" marsh on which the smallish Hôtel Bourrienne is now located. The buyer, Mrs. de Dompierre, immediately launched the construction of a townhouse, but left its completion to her successors. In 1790, Mr. Lormier-Lagrave, owner of a sugar refinery in the French West Indies, purchased the property. Two years later, his daughter Fortunée Hamelin inherited it. She hired the architect Bellanger to carry out the initial embellishments, but her expensive tastes drove her further and further into debt. By 1801, she was forced to sell, and the little mansion was acquired by a member of Bonaparte's circle, Louis Antoine Fauvelet de Bourrienne, the man whose name the dwelling would finally inherit. The splendid interior design he planned with his architect Leconte remains appealing to this day.

After the place was sold in 1824, it had a series of owners before Charles Tuleu took possession of it in 1886. He was the one who built the brick building stealing footage from the garden space. Still standing today, the building was occupied by a type foundry (visible from 21 bis rue de Paradis). The mansion has remained in the family all these years. It presently belongs to Charles Tuleu's grand-nephews, who take special care of it.

We should not be too surprised by the cattycornered entrance in the far north end of the courtyard. The main entrance actually used to be through number 60, now blocked by newer buildings. The drawing rooms, the dining room with its

▲ Living room in Empire style,
Hôtel Bourrienne,
58 Rue d'Hauteville
(© Gilles Targat)

beautiful marquetry floor, inlaid with rosewood, oak, and lemon wood, the study, the bedroom, and the bathroom are open to the public from July 1-15 and from September 1-30 daily from 12 noon to 6:00 pm, or by appointment the rest of the year (telephone: +33 (0)147 705 114)

► Cité Paradis

care center designed by Marc Béri and Philippe Gazeau. The mansion opposite it dates from the end of the First Empire. It has been renovated several times, but its projecting portico supported by four paired Ionic columns attests to the sustainability of the first owner's taste for classicism.

As we exit and continue on our way, off to our right at **26** is the Hôtel Davout, another small mansion dating from the first quarter of the 19th century. Its second floor houses a handsome vestibule listed on the historic register. Let's go to **24** now to take a look at the small townhouse at the far end of the courtyard. Built in the same era as its neighbor, its architecture is more rudimentary.

On weekdays, Rue d'Hauteville, like the neighboring Rue du Faubourg-Poissonnière, bustles with intense activity. Unaware of any attraction for strollers, workers hurry out of the garment shops, shouldering a pole on which an order of identical shirts hangs, like game on a spit. Early in the day, vans pull up and drop off kilometers of rolled-up fabric. The fur trade was what kept this neighborhood alive during the Belle Epoque. Today, however, with the fur industry is in recession, the wholesale ready-to-wear business has moved in to replace it. There is quite a large number of wedding gown shops.

From Rue Gabriel-Laumain to Boulevard de Bonne-Nouvelle

Let's retrace our steps and take the next left onto the picturesque **Rue Gabriel-Laumain**. In the constant hubbub of this quarter, this street has a soothing effect on one's soul. Construction of the street began in 1820. It cut through the old Hôtel Tabary belonging to Jean-Baptiste Léonard Violet, an entrepreneur. Passage Violet was therefore its name until the end of World War II, when it was rechristened in honor of Gabriel Laumain, a Gare de l'Est postal worker who was shot by the Nazis for his Resistance activities. This lane used to be closed by iron gates at each end. Up and down the street, the architec-

ture of the houses is harmonious. Most are three-storied structures with small courtyards and six bays, crowned with Mansard roofs. Symmetry is the rule.

Midway down, the short street widens and forms a tiny square. Here, at **6 bis**, we discover the Hôtel Mignon, dating from the 1840s, the last single-family dwelling of its size and pretension to go up in the neighborhood. It was erected in an already-developed area, and thus never had any grounds. The four-floor high façade rises to a curvilinear pediment and has lovely proportions. Notice the floral patterns in the quoins (corners) of the ground-floor windows. Stepping up closer, we can tell there is a large vestibule here. At the back end of it is a lovely, half-circle staircase.

Rue Gabriel-Laumain leads west to **Rue du Faubourg-Poissonnière**, through a tastefully decorated carriage porch. Here, we will turn left. At **34**, a plaque commemorates the birth of poet Sully-Prudhomme in this house.

Numbers **32 and 34** date from 1773-1776. Originally, they made up one property owned by Leprince, who traded in faux-marble. In those days, plaster-making was one of the primary businesses in the neighborhood. Notice the bas-reliefs along the noble floor at **34**.

Let's spend a moment looking at **30**. Known as the Hôtel Benoît de

▾▾ Rue Gabriel-Laumain
▲ Rue du Faubourg-Poissonnière

◀ 34 Rue du Faubourg-Poissonnière

Sainte-Paulle, this was one of the quarter's major architectural undertakings. Unfortunately, it has been scarred by alterations. Soon after Air France moved out of its offices in this building, a major rehabilitation program was launched creating fifty-one apartment units and two artists' studios.

Construction of the original residence began in 1774. The plans were drawn up by architect Samson Nicolas Lenoir. Before the home was completed, Benoît de Sainte-Paulle sold it to Jean-François Caron, who enlarged

▼ 6 bis Rue Gabriel-Laumain

it. He designed the wings overlooking the street. In fact, most of the structural transformations date from the period between the two world wars, when the building went from residential to commercial use.

The street-side building's long ground floor has only one upper floor and a Mansard roof. In the middle, two Tuscan columns support the pediment over the main doorway, decorated with symbols of military life: a two-edged sword, a plumed helmet, and an olive branch. Crossing the threshold of the main entrance, let's take a moment to glance up at the coffered ceiling. On the reverse side of the exterior façade, beneath the portico with its Doric columns, two bas-reliefs pay homage to Prudence and Abundance, undoubtedly sound advisors for a successful businessman like Benoît de Sainte-Paulle. The monumental façade on the courtyard of the main hall is composed of a peristyle incorporating four Ionic columns. We will walk through them and go up the steps. The raised roof-space over the attic floor was a later addition. Behind this, there was once a garden that went as far as Rue d'Hauteville.

Another great late 18th-century architect in this quarter was Jean Vincent Benoît Barré. He designed four homes and mansions in the Faubourg-Poissonnière. Only one of them, the house at **28**, has survived, albeit greatly altered. Made up of four bays, it a rather bourgeois-looking home. The four upper floors are more recent.

Our walk comes to its end as we amble down Rue du Faubourg-Poissonnière and return to our starting point on the boulevard de Bonne-Nouvelle.

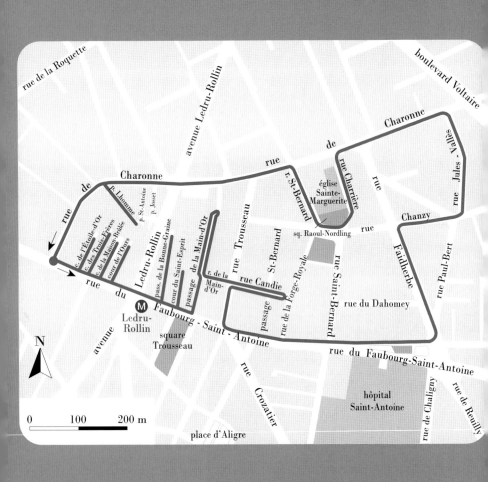

rue de la Roquette

boulevard Voltaire

avenue Ledru-Rollin

Charonne

de

rue

Charonne

rue Charrière

église
Sainte-
Marguerite

rue Jules - Vallès

rue Paul-Bert

de

rue

Charonne

rue

r. St-Bernard

rue

Chanzy

Faidherbe

p. Lhomme

p. St-Antoine

p. Josset

c. de l'Étoile-d'Or

c. des Trois-Frères

c. de la Maison-Brûlée

cour de l'Ours

Ledru-Rollin

pass. de la Bonne-Graine

cour du Saint-Esprit

passage de la Main-d'Or

rue Trousseau

St-Bernard

rue Saint-Bernard

r. de la
Main-
d'Or

rue Candie

rue de la Forge-Royale

passage

sq. Raoul-Nordling

rue du Dahomey

rue de Chaligny

rue de Reuilly

N

rue

du

Faubourg - Saint - Antoine

M

Ledru-
Rollin

avenue

square
Trousseau

rue

Crozatier

rue du Faubourg-Saint-Antoine

hôpital
Saint-Antoine

0   100   200 m

place d'Aligre

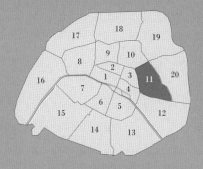

11th

In the Heart of Faubourg Saint-Antoine

▶ Start and finish: at the corner
of Rue de Charonne and Rue
du Faubourg Saint-Antoine,
metro Ledru-Rollin

The particularity of the 11th arrondissement is its craft industry – one might even say it was a calling. Long ago, in the 13th century, the craftsmen of the Faubourg Saint-Antoine were granted exemption from guild membership (and the fees and taxes incumbent thereon). Attracted by the exemption, which lasted for centuries, families of artisans flocked to the quarter. By the early 18th century, the Faubourg had a population of about 40,000. There were carpenters, cabinetmakers, ironworkers, blacksmiths, etc. Businesses set up in the freshly laid-out secondary streets intersecting with the thoroughfares. Factories generally had courtyard locations, while workshops were upstairs, alongside cramped and modest living quarters. This neighborhood walk will take us into some of the most charming alleyways and dead-end passages in the district.

Rue du Faubourg-Saint-Antoine between Rue de Charonne and Avenue Ledru-Rollin

For furniture and interior décor, the Faubourg Saint-Antoine has long been the place to come. This is particularly true along the block we are about to explore up to its eastern end at Avenue Ledru-Rollin. We'll begin our walk at the corner of Rue de Charonne and **Rue du Faubourg Saint-Antoine**, lined with furniture showrooms full of polished reproductions of period pieces or modern designs, vying for the attention of the passer-by.

The first of four alleyways we'll stroll into is the **Cour de l'Étoile-d'Or** (Golden Star Courtyard). Simply go

◄ Cabinetmaker's sign, Cour de l'Ours

through the door at **75** Rue du Faubourg Saint-Antoine (note: on weekends, it is locked). The passage dates from the 18th century, and until rather recently, like many other passages nearby, its old façades sheltered the workshops that were long the pride of the Faubourg.

A four-story brick building dating from the 19th-century straddles the entrance to the courtyard. Inside, to our right, we'll find a little two-story house with ochre walls covered in ivy and honeysuckle, built in the early 19th century, known as the "Pongor House" for its turn-of-the-twentieth-century owner. The other buildings in this courtyard are actually 18th-century, despite appearances.

Before moving on to the second courtyard, we can see vestiges of a

▼ Cour de l'Étoile-d'Or

◄► Cour de l'Ours

Once back on **Rue du Faubourg Saint-Antoine**, we will stop in at **81**. This is the entrance to the **Cour des Trois-Frères**. Several workshops and galleries of more recent date line this long cobblestone alley, partially covered by a glass awning.

Let's continue on our way, and take a look inside at **89** for a glimpse of **Cour de la Maison-Brûlée**. At **95**, **Cour de l'Ours** can be admired on weekdays (it's locked on weekends). Some of these two- and three-century-old walls recall a time when this area of town was teeming with woodworkers, cabinetmakers, wood and metal gilders, inlayers, weavers, upholsterers, bronzesmiths, varnishers, marble workers, etc.

This brings us to **Avenue Ledru-Rollin**, which is less than a century old at this location, and therefore of no particular interest for today's stroll. We might only point out that until 1906, the city's most picturesque all-day furniture market was held every Saturday at this intersection, and was referred to as *le marché de la trôle* (a freelance craftsmen's market). In the 19th century, certain artisans received orders straight from furniture dealers. Others, however, were not so fortunate; they produced furniture for the general public in home workshops. Having no galleries or showrooms, they conducted their business out on the street.

much older lodge built in the second half of the 17th century in the middle of a small garden. It underwent major remodeling. At one point, the third floor was removed, and a passageway was cut through the ground floor, which we will now take to reach the second courtyard. Despite the changes, it has kept its lovely 17th-century interior staircase, with carved wooden balusters and reclining figures representing the four seasons. To the right is a sundial with the year 1751 engraved on it.

In the rear of the courtyard, we will also see early 19th-century buildings which have also undergone major changes. Lastly, let's take a look at a large five-story workshop building, designed by the architect Chabot in 1882. It is a mix of brick and stone.

From Passage de la Bonne-Graine to Rue Trousseau

Let's continue walking down **Rue du Faubourg Saint-Antoine** and enter **115**, which contains **Passage de la Bonne-Graine**, yet another of the many hidden alleyways previously known and used only by residents of the Faubourg.

A little further down the street, we reach the **Cour du Saint-Esprit** with its typically Parisian buildings. At **133**, we will enter **Passage de la Main-d'Or** which, one third of the way down, unexpectedly becomes Rue de la Main d'Or, a craftsmen's alley belonging to the Paris of yesteryear. In 1987, the new Théâtre de la Main d'Or opened in an old cabinetmaker's workshop at **15**.

At numbers **17, 19, and 21,** as in many other places in the neighborhood, the workshops here were torn down and replaced by a modern condominium and business complex. This one, in pink and white, is reminiscent of an ocean liner. The balconies are sheltered by white latticework, and the white-ceramic-tile façade curves to connect with the adjacent buildings - hence the nautical feeling.

Let's backtrack and veer to the left onto **Rue de la Main-d'Or,** which has preserved its old Faubourg ambience, thanks to its two wine bars. L'Ami Pierre, at **5**, is also known as "À l'Ancien Rebouteux," because it was also a waiting room of sorts for one of the last healer-bonesetters in Paris, men without formal medical training, but reputed to have special "magnetism" in their hands.

Let's move ahead to **11 Rue de Candie**. November 1992 saw the opening of a new neighborhood gymnasium with a sound architectural design blending in harmoniously with the 18th- and 19th-century façades around it.

We'll backtrack again, this time to move onwards to **Rue Trousseau**, formerly named Rue Sainte-Marguerite. At **22**, we come upon a building erected in 1904. The façade is decorated with delightful Art Nouveau sunflowers. Their freely-interpreted stems frame the door as well as the

sixth-floor balconies. The sculptor preferred daisies, however, for the third-floor balconies. The lobby has a colorful mosaic mural. Note also the plant-inspired motifs in the ironwork, typical of the early 20th-century.

Back to Rue du Faubourg-Saint-Antoine

▶ Detail of the Petite-Halle fountain, Rue du Faubourg Saint-Antoine

▼ Plaque commemorating Jean-Baptiste Baudin, 149-151 Rue du Faubourg Saint-Antoine

We'll take Rue Trousseau to reach the very spot on **Rue du Faubourg Saint-Antoine** where tragic violence occurred in December 1851, following the coup d'état by prince-president Louis-Napoleon Bonaparte, set on becoming Emperor Napoleon III. A commemorative plaque placed **between 149 and 151** Rue du Faubourg Saint-Antoine pays tribute to Jean-Baptiste Baudin, who died of a gunshot wound. He was shot when he scaled a barricade to show citizens how a parliamentarian would stand up for them and face death "for twenty-five francs a day." He was referring to the meager salary the people's representatives were being paid, while workers and artisans generally believed them to be well-off and too bourgeois to understand their cause.

Glancing left as we pass by, we see Rue de la Forge Royale (created in 1770) and then Rue Saint-Bernard, a path opened in the 13th century from the Saint-Antoine abbey (on the site of today's hospital) to the Courtille [gardens] du Temple.

Ahead of us is the fountain at **211** Rue du Faubourg Saint-Antoine, directly across the street from the hospital, on a traffic island formed where Rue de Montreuil angles in. Called the Petite-Halle fountain because of a now-gone market that

was nearby, it and four other fountains in the Faubourg Saint-Antoine were built after the Council of State issued a decree on June 1, 1719 and patent letters one month later. This fountain does indeed date from 1719 and was restored in 1963. The neoclassical edifice has a square plan. Its four sides are endowed with pilasters with no capitals. They support a cornice surmounted by a triangular pediment. The whole is crowned by an acroterion. Two sides have niches with spigots. This fountain operated commercially from 1774 to 1782, when companies went into business supplying water to individuals at a rate set by city officials.

Petite-Halle means "little marketplace." This covered market survived until 1940 and took up the triangular strip between Rue du Faubourg Saint-Antoine and Rue de Montreuil. In the 17th century, it was the location of the sole neighborhood butcher shop, a monopoly under the control of each successive mother superior governing the Abbey of Saint-Antoine-des-Champs.

From Rue Faidherbe to Rue Jules-Vallès

At the next intersection, we will take a left and head into **Rue Faidherbe**. The building at **11-bis** has a façade decorated with pilasters topped with young ladies' faces. The doorway itself also features low-relief female faces mingled with flowers. Notice the keystone over the door, also carved with flowers and a dog's face. This Art Nouveau building was designed by Jean Falp in 1907.

Across the way, the industrial building at **22 and 24** is home to the research department of the RATP (the Paris mass-transit company). It was designed in 1926 by Achille Champy. After a respectful renovation in 1989, today's building has new large windows underscored in blue. The architectural unity of the original has been faithfully conserved. Even the engraved name of Mr. Boutet, who commissioned the building as a plywood factory, is still on the façade.

The Boutet factory spells out its specialties for us with a mosaic in blue and gold letters against an ochre background: local woods, exotic woods, sawing, sanding, veneering, etc. The façade has kept its original colors, and its cornice is decorated with a floral frieze in mosaic, on a golden background. Yellow and blue glass add cheerful touches of the house colors to the awning.

We will soon cross **Rue Chanzy** and make a right to reach **Rue Jules-Vallès**, only steps away. The latter has a bend in its middle section. Like its neighbor, it was built on lands that once belonged to the Traisnel priory.

We will sample more early-20th-century architecture at **1**. This build-

ing was erected in 1908. Lovely carved heads and floral patterns appear beneath some of the windows. A 1900s restaurant takes up the ground floor. It has a wooden exterior and a glass awning. The interior décor was inspired by rocaille style; the ceil-

◄ 11 bis Rue Faidherbe
► 1 Rue Jules Vallès

▼ 22-24 Rue Faidherbe

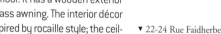

Views of the Faubourg Saint-Antoine

"He pointed to where Rue de Charonne came in, with its old windows, mansard roofs, and walls ornamented with bas-reliefs; the public fountain with its dreams of majesty; then, as they retraced their steps, he gestured towards the entranceways to deep, tortuous, cluttered inner passages and courtyards: 'All that is full of workshops, glue-pots, varnish-pots, and irascible skilled laborers, who still believe the twentieth century will see the rule of justice and peace...'
The sidewalks were crowded. Surprisingly enough, there were still signs of activities belonging more properly to the morning. Housewives were shopping for the day's provisions from fruit sellers and pushcart vendors. Most of the passersby were workers on their lunch break. Those who strolled at a leisurely pace were on their way to purchase a meal from one of the neighborhood rôtisseries. Others were hurrying, probably trying to reach home, at some distance. A few lingered, seated or standing, in doorways. They'd no doubt eaten a sandwich on the spot, because they were smoking and telling jokes until it was time to return to work. On the whole, they seemed rough and sturdy. This tribe appeared to be quite at home on the street, which had been the main thoroughfare of their territory for centuries. If one paid close attention, one might have detected a vague whiff of discontent, of complaint. But it was covered over by a hearty roguishness, a swaggering, ironic wisdom about life. Naturally, riot and revolution are still part of the legend, and the future may also be entitled to be legendary. But the Faubourg Antoine has nothing in common with the zone, with its papier-mâché shacks, damp bedding, and smoldering rages. The Faubourg believes in square angles, strong glue, and joints that fit to within a hair's breadth, like a crust of bread ready to be eaten, with cheese and red wine.

Jules Romains,
Les Hommes de Bonne Volonté, Flammarion, 1958.

ing and the mirrors have stucco ornaments. Etched glass framed in mahogany paneling separates the dining room from the bar. The zinc counter top sits atop polychrome marble.

And since this street was named after the man famous for his novel *L'Insurgé*, let's close this section with a quote from his *Tableau de Paris* (1882-1883), "Under the Second Republic, the Faubourg Saint-Antoine still looks and smells revolutionary. It may no longer ram its way into the city, but it stands its ground and fights with the fury of a wild boar. The paving stones here are still branded with the red letters of the Revolution."

Going Down Rue de Charonne

Once we reach the end of Rue Jules-Vallès, we will enter **Rue de Charonne**, one of the oldest streets of Paris. It used to be the main road from the capital to the village of Charonne. Several convents moved out of the city to this country road in the 17th century, seeking peace and quiet. The first to come were the Dominican sisters of the Cross. Cyrano de Bergerac's aunt joined this congregation and, according to legend, Cyrano's body was laid to rest in their convent. Then came the Dames du Bon-Secours who took in wayward women, followed by

◀ 102 Rue de Charonne

the Benedictines de la Madeleine de Traisnel, who had been run out of the Champagne region in a time of war.

Let's turn left onto this street which, after several justified detours, will lead us back to our starting point on this Faubourg-Saint-Antoine tour.

The buildings at **102 and 100** that we are walking past sit on land that once belonged to the nuns of the Madeleine de Traisnel convent. The sisters took up quarters here in 1654. Half a century later, they owned nearly forty hectares (100 acres) of gardens, vineyards, orchards, and buildings in a section between today's Rue de Charonne, Rue Léon-Frot, and Rue de Montreuil.

Certain little houses sheltered behind the convent walls were rented out to women of high society who wished to withdraw from the world. Such was the case of the Duchess of Orléans. On June 9, 1744, her guest for supper and for the night was none other than Queen Marie Leszczynska. The convent was listed as national property during the Revolution, resulting in its closure. Little by little, the buildings were abandoned.

In the early 19th century, part of the estate was purchased by citizens

François Richard and Jean-Daniel Lenoir, who had been operating a spinning factory for some time on the other side of the street in the old Notre-Dame-du-Bon-Secours convent. In 1824, the Richard-Lenoir factory went bankrupt and had to sell off its converted convent buildings. In 1832, the same buildings became home to the school of industrial arts. From 1846 to 1848, they housed a hospice. Finally, they were purchased by lawyer and one-time radical leftist Alexandre Ledru-Rollin, who owned numerous other neighborhood properties.

Describing the Faubourg cabinet-makers in his *Tableau de Paris*, Jules Vallès informs us, "Some of these craftsmen are called "Ledru-Rollins," because their shops are located in the buildings which belonged to the old Montagnard of 1848, and are still the property of widow." Upon her death in 1888, she made the city of Paris her sole legatee, and the buildings were sold to individuals. Around 1910, a series of fires damaged the convent buildings so badly that they had to be torn down when land excavation works began a little later.

Number **102** was completely transformed in the early 20th century for Wilfrid Bertin's workshops. Notice the large expanses of glass made possible by the building's iron framework, providing natural light in the vast shop. Unfortunately the last vestiges of **100** were not preserved by the contractors who rebuilt the lot in 1980, despite protests by associations of concerned neighborhood residents.

Further down, at **94 Rue de Charonne**, where it crosses Rue Faidherbe, is the impressive Palais de la Femme, erected in 1910 by architects A. Labussière and C. Longerey. The building's brick upper floors sit on a massive millstone base which contains the main entrance and the offices for women's services. The pale brick surface is interspersed with vis-ible structural design elements in "reconstituted stone." They are either outlined or framed by red and blue brick. The gables are oddly embellished with blue enameled bricks. Entrance is through the angled face of the building on the corner of Rue Faidherbe. A triple arcade with a vaulted porch frames the doorway. Notice the allegorical bas-relief by Camille Garnier showing a woman reaching out to a family.

The Palais de la Femme is a refuge for single women, particularly young workers or students, run by the Armée du Salut, the Salvation Army. It has several hundred dormitory rooms, a 500-seat restaurant, a library, a tea room, meeting rooms, a lounge, and a TV room.

This same site was the location of the convent of the Dominican nuns, the Sœurs Dominicaines de la Croix. The Revolution forced them out of their convent, without actually expropriating them. When a 1904 law banned religious communities' teaching institutions, the nuns left France and the convent was demolished. Today's building was erected in 1910. It was originally designed as a hotel for single workers. The men could stay year-round or just one night. It had a large dining hall, drawing rooms, meeting rooms, and more. The complex also featured essential services such as a laundry, tailors, barbers, shoe repair, etc. The goal was to take them out of their squalid boarding rooms and cabarets, by giving them a social life. When war broke out in 1914, the building was turned into a military hospital. By 1926, the property was sold to the Armée du Salut, which converted it into today's Palais de la Femme.

▼ Palais de la Femme, 94 Rue de Charonne

Around Sainte-Marguerite's Church

Let's head down Rue de Charonne to number 88 and make a left on **Rue Charrière**, which runs beside the apse of Sainte-Marguerite, the neighborhood's parish church, and carries on to **Square Raoul-Nordling**, which provides a pleasant view of the church. According to legend, the small cemetery of this endearing little parish church was the burial spot of "the child who died in the Temple dungeon" (an obvious allusion to Louis XVII).

The sober façade of Sainte-Marguerite stands at **36 Rue Saint-Bernard**. It rises to a simple cross and has a trinity of brown doorways. The church dates back to 1625. At that time, it was but a simple chapel with a classic Latin cross floor plan. It was commissioned on land belonging to Jean de Vitry, lord of Reuilly, by Antoine Fayet, the priest at Saint-Paul's, as a burial plot for members of his family. Upon Fayet's death in 1634, at the request of neighborhood residents, the chapel was upgraded to the status of branch church of the Saint-Paul parish, allowing regular church services to be held within its walls. The tiny church grew and was endowed with a sacristy and a presbytery. Improvements were made in 1669 and in 1678. A chapel was added in 1703. In 1712, with the Faubourg Saint-Antoine's population growth, the Cardinal de Noailles elevated its rank to a cure.

In 1764, Victor Louis, the architect of the Palais Royal, was handed a commission for the Chapelle des Âmes du Purgatoire (souls in purgatory chapel), which projects from the left side of the church. Trompe-l'œil virtuoso Paolo Antonio Brunetti was commissioned to paint it, giving it two rows of fake white marble columns and a frieze depicting the death of Jacob and his funeral. In the center of the ensemble, behind the altar, is a canvas by Gabriel Briard (prix de Rome 1749), *Passage des Âmes du Purgatoire au Ciel*, completed in 1761. It depicts a group of bodies leaving the fire for the heavenly journey. This trompe-l'œil masterpiece was restored twice, once in 1846 by Pierre-Luc Charles Ciceri, who repainted the white figures on the black background, and in the 1960s by the Atelier Malesset, commissioned by Minister of Culture André Malraux to restore it to its original state.

▼ Sainte-Marguerite Church

▲ *Le Christ descendu de la Croix* (*Descent from the Cross*) by Charles Dorigny, 1546, Sainte-Marguerite Church
(© City of Paris, COARC/C. Fouin)

◂ Plaque in memory of those guillotined in 1794 and buried in the old Sainte-Marguerite cemetery

side is *Pèlerins d'Emmaüs* (pilgrims from Emmaus).

Two funerary elements from the tomb of Catherine Duchemin (wife of the sculptor Girardon) were remounted in the apse behind the high altar in the early 19th century. They originally belonged to the Saint-Landry church (then on Île de la Cité). One is a descent from the Cross and the other is a Mater Dolorosa; both white marble sculptures date from 1705-1706 and were based on drawings by Girardon and carved by his students Eustache Nourrisson and Robert Le Lorrain.

The church also contains four beautiful paintings recounting the life of St. Vincent de Paul, by Louis Galloche, Brother André, Jean Restout, and Jean-Baptiste Féret, which came from the Maison de Saint-Lazare located on Rue du Faubourg-Saint-Martin.

During the Revolution, the church was turned into a meeting hall. Many of its artworks and statues were lost. In 1792, the congregation was shaken by a great scandal when its vicar, Father J.-F. Aubert, married. The church was closed by the Revolution in 1793, but reopened in 1795 under the name of "Temple de la Liberté." It was handed back to the Catholic Church in 1803, and two years later, Pope Pius VII celebrated a Mass here.

The nave, the oldest part of the church, is simply lit by oculi, leaving it rather dark. The pulpit dates from 1704. It has four bas-reliefs depicting the Sermon on the Mount, St. John the Baptist preaching in the desert, St. Peter, and St. Paul. On the left side in the nave, against the façade wall's interior side, we will see a splendid descent from the cross, painted on wood by Charles Dorigny (1546). If you look carefully at the painting, you may notice that the model for the Joseph of Arimathea holding the body of Christ was King Henri II. Further down on this wall, to the right, and over the doorway, is a painting of Herod's Massacre of the Innocents (circa 1650) by Francesco de Rosa (also known as Pacecco de Rosa).

The two gables in the transept are graced by elegant bas-reliefs executed in 1724 by an abbot and church priest named Goy. On the south side is a Virgin and Child, and on the north

But the real historical curiosity at Sainte-Marguerite's remains the little cemetery that surrounded it. On June 10, 1795, at nine in the evening, with no religious service whatsoever, the body of the "child who died in the Temple dungeon" was laid to rest. Many believe this referred to the young Louis XVII, then ten years old, son of Louis XVI and Marie-Antoinette.

For over a hundred and fifty years, the mystery of the missing Dauphin was taken up time and again by amateurs of historical enigmas, leading to several appearances of impostors of the prince. Some people claimed the coffin had been placed in a common grave, but that during the night, royalists had removed it to another freshly dug grave, and that it was later secretly carried away by the Comité de Sûreté Générale (security forces).

In any case, evidence collected during the digs of 1846 and 1894, and data collected during drilling on church grounds in 1979 indicate that the remains exhumed could not have been those of the heir to the throne. The individuals are older. More importantly, however, the bones were not scarred by the tuberculosis infection Louis XVII was known to have.

What we do know for sure, however, is that from June 9-12, 1794, a guillotine was set up on Place de la Bastille, and during those three days, the time required to execute seventy-three citizens, the bodies were carted to Sainte-Marguerite's cemetery for burial. The graveyard was closed in 1806, three years after the death of Georges Jacob II, son of Georges Jacob, the famous cabinetmaker, who lived and worked in the Faubourg. A bronze bust still stands over his tomb.

▲ A 1990 fresco by Christian Zeimert, 50 Rue de Charonne (© Adagp, Paris 2009)

From Rue Saint-Bernard to Rue du Faubourg-Saint-Antoine

The elementary school located at **31 Rue Saint-Bernard**, across the street from the church, was built on land where the church's presbytery stood until 1912. The nursery school at **33** was built on the site of a refuge for invalid workers, founded in 1865.

Rue Saint-Bernard leads us back onto **Rue de Charonne**. At **50**, we see a huge blue mural covering the back wall of a building facing Avenue Ledru-Rollin. It was commissioned from Christian Zeimert in 1990 to replace a fading advertisement for bouillon cubes. The artist incorporated typical neighborhood places and characters in his design. There is the Balajo nightclub and, of course, the Faubourg's ever-present furniture makers. They appear right on the cubes, looking a lot like a children's construction set. Paying homage to the original mural, the artist incorporated the advertiser's name in three gigantic letters, spelling out "KUB."

On the other side of the prow-shaped building, on the corner of Rue de Charonne and **Avenue Ledru-Rollin** at **116** of the avenue, is the Bistrot du Peintre, an Art Nouveau bar dating from 1902. The ornate front, framed out in fine, varnished wood, is topped by an awning (or mar-

▶ Le Bistrot du Peintre, 116 Avenue Ledru-Rollin

▼ Passage Lhomme

quise). The interior décor dates from the 1930s and is in "modern style," as it is called. The frescoes are all original, and so is the stucco ceiling with its little angels. Twin ceramic panels in a style reminiscent of Mucha's work depict Spring and Summer as scantily clad nymphs with long, flowing hair, in fields of flowers.

We will now cross Avenue Ledru-Rollin and continue walking down **Rue de Charonne**. On our left, we have Passage Josset and Passage Saint-Antoine, which both act as extensions of Passage de la Bonne-Graine after it crosses Avenue Ledru-Rollin.

At **26** we come to **Passage Lhomme**, with its old paving stones and its small, modest, ivy-covered four- and five-story buildings. The ground floor has narrow workshops, all alike.

Let's go all the way to the end of **Rue de Charonne**. In a few minutes, we reach our starting point on the corner of **Rue du Faubourg-Saint-Antoine**.

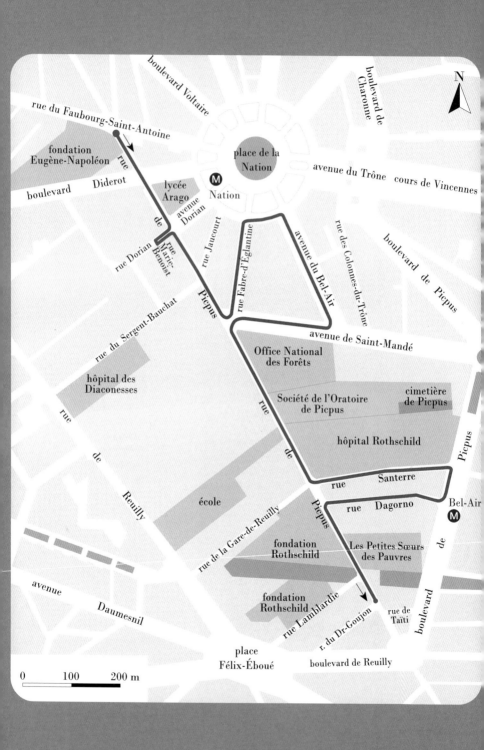

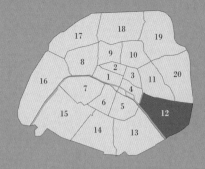

12th

Along
Rue de Picpus

▶ Start: **Rue du Faubourg-
Saint-Antoine, metro Nation**

▶ Finish: **Rue de Picpus,
metro Bel-Air**

Rue de Picpus was named for the small village it served. The street's name dates back to 1540 at least, with spelling variations over time ranging from *Picpuce*, *Piquepus*, and *Piquepusse* (all pronounced alike but with variable interpretations, e.g. "flea bite" and "pricked pus"). The place name could refer to an inn located on the pilgrimage path from the abbey of Saint-Maur to Saint-Denis, which ran through Rue Picpus. The establishment might have been infested with fleas, leaving travelers with painful memories. Thiéry's *Guide des Amateurs et des Étrangers Voyageurs à Paris* (1787) gives another explanation, "This hamlet got its name from the fact that its residents, afflicted with a skin disease which caused the formation of blisters, lanced them with needles to let the pus ooze out, thus the name '*Pique pus.*'"

The street was partially paved in 1728. In addition to the thirty or so houses which lined it at the time, it led to vineyards, orchards, and fields where vegetables were grown for sale in the nearby city.

It was a thoroughfare angling off the Faubourg Saint-Antoine, taking traffic to the town of Charenton. In the 18th century, it and its sister street Rue de Reuilly ended at Rue Lamblardie. The Reuilly toll gate stood at the crossroads of Rue de Picpus, Boulevard de Picpus, and Boulevard de Reuilly. It marked the Paris city limits of 1785. In 1863, Rue de Picpus was extended when the city of Paris absorbed the peripheral communities as far as today's Boulevard Poniatowski.

The Eugène-Napoléon Foundation

The Fondation Eugène-Napoléon was erected at the **corner of Rue de Picpus and Rue du Faubourg Saint-Antoine, at 254**, between 1853 and 1857. It was designed by Jacques Ignace Hittorff (1792-1867), the architect of the Cirque d'Hiver (winter circus) and the Gare du Nord (the city's northern train station).

It owes its existence to a diamond necklace the city of Paris had planned to give as a wedding present to Empress Eugénie, bride of Napoléon III.

▲ Statuette of the Virgin Mary in a garden of the Fondation Eugène-Napoléon

◄ Chapel, Fondation Eugène-Napoléon
(© AFP/Jean Ayissi)

▲ Façade, Fondation
Eugène-Napoléon

ber 1953. The foundation was named after Prince Eugène Napoléon, born on March 16, 1856. The Empress entrusted management of the institution to the Sœurs de la Charité. The ribbon-cutting ceremony was held on December 28, 1856.

The buildings were laid out in a hexagon to meet two constraints: the shape of the lot and program requirements. Respecting the Hospitaller tradition, the chapel was placed in the center. Three courtyards separate the various buildings, which were interconnected, offering protection from bad weather.

Hittorff built the main façade and the chapel in stone, but he cut costs by using brick for less important façades. The two-story buildings' façades have the same running pattern of arched windows on both floors. The architect borrowed from the vocabulary of Italian Renaissance design and 18th-century French architecture.

Despite the narrowness of the lot, the architect gave the main façade a courtyard, complete with two very small side wings. A portico in the center led to the Empress's reception hall.

The chapel shows the evolution of neo-classical style towards a return to medieval traditions. The main façade is dominated by a bell tower, a mainstay of medieval architecture. Abandoned by the neoclassical architects, bell-towers had been revived again in religious architecture by 1830. Notice the three statues to Faith, Charity, and Hope, executed by Nanteuil (pseudonym of Charles-François Lebœuf, 1792-1865).

While the rectangular chapel has no choir, it offers the curiosity of a second façade influenced by Early Chris-

A budget of six hundred thousand francs had been set aside for the gift on January 26, 1853. Eugénie, however, wisely refused to have so lavish a gift taint her marriage. She asked that the funds be allocated instead to the creation of a school for orphaned and underprivileged girls. The city of Paris granted additional funds to take the establishment from an initial student body of sixty to three hundred.

The site selected was an old hay and fodder market. Hittorff submitted five projects to city authorities. One of the designs presented in parallel the outline of the necklace and that of the foundation. The city of Paris accepted the fifth project in Decem-

tian architecture. A peristyle rules the ground floor level and the side façades. Inside the chapel, the ceiling is supported by exposed wooden beams, as can be seen at Saint-Vincent-de-Paul (off Rue Lafayette in the 10th arrondissement), yet another example of a return to Early Christian inspiration. The painting in the apse by Félix-Joseph Barrias (1822-1906), shows Empress Eugénie visiting the foundation and symbolically offering her necklace to the orphans. Barrias was also commissioned for the interior decoration on the Cirque d'Hiver.

Today, the state-approved foundation is made up of a nursery and a primary school, a vocational high school, and a girls' dormitory. It also houses a middle school and the boarding school for the Petits Chanteurs à la Croix de Bois. These young singers spend half their time in school work and the other half receiving vocal and musical training. The foundation also offers concerts and lectures. The garden along Rue de Picpus was opened to the public in 2007.

Rue de Picpus: from Rue du Faubourg-Saint-Antoine to Rue Dorian

Numerous boarding houses and sanatoriums were attracted to Picpus, a quiet country road. Convents also moved here, only to be ousted by the Revolution. In 1740, the home of Léonard Bounaud de Tranchecerf, a squire and count of the Holy Roman Empire, stood at **4 Rue de Picpus**. Around 1780, Mrs. de Sainte-Colombe turned it into a home, which in 1786 admitted 19-year-old Louis de Saint-

Gérard de Nerval's Days in Picpus

Poet Gérard de Nerval (1808-1855) had his first fit of madness in late February 1841 in a house on Rue Miromesnil, in the course of which he smashed chairs and a mirror. He was taken away to the clinic at 10 Rue de Picpus run by Mrs. de Saint-Marcel. He received care from the clinic's Dr. Pierre Édouard Vallerand de la Fosse, one of the doctors to King Charles X between 1827 and 1830, and an acquaintance of writers Alexandre Dumas and Gustave Flaubert. On March 5, 1841 (at the age of 32), Nerval wrote home, *"Dear Father, At last they are allowing me to read and to write. I believe I have fully recovered my health. Dr. Vallerand saw me yesterday and was satisfied. We strode through the garden in high spirits. I was told yesterday you were coming. There is really nothing else to prescribe for me but good, nutritious meals, but I am angry that I haven't seen you come as soon as possible. I have much to tell you. I would like to recount all the wonderful things that have happened to me thanks to our friends and the kindness of the minister. Since my fever, I have not been able to see you longer than a few instants and only to discuss the practicalities of clothes and money, which is hardly amusing. Thanks to you and all who are dear to me, I have what I need to stay and to leave. Henceforth, it is important that I not waste a moment, and that you yourself come set up the date for my release. I do wish to avoid compromising the lovely position I now enjoy. While I shall not be leaving the home until I have been completely cured, I could still be allowed out for necessary visits."*

Nerval was released on March 16 only to be admitted five days later, after a relapse, to a clinic run by Dr. Blanche on Rue Norvins in Montmartre.

Just (1767-1794, a fierce French Revolutionary). He was locked away for having stolen his family's silverware and jewelry. His mother, who made his shirts, requested that they be doled out to him only two at a time, to keep him from selling them. The institution was demolished in 1908.

Mrs. de Saint-Marcel's clinic was located off Boulevard Diderot at numbers **8 and 10 Rue de Picpus**. The property lost part of its grounds when Boulevard Diderot was created in 1850. The 1840 edition of the famous Bottin business directory listed the establishment in these terms: "Health institution founded over a century ago for mental illnesses, ideally located, vast, pleasant, healthy, lovely landscaping, a home for expectant mothers and patients with diseases requiring particular treatment [...], at Rue de Picpus, 6." The street numbering was changed in 1851, resulting in the old 6 becoming today's 10.

Writer Gérard de Nerval, the author of *Aurélia* and *Nuits d'Octobre*, was a patient in this establishment in February 1841. The sanatorium closed in 1912.

The lot at **12** may have been the site for a country home owned by Ninon de Lenclos (1616-1706), famous for the literary circle that met in her townhouse at 36 Rue des Tournelles in the Marais. Her guests were such luminaries as Boileau, Mignard, and Lully. One of her lovers, the Marquis Henri de Sévigné (husband of the famed letter writer), fought a duel with Chevalier d'Albret over Mrs. de Gondran. It took place in nearby Picpus. The Marquis died from his wounds two days later. Twenty years later, his son, Charles de Sévigné, became involved with Ninon.

Mr. Audet de La Mésangère, a former professor and member of the Académie des Sciences et Belles-Lettres in Châlons-sur-Marne, turned this property into a boys' boarding house. Tuition costs ran five hundred francs for children up to the age of ten, and six hundred francs for those over ten.

"This price includes the study hall supervisor, reading and mathematics teachers, laundry, lighting, and firewood. Paper, quills, ink, powder, and pomade for everyday use cost twenty-four livres a year. Twelve livres shall be paid as a way of welcoming the teachers and the servants." (Thiéry, *Guide des Amateurs et des Étrangers Voyageurs à Paris*, 1787).

In 1826, Adélaïde d'Orléans bought the lot with house and garden opening onto 77 Rue de Reuilly to establish a new Hospice d'Enghien, the original having been founded in

1819 on Rue de Babylone by her aunt, the Duchess of Enghien. She hired Pierre François Léonard Fontaine for the renovation. The hospice was demolished in 1904. A year later, the extension of Rue Dorian was completed.

In 1905, Jean Falp designed a building in pure Art Nouveau style for a corner lot with two addresses, **12 Rue de Picpus and 2 Rue Dorian**. A crenellated corner tower ornamented with the heads of mythological animals stands watch over the entire structure. The carved embellishments

► Building on the corner of 12 Rue de Picpus and 2 Rue Dorian

▼ Detail, 2 Rue Dorian

include female faces with long flowing hair, influenced by Botticelli and the Pre-Raphaelites. Falp also drew inspiration for other decorative motifs from the animal and plant kingdoms.

The Art Nouveau style is matched by two neighboring buildings designed by Falp in 1909, at **4 and 6 Rue Dorian**.

Around Avenue de Saint-Mandé

We come to a second corner building with dual addresses: **22 Rue de Picpus and 42 Rue du Sergent-Bauchat**. During the Bourbon Restoration (1814-1830), it served as a military hospital and was a branch of the Val-de-Grâce military hospital (5th arrondissement). It was converted into barracks in 1860, only to be shut down shortly thereafter. The Sainte-Clotilde convent gardens used to take up **42**, sweeping all the way to today's 101 Rue de Reuilly.

We will slip away from Rue de Picpus for a moment by taking a left on **Rue Fabre-d'Églantine**. In 1896, G. Lobbé built a rental house at **9** in neo-Gothic style. The brick and stone

façade is a mixture of Henri IV with Louis XIII styles, with a bold borrowing from the vocabulary of medieval French architecture: arches with doubly curved sides and foliated capitals on small columns framing the windows, trefoil arches, crockets, and imaginary animals carved in Gothic style. The doorway is topped by an ogival tympanum with a bas-relief showing a pensive alchemist in his laboratory, in the company of his cat.

Once we reach **Place de la Nation**, we will turn right onto **Avenue du Bel-Air**, a broad street dating back to 1667, a time when *jeu de paume* was played here. This avenue will take us directly from today's Place de la Nation (formerly named Place du Trône) to the promenade along Avenue de Saint-Mandé.

In 1905, Jean Falp designed a rental property at **17** in high Art Nouveau style. As Falp lived in this building, he hired sculptor Georges Ardouin, whose work he greatly appreciated. Taking inspiration from the Pre-Raphaelite movement, Ardouin ornamented the façade with ladies' faces, framed by swirls of flowing hair. Other design elements include animals (cats, squirrels, monkeys) and plants. The front door is crowned by a profusion of loving faces of mothers and their children, as a celebration of maternal love.

We will veer to the right on **Avenue de Saint-Mandé**, which was created by Cardinal Mazarin, executing orders he had received from Louis XIV in 1658 to carry out embellishments to the Château de Vincennes, its grounds, and surrounding area. Mazarin planned two parallel roads running from the royal castle into Paris. The first, Cours de Vincennes,

▲ 4 Rue Dorian
▼ 17 Avenue du Bel-Air

◄ 9 Rue Fabre-d'Églantine

was not completed until 1669. The second, Avenue de la Ménagerie - later to become Avenue de Saint-Mandé - was laid out here between 1658 and 1662, "leading to the royal menagerie at Picpusse."

The royal menagerie was set up in 1211 during the reign of Philippe Auguste. It was located on the western edge of the Parc de Vincennes. In its cages were wild animals for the king's hunting parties. As Dulaure, a 19th-century historian, informs us in his *Description de Paris et de ses Environs*, it also contained, "caged lions, tigers, and leopards, which were kept for fights in an arena in the middle." The menagerie was transferred to Versailles in 1706, then, during the Revolution, to the Jardin des Plantes. In the 18th century, Parisians greatly appreciated a stroll on the Avenue de Saint-Mandé, known for its wide lawns, peace, and quiet. All non-pedestrian traffic was banned.

The Centre Technique du Bois et de l'Ameublement is located at **10-14**. Its façade is ornamented with exotic woods. The center publishes scientific and technical data about wood and wood products.

Still in the wood theme, number **2** was built in 1976 for the Office National des Forêts (the national forest service) by architects Deschler, Thieulin, and de Vigan. Rising thirty-one meters high, it is a forty-sided polygon shaped somewhat like a tree trunk.

A left turn will put us back on **Rue de Picpus**. The Agriculture Ministry built offices from 1950 to the 1990s at **33**, on the site of the old Institut des Sacrés-Cœurs, founded in 1804 by Father Coudrin for the training of clergy. Coudrin also founded the Congrégation des Sacrés-Cœurs, whose convent buildings are next door. The three-story building has a rhythmic series of windows slightly, arched at their tops, string courses and corner chains. It is the only vestige of the old seminary.

Cimetière de Picpus

The small Picpus cemetery is at **35**. In the 17th century, it was the old Chanoinesses Régulières de Saint-Augustin convent, called Notre-Dame de la Victoire de Lépante. Every October 7, the religious community was required to celebrate Don John of Austria's victory over the Ottoman navy in the 1571 Battle of Lepanto.

The nuns, originally from the city of Reims, moved to Picpus in 1640. Tubeuf, Queen Anne of Austria's finance minister, granted them a house. A century and a half later, Revolutionary authorities confiscated the convent, assigned it a rental value of 1,730 livres, and leased it to one Antoine Riédain starting October 1, 1792. He then sublet part of the property to a certain Coignard, who planned to capitalize on the local fresh air and the gardens to set up a clinic. But the events of the Revolution were in full swing. On June 14, 1794, the guillotine was set up on Place de la Nation. The municipality ordered a cemetery be created nearby. The next

day, Poyet, the town architect, accompanied by Coffinet, an inspector, and Delépine, a public works administrator, requisitioned the garden and had it converted into a cemetery, despite Riédain's protests. They created a wide carriage door to accommodate carts hauling decapitated bodies in for burial.

The guillotine on Place de la Nation operated for seven weeks, from June 14 to July 27, 1794. Among the 1,306 people executed were Prince Friedrich III von Salm-Kyrburg, the Duchess of Ayen, the Marshal and Viscountess of Noailles, poets Antoine Roucher and André Chénier, as well as Eugène de Beauharnais, Empress Joséphine's first husband.

The victims were hastily buried in two common graves dug in the garden. Riédain and his neighbors (wine growers, farmers, boarding house operators, and directors of clinics), drew up a petition demanding the cemetery's removal. But the cadavers continued to be carted in at all hours of the day and night.

The executions ended after the fall of Robespierre, on July 27, 1794. Nevertheless, burials continued up to August 16. During the Directoire, Princess Amélie de Hohenzollern wanted to locate her brother's grave. On November 14, 1796, she bought the cemetery parcel. It was twenty-seven meters long and twelve meters wide. In 1802, upon their return from exile, the Marquise of Montagu and Marie-Adrienne de Noailles (the wife of General Lafayette) wanted to locate the burial places of their grandmother, mother, and sister. They started a fund, inviting others who had lost a relative to the guillotine to contribute, and created the Oratoire society. By 1803, the society was able to purchase the convent and to open a second cemetery in the garden, reserved for direct descendants of the guillotined.

▲ Chapel, Picpus Cemetery

▸ Commemorative plaque to the Carmelites guillotined during the French Revolution and buried in Picpus Cemetery

◂ Tomb of General La Fayette, Picpus Cemetery

General Lafayette died in 1834 and was buried beside his wife in the small Picpus cemetery. For over a hundred years, every July 4, on the occasion of America's Independence Day, the US flag has flown over Lafayette's grave, even during the German occupation. In 1917, General Pershing, commanding an American expeditionary corps in France, paid his respects here and said the now very famous words *"Lafayette, nous voilà"* (literally: here we are, Lafayette), which France's Marshal Joffre applauded.

By 1805, the convent buildings had fallen into a state of neglect. An order founded by the Abbot Coudrin and Henriette Aymer de la Chevalerie, the Congrégation Perpétuelle du Très-Saint-Sacrement et des Sacrés-Cœurs de Jésus et de Marie, moved in and gradually replaced the dilapidated buildings with new ones.

In 1841, Joseph-Antoine Froelicher (1790-1866), the architect of a dozen chateaux including Bonnelles in the Yvelines, built a memorial chapel in neo-classical style. Inside, is a statue of Notre-Dame-de-la-Paix which

belonged to Father Ange, born Duke Henri de Joyeuse. He donated the statue to the Capucine convent on Rue Saint-Honoré in 1608. The sculpture was bequeathed to Henriette Aymer de la Chevalerie in 1806. The statue is believed have prompted numerous miraculous healings.

Built in 1850 in neo-Louis XV style (particularly the cartouches and seashells over the door), the convent building at **37** Rue de Picpus belongs to the Congrégation des Dames du Sacré-Cœur. It is crowned by a gabled pediment buttressed on either side by reversed console volutes. The tympanum is carved with two hearts, the symbol of the congregation.

The old boarding house once managed by the nuns of the Congrégation de la Mère de Dieu at **45** now houses the Paul-Dukas music conservatory. The neo-Romanesque façade built in 1880 features arched windows and a cornice supported by modillions.

Rue Santerre and Rue Dagorno

At this point, we will take a left onto **Rue Santerre** bordering **Hôpital Rothschild**, which has an exit on 33 Boulevard de Picpus. The hospital was founded by Edmond de Rothschild (1845-1934), carrying on the family's charitable activities through the foundation which had been set up by his

father, James Mayer de Rothschild. Lucien Bechmann (1880-1968), architect of the Maison Internationale at Paris's Cité Universitaire, designed the new hospital in collaboration with Dr. Léon Zadoc-Kahn, who administered the establishment until he was deported to Auschwitz, where he died in 1943. Bechmann opted for a system of separate buildings for individual, autonomous hospital units. This layout was based on the state of medical and therapeutic knowledge in the early 20th century. Isolating patients by disease groups prevented the spread of infectious diseases.

With its flowerbeds and pert pavilions, the hospital resembled a pretty, landscaped suburban development. During World War I, on the night of June 16, 1918, bombs damaged the hall on the site of today's general practice building. During World War II, the Germans used the hospital as a prison from 1941 to 1944. Jews suffering from any disease were brought here under the surveillance of the French police and were then deported to extermination camps.

On January 1, 1954, Guy de Rothschild donated the hospital to the city public-hospital system for the token sum of one franc. The establishment has grown greatly since then. Between 1971 and 1993, new buildings containing operating rooms and laboratories were erected. Today, the hospital mainly provides neuro-orthopedic re-education, dental, and geriatric care.

A turn right will put us back on **Boulevard de Picpus** for a short block. Then we will turn the corner onto **Rue Dagorno**, named after Nicolas-René Dagorno, a farmer. In 1791, Dagorno owned a parcel stretching from today's 23 Boulevard de Picpus to 61 Rue de Picpus. A private road laid out in 1899 was soon lined with homes. In 1914, the Germans bombed the neighborhood. An unexploded bomb was found at **13** Rue Dagorno.

Back to Rue de Picpus

This street will lead us back to **Rue de Picpus**, which we'll follow to the end of our stroll. Number **61** was the location of the convent of the Pénitents Réformés du Tiers-Ordre de Saint-François, so named because it was the third (tiers) set up by St. Francis of Assisi in 1221. The members set up a convent in Picpus in 1601. Louis XIII laid the chapel's cornerstone in 1611.

Having become a royal foundation, the convent was endowed with numerous pieces of art. *Le Serpent d'Airain*, a painting by Le Brun, hung in the refectory, where it was unfortunately damaged by damp. The spacious garden was embellished with

◄ Hôpital Rotschild
► Townhouses on Rue Dagorno

grottos and rock gardens, seashells, and statues. The library collections included precious books, some of which are now in the Bibliothèque Mazarine. An apartment was reserved for Catholic ambassadors and foreign dignitaries, who stayed here before beginning their highly ceremonial entrance into Paris with a sumptuous procession. In 1772, Picpus was dispensed of the requirement to host ambassadors.

A retirement home for the poor at number **65** was run by the Petites Sœurs des Pauvres. Empress Eugénie presided over the ribbon-cutting ceremonies on November 29, 1853. The congregation's founding mother was Jeanne Jugan (1792-1879), a modest servant beatified in 1982. In 1839, in the town of Saint-Servan, in Brittany, she began taking in penniless elderly women, and from 1842, a growing number of elderly men.

Across the street at **76-78** is the Rothschild Foundation retirement home. James de Rothschild (1792-1868), who set up the French branch of the Rothschild bank, was an active philanthropist. This retirement home

was for the Jewish community. The foundation started out in 1852 with a 50-bed hospital, a hospice for the aged, and an orphanage. The buildings soon proved to be too crowded, and a new orphanage able to house two hundred children was erected in 1874 at the nearby 7 Rue Lamblardie. In 1914, the hospital was transferred to 33 Boulevard de Picpus. During World War II, the children in the orphanage were deported.

Today's Rue Lamblardie was officially the southernmost limit of Rue de Picpus in the 18th century. Its

name at that time was Ruelle Picquepuce ("Flea Bite Alley"). Beyond this point, travelers left the Faubourg Saint-Antoine and entered the countryside. In order to maintain security and avoid overextending the police forces, royal authorities tried to dissuade new construction beyond the city limits. From 1724 to 1726, they erected physical markers. In 1727, one such marker was placed on a house, then the only one on the street, at what is today's corner lot at **30 Rue Lamblardie and 88 Rue de Picpus**. The house was torn down in 1914 and the marker was placed in the Musée Carnavalet. Translated into English, the engraved regulation reads, "1727. In the reign of Louis XV. By the King's order, nothing may be built on this street past this marker."

◄ Paris city limit marker at 304 Rue de Charenton, similar to the one that was placed on the corner building 30 Rue Lamblardie and 88 Rue de Picpus

► 76-78 Rue de Picpus

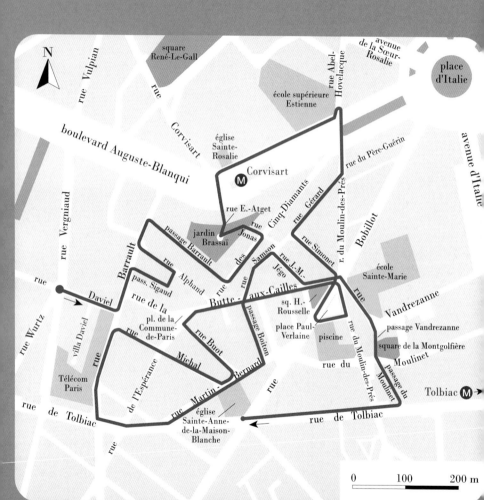

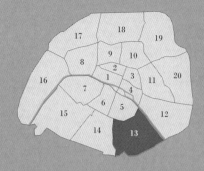

13th

Butte-aux-Cailles

▶ Start: Rue Wurtz,
metro Corvisart
▶ Finish: Rue Bobillot,
metro Corvisart or Tolbiac

Compared to Montmartre's and Belleville's elevations of nearly 130 meters, the Butte-aux-Cailles's sixty-three meters are hardly impressive. This hill is not much higher than Mount Sainte-Geneviève, and it does not match either Montparnasse ou Montsouris. What made it seem high was the spectacular cut the Bièvre River made through this quarter. Today, however, the Bièvre river has been engineered and driven underground, and its valley has been leveled. The Cailles were a family of farmers and millers for whom the quarter was named as early as the 16th century.

By 1750, an increasing number of windmills were being erected at the top of the Butte-aux-Cailles and along the plateau of present-day Avenue d'Italie, which then was very simply called *la route de la Butte aux Cailles*.

Until 1850 or so, however, there were practically no constructions on the Butte aside from a few light farm buildings and perhaps a few shacks beside the numerous entrances to clay and limestone quarries. They were generally dug about twenty-five meters deep, just enough to cut through the softer layers and reach good rock. An already dirtied Bièvre River wound its way past the mount and Rue Vergniaud, down in the steep ravine that had a forty-percent grade, far more than today's already quite steep Rue Daviel.

After this part of Gentilly was annexed by the city of Paris in 1860, the Butte-aux-Cailles saw its first real urban development. It became home to laundrywomen, ragmen, shoe-industry workers, and others desperately trying to eke out a living. Housing for these classes was slowly built

The Butte-aux-Cailles as Viewed in 1876

"The Butte-aux-Cailles will soon lose its unusual and picturesque character. Wide, airy new streets are being cut through it; every morning, it gets a fresh grooming, swept as tidy as the Opéra quarter. Little by little, the ragmen are being pushed out, seeking digs elsewhere. Cleanliness! But don't you understand that cleanliness is a nuisance for them, an insult to their dirty rags, to their birthright to filth! Leave them their narrow, winding alleys, veritable gutters of garbage and grime where mangy dogs, shivering from hunger, scratch the muddy pebbles for crumbs. Stop demolishing the blocks of ramshackle houses that seem to lean against each other like two drunks trying to regain their balance - perhaps for mutual support, perhaps to collapse in like company. Pretend to ignore the unhealthy one-room flats where father, mother, sons, and daughters sleep pell-mell with their pets and no shame. If you knock down these already-caving-in walls; if you lay out boulevards and squares in these places where children smoke home-rolled cigarettes; if you replace the smudged oil lamps with garlands of gas lights, what an incredible loss it will be for engravers and amateurs of twisted skylines and baroque squalor! City of Paris, respect the Butte-aux-Cailles!"

Pierre-Léonce Imbert, *À Travers Paris Inconnu*, 1876

on the Butte. The area had been so heavily quarried, it was not always safe. No real urban development plan could be worked out until the Bièvre was channeled and covered over in the period between 1900-1910.

The Butte became trendy in the 1990s. Today's bars and restaurants are doing a booming business. Tourists flock here to sample the village-like ambience of a relaxed and convivial working-class area historically known for its anarchist residents. Becoming fashionable, however, has reversed the social climate.

▶ Antoinist Temple,
34 Rue Vergniaud

◀ The Petite Alsace area,
10 Rue Daviel

▼ Villa Daviel

The little houses have been renovated and the neighborhood gentrified. The new residents are generally well-off, in love with their romantic illusions of "authentic" Paris. The influx of bourgeois-bohemians has driven rents sky-high. Much of the quarter is on the historic register and zoning regulations proscribe any new high-density construction.

From Rue Wurtz to Rue des Cinq-Diamants

Our stroll begins at the lowest point in the Bièvre valley. **Rue Wurtz** was built atop an old arm of the river. At a bend in the river, now traced by the junction of Rue Wurtz and Rue Vergniaud, is an **Antoinist temple** consecrated in October 1913. The intersec-

tion here had to be raised nine meters, given the valley's slope. This small chapel is one of three Antoinist places of worship in Paris. Founding father Louis-Joseph Antoine died in 1912 (although Antoinism was a Spiritist movement believing in reincarnation), and his followers have focused

on charity work and healing the sick. Further up the street, on the eastern corner of the intersection with Rue Daviel, we have a 1900s **bakery** with a pretty interior décor.

Let's walk up **Rue Daviel** now. Villa Daviel and the neighboring low-income housing project at **10** were finished almost simultaneously in 1912. Often called "Petite Alsace," number **10** features a faux farmyard framed by brick and half-timber houses, their façades enlivened with roofs and gables. The ensemble is charming but has no particularly orig-

inal features. Let's cross the street to **Villa Daviel**, a typically Parisian private lane. The properties were harmoniously developed and designed. Most of the townhouses here are very well maintained and boast small front yards. All sorts of flowers, bushes, and trees are nurtured on the postage-stamp-sized lots. There's at least one fig tree, and, more surprisingly, a banana tree.

Exiting the lane, we continue to **Rue Barrault**, at the end of the block, where two well-designed modern townhouses stand at **35** and **37**. After our left onto Barrault, we'll turn right on **Passage Sigaud**. The Marxist library used to be at **21**. According to legend, it was located on the site of an old bordello known for the way its girls called out to passersby from the balcony. From **17 to 7**, we will see some lovely little townhouses, completely renovated.

Curious Art Nouveau grotesque masks stare down at us from the third floor of **11 Rue Alphand**. Pleasant greenery in the courtyard adds to the charms of this apartment complex. We'll follow Rue Alphand to where it meets **Rue Barrault**, and turn left. Our next right is **Passage Barrault**. With

▲ 21 Passage Sigaud

its old-fashioned cobblestones, the lane is irresistibly attractive. Until recently, a sign informed motorists that this private passage could not admit vehicles over three tons, as deep quarry tunnels below haven't always been filled in properly.

Several tiny houses line the street, which climbs the hill. Notice the pretty property that can be partially seen when viewed through the iron gates at **11**. Until rather recently, **6 bis** across the street housed a small rubber-washer factory. Its next door neighbor, number **6**, formerly a shack, is a prime example of gentrification

◄◄ Rue Alphand
◄ Passage Barrault

and the rapid shifts in the social fabric of the Butte-aux-Cailles.

We reach **Rue des Cinq-Diamants**. This name once belonged to a short street south of Rue Quincampoix (4th arrondissement), the five diamonds referring to the wares of a 16th-century jeweler who had a shop there. In 1851, however, it was merged with Quincampoix, leaving the name "Cinq-Diamants" available for the street where we now stand in the 13th.

Let's turn left. **46** is still the headquarters of the "Amis de la Commune de Paris 1871." Founded in 1882, it is

the oldest existing workers' organization in France. They were the ones who fought to have the triangular Place de la Commune de Paris at the top of the Butte named in honor of that historical revolt of 1871, in which residents of the Butte-aux-Cailles valiantly defended their ideals. Communard General Valéri Wroblewski had moved artillery to the top of the hill, and for several hours, the Butte held off the Versaillais, who had made a deal with the victorious Prussians to quell the rebellion in Paris. At least the pummeling from the artillery gave the doomed Communards enough time to flee to the Right Bank.

A café-hotel sign at **39** proudly announces that it has been in business since 1927. A small courtyard at **40** is still used by one of the workshops that were ubiquitous here until

the 1970s. Several shops have kept their original storefronts; one good example is the one at **29**, with its painted wooden panels. Opposite the famous "Chez Gladines" is a convivial café at **23** called "Le Passage des Artistes," an ironic way of referring to tiny Rue Jonas. It led to an alley called Cité Jonas, which, in the old days, was haunted by beggars, fake cripples, and thieves. It is now a small park named for the photographer Brassaï.

Around Boulevard Auguste-Blanqui

Let's take **Rue Jonas**, which becomes **Rue Eugène-Atget** at the entrance to the square. The flight of stairs taking us down to Boulevard Auguste-Blanqui gives a clear idea of the steep path to the Butte, which was outside the city limits back in 1860. When the semicircular condominium complex you see was being built, its developers claimed it followed the course of the Bièvre River. In reality, however, the riverbed was a good hundred meters away, and ran perpendicular to the street. This building wiped out a magnificent view.

At this point, we'll cross **Boulevard Auguste-Blanqui**, under the elevated metro line, to reach **Sainte-Rosalie's Church**. Founded in 1859, it was named in memory of Sister Rosalie, as was the street where it stands. Erected on the orders of Father Le Rebours, it has been served by Lazarist fathers. Two years later, a school and an employment office for local young men were added. Expropriated in 1867 to make room for the new boulevard, the church had to be moved. It was consecrated on its present-day site in 1869. The plans had called for a bell tower on the northwest corner but the funds were never collected for its construction. Lack of funds affected other 13th-arrondissement churches; there was a decade-long halt in tower construction at both Saint-Hippolyte and Saint-Marcel. Sainte-Rosalie did not become a parish church until 1963. The Lazarist fathers stayed on for another eight years. A plaque commemorating their service is inside this small church, on the left wall of the nave. The stained-glass window over the choir has a panel to the right showing Sister Rosalie presenting her patron saint with a model of the church, bell tower included.

Let's walk up Boulevard Auguste-Blanqui as far as the **École Supérieure Estienne des Arts et Industries Graphiques**, where graphic arts and printing have been taught since 1896. The main building is mostly in brick. The walkway lined with flowerbeds and beautiful magnolias takes us up to the main entrance, topped by the coat of arms of the city of Paris. The campus was designed by architects Manjot and Dammartin, and the steel framework for the main print shop was produced by the Gustave Eiffel factory.

Crossing back to the south side of the boulevard, past the arrondissement's only 1900s **bandstand**, we are headed for **Rue du Moulin-des-Prés**. The corner building, number **1**, was Auguste Blanqui's place of death (his motto: "no God, no master!"). He died in a fifth-floor apartment in 1881, after three years' residence. A plaque that is both too small and too high informs us that he remained faithful

◄ Sainte-Rosalie church

► Bandstand, Boulevard Auguste-Blanqui

▼ École Estienne, 18 Boulevard Auguste-Blanqui

▶ Old shoe factory sign,
Place Paul-Verlaine

to the workers' cause during his forty years in prison.

A little farther up Rue du Moulin-des-Prés, off to the right, is **Rue Gérard**. Small *faubourg*-style houses line the street from **40 to 48**. At the next corner, let's turn left onto **Rue Simonet**, which once ran between rows of workshops. Only a few decades ago, it was still home to a brewery, three factories, and a charity organization. The street will take us to **Place Paul-Verlaine**.

Around Rue de la Butte-aux-Cailles

To our left, on the corner of Place Paul-Verlaine, a gabled façade's recently restored **sign** informs us that H. Lefèvre made shoes and galoshes here. The little factory has been converted into apartments.

At the other end of this square is the famous **Butte-aux-Cailles baths**. Behind the curious brick façade are two outdoor pools, and an indoor pool under a concrete cathedral ceiling. This remarkable sports complex designed by architects Bonnier and Hennebique was recently restored.

▼ Turreted house,
Place Paul-Verlaine

The establishment's history is connected to that of an old artesian well, marked today by a **modern fountain** on the square. In the 19th century, Paris Prefect Haussmann ordered this well to be dug to supply water not only to residents on the Butte but also to fill the Bièvre River, which often ran dry in the summer. Drilling began in 1866. It continued for the next six years, but 532 meters down, the bottom was still dry. The site was then closed for nearly twenty years. Finally, in 1903, at a depth of 582 meters, water sprang up. But by that time, plans were underway to cover the Bièvre, and running water had already been piped in to every building in the neighborhood. What was to be done with the 6,000 cubic meters of water gushing out daily from the artesian well? A small bathhouse was opened in 1908, but it was not until 1924 that the present-day public swimming pool complex was opened. The water was 28°C (82°F) and contained a small amount of healthful sulfur. This establishment created a veritable revolution: not only was the water supplied by an artesian well, the complex offered showers for hygiene and a pool for sports, encouraging locals to learn how to swim. It was also the first in France to require swimmers to shower before taking a dip. In 1922, France only had twenty year-round pools (seven of

which were in Paris), compared to 806 in England and 1,362 in Germany.

To the left of the pool is an odd **house with a turret**, known in the quarter as the "petit chateau." It was restored and incorporated into a real-estate project. A left turn will put us on **Rue de la Butte-aux-Cailles**. This ridge is the quarter's busiest spot. Back in 1850, a windmill operated at today's **12**. In July 1976, a restaurant opened at **16**. It was set up by a workers' collective called "Le Temps des Cerises," in reference to the famous song by Jean-Baptiste Clément (see inset), the melody that rallied the Communards who spilled their blood here. The restaurant, a gathering place for over a generation of free-thinking libertarians, anarchists, and post-May-1968 artists — a jolly mixed bag — foreshadowed the attraction the Butte would have for intellectuals and social activists. The main hall displays a handsome cast iron service elevator. Two other cafés on the street borrowed their names from the lyrics of the same song; both Le Merle Moqueur at **11** and La Folie en Tête at **33** host concerts. Many businesses have moved away over the past two decades, as more and more restaurants have moved in. A subscription library at **17** is run by the Bienvenue Association. The bar-cum-tobacconist (*bar-tabac*, as the French call such places) at **23** is popular with every-

Le Temps des Cerises

Le Temps de Cerises is a song nearly every French person knows. Composed in 1867 by Jean-Baptiste Clément, it has been performed by many popular artists, including Yves Montand. In this land of uncountable insurrections and counter-insurrections, it is a revolutionary hymn. It became a poetic protest to the military might from Versailles that crushed the Commune revolt, which was as sweet and fleeting as cherry season. Clément is the composer of a few other equally well-known songs, like *Dansons la Capucine*, *La Grève*, and *Le Premier Mai*.

Quand nous chanterons le temps des cerises,
Et gai rossignol et merle moqueur
Seront tous en fête.
Les belles auront la folie en tête
Et les amoureux du soleil au cœur.
Quand nous chanterons le temps des cerises,
Sifflera bien mieux le merle moqueur.

Mais il est bien court le temps des cerises,
Où l'on s'en va deux cueillir en rêvant
Des pendants d'oreilles,
Cerises d'amour aux robes pareilles
Tombant sous la feuille en gouttes de sang.
Mais il est bien court, le temps des cerises,
Pendants de corail qu'on cueille en rêvant.

Quand vous en serez au temps des cerises
Si vous avez peur des chagrins d'amour,
Évitez les belles !
Moi qui ne crains pas les peines cruelles,
Je ne vivrai point sans souffrir un jour.
Quand vous en serez au temps des cerises,
Vous aurez aussi des peines d'amour !

J'aimerai toujours le temps des cerises,
C'est de ce temps-là que je garde au cœur
Une plaie ouverte.
Et dame Fortune, en m'étant offerte,
Ne pourra jamais fermer ma douleur.
J'aimerai toujours le temps des cerises,
Et le souvenir que je garde au cœur.

▲ A Wallace fountain, Place de la Commune-de-Paris

◄ 27 Rue Michal

one in the neighborhood. In a community which is such a social and cultural crossroads, this is especially meaningful.

Continuing our stroll along Rue de la Butte-Cailles, we come to **Place de la Commune-de-Paris**, where small groups often gather on pleasant summer evenings. It is graced by a Wallace fountain. As we exit via Rue de l'Espérance, try to imagine that around 1850, this spot was home to the Butte's last two windmills.

From Rue de l'Espérance to Passage Boiton

We will take a few steps down Rue de l'Espérance, then make a left on **Rue Buot**, which will take us to the apse of Sainte-Anne's church. Notice this street's charming little house at number **11**. We soon reach **Rue Martin-Bernard**. Right across the street, a brick warehouse once stood beside the church. It was long used as a movie theater. Prior to that, an entire century ago, it housed a charity organization which was run by a

group of students. In October 1915, a hand grenade factory located at 164-172 Rue de Tolbiac exploded. The bodies of the forty-three victims were brought here. Eventually, the warehouse, not being of any particular interest, was demolished.

Let's move up the street. Off to our right is **Rue Michal**, even more picturesque than Rue Buot. It is lined with village-type houses on both sides. The one at **27** is certainly one of the oldest in the quarter. This one-story structure's low, slanting roof is typically rural, a rarity in Paris. Rue Michal also has an elegant modern house at 18 as well as several **artist studios**. The quiet neighborhood's old working-class homes have been renovated and remodeled. At the corner of Rue de l'Espérance, we will see a **shop with wooden shutters**. From here, we will continue our stroll along Rue Michal and cross the intersection. **8** is a small building of pleasing proportions with a nicely rounded central staircase projecting from the façade. In 1994, a committee for the homeless set up offices at this address.

At the end of the block, we wind up on **Rue Barrault** again, take a left. A university building occupies **42-46**; formerly the École Nationale Supérieure des Télécommunications, it is now called Télécom ParisTech. It has a sweeping concave façade of

▼ Rue Buot

graceful design, created by the architect Chappey in 1962, ornamented by a large bas-relief by Joffre, entitled *De la terre au cosmos / L'homme au cours des âges utilise les forces élémentaires pour les transmissions* (literally: From Earth to the Cosmos / Throughout the Ages, Mankind Uses Elementary Forces for Transmissions). It is a powerful ensemble, created in a period when technological progress was the guiding light of many nations.

We now meet up with **Rue de Tolbiac**. We will turn left and go two short blocks to the intersection with **Rue Martin-Bernard**. At the corner is an Italian restaurant that managed to salvage part of its old 1900s café décor, by the Reybaud studio. It is the pretty wrought-iron floral frieze along the awning on the façade. Let's head up Rue Martin-Bernard until we reach **Passage Boiton** on our left. It is another of the Butte's charming lanes, lined with small houses with quaint front yards.

From Rue Samson to Sainte-Anne Church

Crossing Rue de la Butte-aux-Cailles now, we will continue onto **Rue Samson** straight ahead. Some two decades ago, an architect built a brick-and-concrete house at **13**. It fits in very nicely with the modest dwellings being renovated on the rest of the street. A right onto **Rue Jean-Marie-Jégo** will lead us back to **Rue de la Butte-aux-Cailles**, where we will take a left to reach **Rue Vandrezanne**. Crossing Rue Bobillot, we again find ourselves on **Place Paul-Verlaine**, on the plateau created at the top of a steep slope.

On November 21, 1783, the first manned flight in a hot-air balloon, or *montgolfière*, landed not far from here, in a bend of Rue Vandrezanne. On that day, Jean-François Pilâtre de Rozier and François Laurent, Marquis of Arlandes, lifted off from a garden in La Muette (today's 16th arrondissement). They flew over the Seine near the Invalides and soon reached Les Gobelins, landing between two windmills on the Butte-aux-Cailles. The neighborhood's recent public park on the southwest corner of Rue Henri-Michaux and Rue du Moulinet, was named Square de la Montgolfière in commemoration of this event.

But let's stay a while longer on **Rue Vandrezanne**, home to the social institutions in this arrondissement. At the corner of Rue Bobillot, an old **arched gateway** is a reminder that in 1828, four nuns of Saint Vincent-de-Paul set up a health clinic on the site now occupied by Sainte-Marie school (at the end of the lane) and part of the Italie 2 shopping mall.

At the bend in Rue Vandrezanne, off to the right, is what remains of **Passage Vandrezanne**, a quaint alley with three restored gas streetlamps.

▲ Passage Boiton
▼ Rue Vandrezanne

▶ Passage Vandrezanne

The far end of this alley seems to sink into the ground after Rue du Moulinet. This is a vestige of its old southern portion, dating back to the days when it had to duck under the Rue de Tolbiac overpass. Bringing these streets up to the same level required pouring in more than 15 meters of fill. Opposite the new entrance to the tiny Square de la Montgolfière is **Passage du Moulinet**, now a pedestrian street. It, too, has several tiny houses typical of the Butte, for example those at **5, 7, 9, 10, and 12**.

Rue de Tolbiac to our right will take us to the intersection with Rue Bobillot and the 13th arrondissement's largest church, **Sainte-Anne-de-la-Butte-aux-Cailles**, formerly called Saint-Anne-de-la-Maison-Blanche. The old Bréa chapel on Avenue d'Italie

▶ Passage du Moulinet
▼ Sainte-Anne-de-la-Butte-aux-Cailles, 186 Rue de Tolbiac

(demolished in 1897) had become too small to accommodate the growing community. In 1865, Haussmann drafted plans for a monumental church atop the Butte-aux-Cailles, but the project was shelved. The land needed for Sainte-Anne's came from the generosity of Jules and Honorine Nolleval who, in 1892, donated the lot where today's church stands.

Bobin, the architect, had in mind a Byzantine-Romanesque style church set upon a crypt and finishing with a monumental dome. Donations poured in and construction began in 1894 under the direction of Father Miramont from the Bréa chapel,

who oversaw the project for two full decades. The church foundations, poured on the backfill of Rue Tolbiac, required seventy-one pillars, ten thousand cubic meters of millstone, and two thousand cubic meters of concrete.

The façade, financed by the chocolate-making Lombart family, was not presentable until 1898. Neighbors soon started calling it the chocolate façade. The stained glass windows and mosaics date from the 1930s and were created by Maumé-jean, the famed master glassmaker.

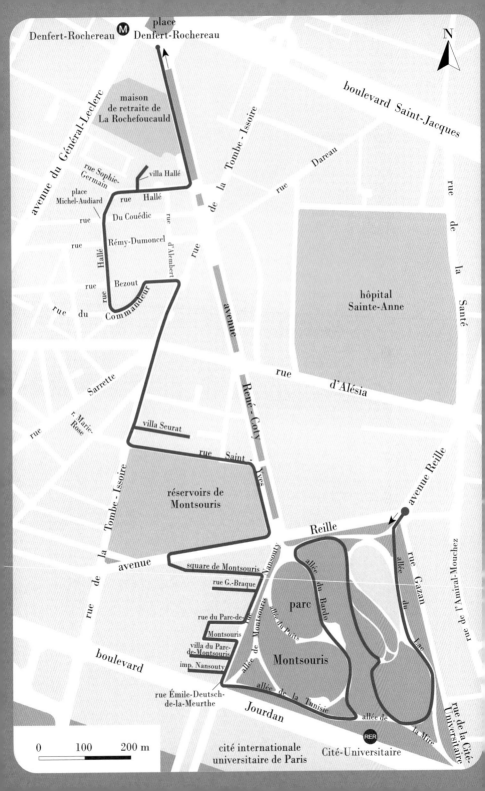

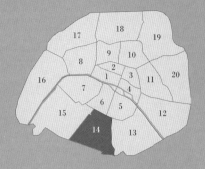

14th

From Parc Montsouris to Place Denfert-Rochereau

▶ Start: Parc Montsouris,
RER Cité-Universitaire
▶ Finish: Place Denfert-Rochereau,
metro Denfert-Rochereau

◄ Parc Montsouris

Ithough the decree for the creation of a park at Montsouris dates from February 22, 1865, the landscaping was not actually completed until 1878. Engineer Jean-Charles-Adolphe Alphand (1817-1891), often dubbed "Haussmann's gardener," the man in charge of city parks, drafted the plans for it. In the minds of Napoleon III and his prefect, Baron Haussmann, what the city needed was a pleasant public park to the south. It would complete a diamond pattern of city parks, with Buttes-Chaumont to the north, the Bois de

Vincennes to the east, and the Bois de Boulogne to the west. The Montsouris field was the ideal location.

Alexis Martin's *Promenades dans Paris* (Éditions Hennuyer, Paris, 1892) described the Parc Montsouris thus, "It is a delightful place, a sort of mirror to the Parc des Buttes-Chaumont, and visited and appreciated just as much, not only by residents of the neighborhood, but by many people out for a stroll. The park's total area, with its clusters of tall trees and its murmuring water, is sixteen hectares [forty acres]. Two rail lines run through it: the Ceinture and Sceaux lines. The Bardo, which had been the palace of the Bey of Tunis at the Universal Exposition of 1867, was moved to the highest point in the park, and now serves as a meteorological observatory..."

The Bardo no longer stands, having been destroyed by fire in 1991.

Inside Parc Montsouris

Today, commuter line RER-B is the railway running through Parc Montsouris. Leafy, flowering, and steep, with some 20 meters (over 65 feet) in altitude, Parc Montsouris is a trapezoid between Boulevard Jourdan, Rue Nansouty, Rue Émile-Deutsch-de-la-Meurthe, Avenue Reille, Rue Gazan, and Rue de la Cité-Universitaire. The park is like a giant aviary. The vegetation is surprisingly lush, rich in plant varieties and in heady scents. Amateur botanists will be able to identify a Judas tree, laburnum, silver lime, Japanese maple, various species of saxifrage, hosta, azalea, ferns, American tulip poplars, a cedar from Lebanon, three catalpas, a snow pear, a twisted dwarf beech, a Siberian elm, a copper beech, a live oak, a sequoia, and even a persimmon tree.

Bird lovers and bird watchers will be thrilled to observe mallards, mute swans, ruddy shelducks, red-crested pochards, black-headed gulls, Eurasian coots, moorhens, gray wagtails, goldcrests, European magpies, and, of course, crows, blackbirds, and European starlings.

Let's enter the park through the iron gate at the **corner of Rue Gazan and Avenue Reille**. The **lake** stretches out before us. We'll take the path to the left, with the lake to our right. It

leads past a lovely **bandstand** reminiscent of the ones in old-fashioned thermal spas. Unfortunately, it has become too rickety and is off limits.

To our left is the **Pavillon Montsouris** restaurant, a veritable culinary institution. The ivy-covered entrance is at 20 Rue Gazan. Dining outdoors here on a summer evening is quite a treat.

Reaching the **guardhouse**, we'll turn right onto the path that climbs the hill. The sculpture to our left is entitled **La Carrière ou Accident de Mine** (The Quarry, or Mine Accident), and was executed by Henri Bouchard in 1906. It reminds us we are walking through an area where much of the stone used to construct the buildings of Paris was quarried.

At the top of the steps, we'll turn right, but, instead of crossing the bridge, we'll go down the path to our

right, between the train tracks and the grassy slope. At the intersection, we will continue in the lane farthest to the left. Soon, we will be able to gaze at a statue of two female nudes by Morice Lipsi entitled **Les Baigneuses ou Les Jumelles** (The Bathers, or The Twins).

Passing the islet of greenery gracing the pond, we come to another group of statues. To our left is **La Mort du Lion** (The Lion's Death), by E. Desca. Two men shoulder the heavy carcass of a big cat.

◄ *Les Baigneuses ou Les Jumelles*, sculpture by Morice Lipsi, in Parc Montsouris

A statue by René Baucourt, off to our right, entitled **Premier Frisson ou La Bergère et ses Moutons ou La Bergerie** (*First Shiver, or The Shepherdess and her Sheep, or The Sheep-Barn*), sits against a background of foliage. A scantily clad young woman nonchalantly leans on a young man's shoulder.

Our path now leads under the railway bridge and to the left, towards the park entrance at the corner of Avenue Reille and Rue Nansouty. The 8.5-meter **Colonne de la Paix Armée** (*Column to Armed Peace*) is a park landmark. It was based on drawings by architect Paul Sédille and is topped by a bronze designed by Jules Coutant (1888).

The playground on our left contains an oddity for a children's area: the **Memorial to Col. Flatters and His Men**. This officer (1832-1881) led a reconnaissance mission for the construction of the trans-Saharan railroad line. He and nearly all the members of his unit were slaughtered by Tuareg warriors near the well in Bir El Garama (southern Algeria).

Do not be overly startled by the ferocious **panther** to our right, caught in mid-pounce, ears flattened and fangs bared. Let's continue down this path to the spot overlooking the train station, and turn right on the path running parallel to Boulevard Jourdan. On either side stand statues that are prime examples of the many surprises this park offers. The first, **La Pureté ou la Grèce** (*Purity, or Greece*) was commissioned by C.-D. Panopoulos from sculptor Costas Valsamis, and dedicated to the city of Paris. Across the way, hidden in the foliage and facing the Maison de l'Argentine on the university campus across the

◀ *Drame au Désert*, sculpture (1891) by George Gardner, in Parc Montsouris

boulevard, is an equestrian statue by Van Peborgh celebrating José de San Martín (1778-1850), liberator of Argentina and Chile and protector of Peru, which owes its independence partly to him.

Further on, a quadrangular pillar called the **Mire du Sud**, erected in 1806 by Vaudoyer, pinpoints the old Paris Meridian, calculated in 1667 by the Observatory, which was replaced by the Greenwich Meridian in 1911. Napoleon's name was originally engraved on the pillar, but it was chiseled off during the Bourbon Restoration.

After passing a small building housing **National Weather Service offices**, we reach the corner of Boulevard Jourdan. A second **small edifice** here was initially designed as a park building, but is now used by an astronomy publication.

▲ The "Mire du Sud" in Parc Montsouris

▼ Park building at the entrance to Parc Montsouris

The Streets beside Parc Montsouris

Exiting the park via the gate on **Rue Émile-Deutsch-de-la-Meurthe**, we shall now explore **Impasse Nansouty**, **Villa du Parc-de-Montsouris**, and **Rue du Parc-de-Montsouris**. In the shade of their tree-lined streets, the charming private houses with their pretty gardens are an island of tranquility in a neighborhood close to the heart of the city. An enviable location, indeed. U-shaped Rue du Parc-de-Montsouris will take us back to **Rue Nansouty**, which is the southern extension of Rue Émile-Deutsch-de-la-Meurthe.

Let's venture down small **Rue Georges-Braque**. The painter's studio was here at number **6**. The build-

ing, designed by famed architect Auguste Perret in 1927, stands slightly back from the street. Braque's studio was on the third floor.

At the corner of **14 Rue Nansouty** is the villa owned by Swiss painter Walter Guggenbühl, a modern structure with pure lines designed by André Lurçat in 1926-1927. Every room in this house has a view of the park. For the interior design, the architect was particularly attentive to his client's needs.

The last in the series of delightful small streets off the park is **Square de Montsouris**, which runs into Avenue Reille. This piece of real estate may be one of the loveliest spots in the 14th arrondissement, with its cobblestones and greenery. The lane is a wonderland for strolls in any sea-

son, but especially on summer days, when the lush foliage resonates with birdsong. Each townhouse is as charming as its neighbor. The artists' studios, gardens, gracious dwellings, and old-fashioned street lamps give this street an English accent — a rarity in Paris.

We come out of Square de Montsouris at **53 Avenue Reille**. Not only was this the studio of the painter Ozenfant, it was the first Paris building designed by Le Corbusier. The architect adopted gentle curves for this structure, providing the corner with stunning bay windows. The ones on the top floor are simply huge.

From Avenue Reille around to Rue de la Tombe-Issoire

Making a right onto **Avenue Reille**, we should stop to glance up at the two elegant pavilions atop the **Montsouris water reservoir**. Graced by ties made of cut rock and multicolored brick arcades, these small, Guimard-style buildings are topped by a glassed-in floor with a fine metal structure. This rare ensemble deserves to be protected.

We are standing upon the old Montrouge quarries. The Montsouris water reservoirs are fed by six streams: the Vanne, the Loing, the

Voulzie, the Dutreint, the Dragon, and the Seine. The massive structure covers several hectares framed by Rue de la Tombe-Issoire, Rue Saint-Yves, and Avenue Reille.

Rue Saint-Yves rises as a ramp road, parallel to Avenue René-Coty. The small door at **2 bis** gives the home a medieval air. The old two-story house at **1** abuts a reservoir wall. This used to be the address of a coal merchant. Let's move on to **Cité du Souvenir** at **11 Rue Saint-Yves**. Founded in 1925 by Father Keller, this housing

▲ Glass pavilion atop the Montsouris water reservoir on Avenue Reille

◄ Amédée Ozenfant's painting studio and home, 53 Avenue Reille (© Adagp, Paris 2009)

▼ 1 Rue Saint-Yves

▸ 11 Rue Saint-Yves

project also includes a chapel in its courtyard. The street offers several good examples of *faubourg* architecture, particularly at **14, 16 and 20** – unassuming dwellings that have escaped the charges of real-estate developers for decades.

The red brick structure on the skyline is that of the Franciscan chapel built in 1936 on Rue Marie-Rose.

We will take a right on **Rue de la Tombe-Issoire** and walk a short distance to **83**, the entrance to a lovely lane named **Villa Seurat**. In a setting which exudes the serenity nec-

◂ Rue Bezout
▸ 3 Villa Seurat

essary for creativity, artists' studios are thick on the ground. To name but a few of the greats who have resided here: Dali, Soutine, Lurçat, Gromaire, Anaïs Nin, and Henry Miller, who lived at **18**.

From Rue Bezout to Place Denfert-Rochereau

We shall follow **Rue de la Tombe-Issoire** across Rue d'Alésia to reach **Rue Bezout**, where a quaint little quarter awaits us. Sandwiched between the busy Avenue du Général-Leclerc and Avenue René-Coty, Rue Bezout is lined with village-style houses – extremely rare items in the prevailing urban fabric, and a relief from its uniformity.

Off to our left is **Rue du Commandeur**, a quiet, semi-circular street. The explanation for its name is that, long ago, this was the location of the residence of the Saint-Jean-de-Latran commander. Postcard-quaint **Rue Hallé** has curves and bends as it runs north. The tall trees in the walled garden on corner, at **23 Rue Rémy-Dumoncel**, might make us think we're in the provinces, not Paris. The intersection with Rue Du Couédic is a small roundabout, lined with faubourg-style houses. We are, in fact, on **Place Michel-Audiard**, rich

◄ Place Michel-Audiard

with authentic Parisian décor, goading us to indulge in quoting unforgettable lines from classic French movies.

As we continue north, **Rue Hallé** suddenly makes a sharp ninety-degree turn, for no apparent reason. The iron gate at **38** is charmingly discreet. It guards the entrance to **Villa Hallé**, a narrow cobblestone lane leading to homes we can only guess are splendid, because their privacy is so fiercely guarded by the walls. A few steps away, at the eastern end of **Rue Hallé**, the townhouses on the half-moon turnaround are also quite attractive.

An impressive **brick townhouse** sits on the corner of Rue d'Alembert. The street names in this quarter honor numerous mathematicians. Behind us, in the western extension of Rue Hallé, is a street named after Sophie Germain (1776-1831), author of *Recherche sur la Théorie des Surfaces Élastiques* in 1821. In fact, Étienne Bezout himself (1730-1783) wrote several studies, including one on the general theory of algebraic equations.

◄ Corner building at the intersection of Rue Hallé and Rue d'Alembert

◄◄ Villa Hallé, a private alley

▶ La Rochefoucauld
retirement home,
Avenue René-Coty

Rue Hallé finishes at its junction with **Avenue René-Coty**. A left here will take us up to Place Denfert-Rochereau. Along our way, the beauty of the secondary façade of the **La Rochefoucauld retirement home** calls out for our attention. Founded in 1780, this hospice, was built on plans drawn up by Jacques Denis Antoine, the architect of the Paris Mint. The small stone structure in the front yard is an old *regard* (an enclosed inspection hole) for the Arcueil aqueduct, which supplied the institution's water.

As for the hospice building, the majestic composition includes a

▶ Enclosed aqueduct
inspection hole, Avenue
René-Coty

façade and two wings designed with gracious architectural rigor in the purest 18th-century style.

With passing years, the retirement home grounds have dwindled. The first portion of land was gobbled up in 1844 by the then-new train company laying track for its Paris-Sceaux line, across the retirement home's grounds. Over an acre was lost thirty-three years later for the construction of Avenue du Parc Montsouris (renamed Avenue René-Coty in 1964).

On the corner of Avenue René-Coty and Boulevard Saint-Jacques, on **Place Denfert-Rochereau**, is the elegant train station erected in 1846, now an **RER station** on line B. Built as the terminal on the Paris-Sceaux line, the station has an original rounded design along the train turnaround. An engineer named Arnoux had just perfected a revolutionary system. His radial axle enabled trains to negotiate tight turns. The invention cut not only operating costs but travel time, for the train could depart in the opposite direction without any need for complicated maneuvers.

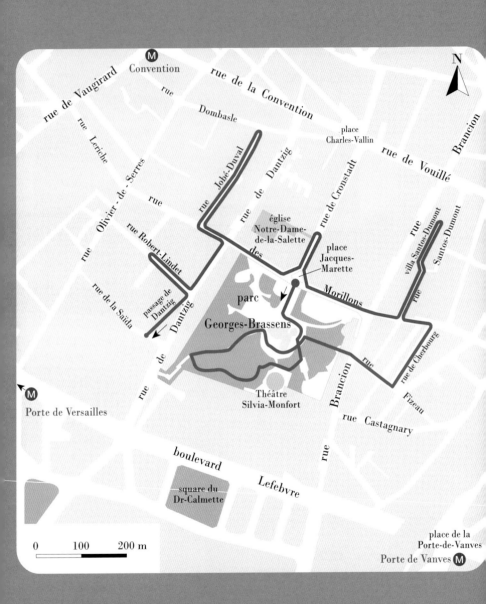

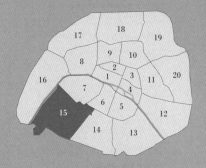

15th

Around the Old Vaugirard Abattoirs

▶ Start: Rue des Morillons,
  metro Convention
▶ Finish: Passage de Dantzig,
  metro Porte-de-Versailles
  or Porte-de-Vanves

O ur stroll begins outside **36 bis Rue des Morillons**, right in front of the main entrance to the lovely Parc Georges-Brassens. Today's park was built in 1977 and 1985 by the City of Paris on the site of the old Vaugirard slaughterhouses (see inset on this page). A powerful pair of bulls, by sculptor Auguste Caïn, watch over the park's main entrance.

Inside Parc Georges-Brassens

Before we even enter the gardens, we will notice **two buildings** dating from the time the slaughterhouses were erected. The ground floor had offices for the superintendent, the watch-

The Old Vaugirard Slaughterhouse

Ceremonially opened by President Félix Faure in March 1898, the slaughterhouses had been commissioned by the city of Paris to replace the ones at Grenelle (Rue Pérignon, Avenue de Suffren, Avenue de Breteuil, and Place de Breteuil). The construction of the Vaugirard complex reduced the inconveniences of meat-packing in town, at a time when each butcher shop had its own slaughtering floor.

One of Vaugirard's many advantages was that it was easily reached from the city's rail links. Nevertheless, the animals had to be led to slaughter on foot, blocking street traffic. Architect Moreau drew heavily on the northern Paris slaughterhouses designed by Janvier and Baltard. He improved on them and modernized the sanitary conditions. 110,000 cows and steers, 70,000 calves, 500,000 sheep and 80,000 pigs were slaughtered and butchered on these premises yearly. The facility's main gate was on Rue des Morillons. There were six groups of buildings arranged around a vast courtyard. Four of them had eighteen scalding rooms apiece, outdoor work areas, stables, cowsheds, and sheep pens, as well as haylofts for fodder, covering a total surface area of 5.8 acres. Supplies were brought in by rail. Tracks ran past the southern end of the facilities. The entrance for traders in pork meats was Rue de Dantzig. It had two iron gates on the main carriage gateway and two pedestrian gates. The pork slaughterhouse section was smaller, taking up only 1.2 acres. The horse slaughterhouse was off Rue Brancion and barely covered half an acre.

After long decades of operation, the slaughterhouses were gradually phased out between 1976 and 1978, beginning with the beef and mutton sections, and ending with the horsemeat section.

man, and a tax bureau. Upstairs, there were offices for the butchers' unions as well as lodgings for slaughterhouse employees.

Landscape architect Daniel Colin and architects Alexandre Ghiulamila and Jean-Michel Milliex planned this green space of 7.7 hectares (19

▶ Sculpture by Auguste Caïn at the entrance to Parc Georges-Brassens, Rue des Morillons

◀ Park building, entrance to Parc Georges-Brassens

▶ The old covered horse market beside Rue de Brancion

▼ Campanile in Parc Georges-Brassens

acres) in 1977 and in 1985, integrating vestiges of the abattoir structures.

Immediately to our left is a little path that leads to a **fragrance garden** containing over eighty species of aromatic and medicinal plants. When they are in full bloom, the whole park is scented. Printed and Braille labels identify each plant. Witch hazel brightens the winter landscape with its long yellow blossoms. The magnolia is one of the first enchantments of spring, and the butterfly bush triumphs in summer. Beyond these flowerbeds is a rose garden containing some

twenty varieties. As we stroll through the grounds, we will soon walk past the **old horse market** beside Rue Brancion. Book fanciers now flock to the covered market for a weekly used-book show and sale.

At the southern end of the park, a gray and red silhouette unexpectedly emerges from the greenery. This architectural folly is the **Théâtre Silvia-Monfort**, which opened in January 1992, six months after the death of the famed stage director. Architect Claude Parent designed this hexagonal pyramid to replace the circus tent the troupe traditionally performed in, and gave them a permanent home after years of wandering the outskirts of Paris.

The theater looks like an unrolled spiral of metal siding, wrapped in a second ribbon of steel painted bright red. Inside, rising twenty-two meters high, the half-circle of bleachers can seat up to 415 spectators. The stage has 225 square meters (2,422 sq. feet) of space.

Walking toward the **campanile** where auction sales were held in the old slaughterhouse days, we will take a little path to the left which leads to an apiary. It crosses a stream we can ford, enjoying the lovely scenery created by the **pond** and the aquatic plants.

▲▶ Pinot Noir vineyard
and climbing wall,
Parc Georges-Brassens

At the top of the hill, beside the **bee hives**, we will reach the park's tiny **Pinot Noir vineyard**, a reminder of the neighborhood's not-so distant past as a wine-growing area. Until the 19th century, it was planted with two varieties of dark, juicy grapes, Morillons and Périchots, the namesakes of two nearby streets.

Let's follow the path bordered with heather, rhododendrons, and azaleas. On our left is a children's **rock-climbing area**. The hewn stone came from the demolished slaughterhouses.

Heading east across the park, we'll leave by the exit on Rue Brancion, and keep walking straight ahead on Rue Fizeau, which leads across Brancion.

From Rue Brancion to Villa Santos-Dumont

At the **corner of Rue Brancion and Rue Fizeau** is a beautiful **bakery** with a splendid 1900s décor, owned and operated by Poilâne. Outside the bakery, the two paintings under glass show bucolic scenes, products of the famous Benoist & Fils studio, which specialized in decorative fittings for shops. On either side of the angled front, the doorway is framed by two panels vaunting the variety of baked goods to be had. The stucco décor is a revelry of garlands and braids. The marble countertops add to the entire Belle-Époque experience.

◀ Bakery at the corner
of Rue Brancion and
Rue Fizeau

Rue Fizeau, like the neighboring streets, used to be lined with wholesale meat businesses. Midway down the street, we come to a junction with no fewer than five streets. Oddly, this shady, tree-lined crossroads has no name.

At this point, we will turn right on **Rue de Cherbourg**, continuing up to Rue des Morillons, where we will have a sweeping view of a 1930s **public school**. The architect was Pierre Sardou, who also designed nearby Notre-Dame-du-Rosaire (14th arrondissement) in 1911 and the "Intransigeant" newspaper building in 1929. His plan for the school was simple. The striped brick façade is harmonious and balanced. The curved upper floor overhangs the 45-degree-angle ground-floor façade on this street corner. Above the bay of glass on the upper floor is a colorful and rather naïve mural depicting various learning activities, an indication of the purpose of the structure. The little turret on the right corner contains a stairwell designed to serve separate floors for boys and girls, but more importantly, the stairs were designed to make up for the sloping lot's varying level.

The courtyard façade (visible from Rue du Lieuvin) received a more sober treatment; its large windows are framed in brick. An article in a 1936 issue of the revue *L'Architecture* stated, "The warm brick colors, the originality in the crowning frieze over the entrance, and the delicately composed iron gates combine to give this ensemble serene simplicity in a cheerful, welcoming ambience. This work defends our art against the current trend to force cold geometric precision on architecture."

◄ Rue Santos-Dumont
◄ Villa Santos-Dumont

Let's take a left on **Rue des Morillons** to Rue Santos-Dumont, named for an aviator who earned the first world airplane record on November 12, 1906 for flying 220 meters in 21 seconds. Take a moment to admire the charming houses on the left side of the street. This row of homes, from 52 to 26, was built in the 1920s. The houses all look alike, with the same curious roof design. Georges Brassens lived in **42** from 1969 to his death in 1981.

The scenery suddenly becomes less typically Parisian as we enter the side street **Villa Santos-Dumont**. It is so calm and picturesque that one is not surprised to learn that it attracted artists from nearby Montparnasse. Famed sculptor Ossip Zadkine owned the house at **3** from 1925 to 1960,

and lived on the ground floor from 1945 to 1952. **10 bis** housed painter Victor Brauner from 1938 to 1945. Mosaic artist Gatti lived at **15**, and writer Jeanne Champion at **17**. To this day, Villa Santos-Dumont is the home of a vibrant community of artists, craftsmen, and writers.

From Rue des Morillons to Rue Robert-Lindet

Let's exit and return to **Rue des Morillons**. At its intersection with Rue Brancion, a **horse head over the gateway** announces this was once the Vaugirard slaughterhouse, providing Paris with horsemeat.

Rue de Cronstadt leads away from the park to an astonishing church, at **38**. This is Notre-Dame-de-La-Salette, designed by Henri Colboc. It was consecrated in 1965.

The exterior and interior are in white cement. Before we enter, notice the solid walnut door panels repre-

◀ Horse head in the pediment of the old gateway to the horse slaughterhouse, now located at the corner of Rue des Morillons and Rue de Brancion

senting Christ on the cross and the Virgin appearing to two children in the town of La Salette (see inset).

Inside, sixteen pillars forming consoles, set up along the ambulatory wall, support the dome. This feat of engineering leaves the choir clear and uncluttered. The dome's stained-glass windows are cleverly arranged

Notre-Dame-de-La-Salette

Devotion to Our Lady of La Salette goes back to 1846 to a mountainside near La Salette-Fallavaux, a town in the department of the Isère, where the Virgin reportedly appeared to two shepherd children, Mélanie and Maximin. By 1853, a small religious community had been established in Paris on Rue Dombasle, with an orphanage and a chapel. Soon, several miracles were attributed to Our Lady of La Salette, and a sanctuary was erected in gratitude. This church's treasures include the rock the Virgin allegedly selected as her mountainside seat, relics of Saint Jean-Marie Vianney, Curé d'Ars, the remains of Father Planchat, who was shot by the Communards, and the hearts of the three founders of the cult. The sanctuary is still standing.

◀ Notre-Dame-de-La-Salette church, 38 Rue de Cronstadt

at a slant, letting sunlight in throughout the day. The light is warm and abundant, despite the nearby high-rise buildings.

Let's exit and return to **Rue des Morillons**. The city's lost-and found, at **36**, is an address well-known to absent-minded Parisians. The decision to collect the objects turned in

to police stations around the city in a single central office dates back to 1804, when Prefect Dubois was in charge. The Rue des Morillons facility

opened in 1932. Items found on the street and in public places, such as buses, metro cars, taxis, shops, train stations, and airports, are registered, tagged, and stored here. Now, a computer database speeds up item identification and retrieval. Right behind this building, at 39 Rue Dantzig, is the city's vehicle impound lot.

Notice the original construction at the corner of Rue de Dantzig. It combines brick and half-timber elements, and tops it all off with a lacy balustrade trimming the eaves.

We continue walking west on Rue des Morillons. In the 19th century, a famous cabaret stood on the next block. Its regulars were quarrymen and local produce farmers. The owner was none other than Mr. Bonvin, a former rural police officer in the hamlet of Vaugirard, and the father of painter François Bonvin, for whom a street in this arrondissement is named.

We will come to a **bakery** near the corner of Rue Jobbé-Duval and Rue des Morillons. The handsome exterior panels are decorated with grisaille landscapes.

A massive brick housing project looms over **Rue Jobbé-Duval**. This

1913 apartment complex is noteworthy for its polychrome brickwork and the blue tile accents beside the arched windows. The overhanging top floor gives the already lively façade even more character.

Returning to Rue des Morillons, we'll retrace our steps to **Rue de Dantzig** and turn right. At the end of this block, we will take a right onto **Rue Robert-Lindet**, where we can admire the lovely curving façade of the building at **19**. The pattern of small orange bricks and green enameled ones produces an elegant effect. The rounded corner is topped by an odd element resembling a hat.

A little further on at **31**, there is another brick building with an original design. Architect Roger Debarnot completed it in 1935. To solve the problems presented by the lay of the land, he endowed the structure with symmetrical, rounded balconies framing a center bay window. Window ledges and balconies give the façade an interesting rhythm.

Passage de Dantzig and La Ruche

▲ Studios, Passage de Dantzig

◀ 19 Rue Robert-Lindet

We are coming to **Passage de Dantzig**, which begins at the intersection of Rue Robert-Lindet and Rue de Dantzig. It is a remnant of the old Vaugirard mill path. The army built fodder barns here in 1840. The passage is now lined with small houses with suburban quaintness (**5 and 7**) and artists' studios. The most surprising and famous of the latter is unquestionably number **2**, known as La Ruche. Formerly the Wine Pavilion at the 1900 Universal Exposition, it was disassembled and then rebuilt here by the Gustave Eiffel crew in 1902, at the behest of the sculptor Boucher.

The School of Paris

Strictly speaking, the School of Paris was not a movement. It was a loose gathering of outsiders from foreign countries or the provinces, in addition to some Parisians, who let their creativity run wild, inspired by the freewheeling atmosphere in the city. "I am unhappy in Paris, but I truly could not work anywhere else," Modigliani privately admitted to Survage. When Henri Rousseau moved to 18 bis Impasse du Maine in 1885, the 15th arrondissement was becoming the hub of a new art scene. It started in 1877 when Gauguin lived on Rue des Fourneaux (present-day Rue Falguière) in a luxurious house. After he returned from Pont-Aven, he moved into a shack at 257 Rue Lecourbe, found for him by his friend Schuffenecker. He befriended Van Gogh, and learned the basics of sculpture from Bouillot in his Falguière studio. Antoine Bourdelle's studio (now the Musée Bourdelle), located on Impasse du Maine, was also a crucible of new talent. Other artists' quarters sprang up around the 15th arrondissement, such as Cité Falguière, which brought together Soutine, Lipschitz, Modigliani, and Foujita. The sculptor Brancusi, however, preferred Impasse Ronsin.

The arrondissement also welcomed the disciples of Cubism, Isaac Pailès from Kiev; Auguste Herbin, one of the founders of the Abstraction-Creation movement; Charcoune, one of Fauconnier's students; Russian sculptor and theoretician Antoine Pevsner; Robert Delaunay, the precursor of Abstraction; Expressionist Jean Fautrier, and others. The Surrealists were also distinguished residents: Spanish sculptor Pablo Gargallo, Catalan anarchist and Dadaist Miró, André Breton, André Masson, and poet Robert Desnos.

◄ La Ruche, 2 Passage de Dantzig

Pure chance brought Boucher to this street during a stroll one day in 1895, and resulted in his purchase of a 5,000-square-meter lot for twenty sous per meter. In memory of the hard times he'd had as a young artist, he erected one of the first artists' communities. Its purpose was to provide cheap housing and studio space, as well as a fraternal work environment for budding talent. Living here was Huysman's dream come true: "To live an oblate of art and beauty within a convent for artists only, isolated from ugliness and, worse still, triteness; to work freely, indulging the imagination, amid fraternal friendships, in an atmosphere of toilsome mysticism."

The name La Ruche (the bee hive) was given to the complex because of the layout of studios around a central staircase, like the cells of a honeycomb. Since its inception, this original edifice has fostered an incredible amount of creativity and artistic energy.

We enter via a wrought-iron gate that came from the Women's Pavilion at the Universal Exposition. The front door, topped by a balcony supported by two concrete caryatids salvaged from the Indonesian pavilion, opens onto the central staircase. The stairway itself is a well of light, channeling sunlight from the belfry on the roof peak. An exhibition hall and the theater where Marguerite Moreno and Louis Jouvet made their debuts operated only for brief periods.

Under Boucher's leadership, La Ruche became a sort of cosmopolitan village welcoming refugee artists from the entire world, especially from central Europe. Léger, Matisse, Henri Rousseau, Chagall, who arrived in 1910, Soutine, who left Lithuania, Modigliani, the only Italian to have come down from Montmartre, Krémègne, Kikoïne,

and Kisling mingled with poets such as Apollinaire, Max Jacob, André Salmon, Blaise Cendrars, etc.

They set up what was soon to be known as the school of Paris. All the artists of this new movement lived and worked in La Ruche.

La Ruche also attracted sculptors, as it offered fine working conditions and room to store materials. Future cubists Csaky and Archipenko appreciated the opportunity. Zadkine, on the other hand, found the confined community suffocating.

The residents of La Ruche certainly did not remain cloistered day and night in their studios. They were regulars at the Dantzig Café, and made the owner so rich he went on to become the owner of La Coupole in Montparnasse.

World War I closed an entire era, and the ambience at La Ruche changed. The death of founder Alfred

▲▲ Studios, Passage de Dantzig

Marc Chagall, La Ruche, and Blaise Cendrars

Chagall moved to La Ruche because of the cheap rent. He recalled these moments in his 1931 autobiography *Ma Vie*: "I had a studio in the rotunda along with the other penniless proletarians. The stone buildings were for the well-to-do, whereas the rich went off to Montparnasse... I was happy to be on the third floor. My window opened onto the sky. It was poetic." He added that a mere hole on the ground floor served as a commode, foul odors wafting through the building. Recalling Apollinaire's first visit to La Ruche, he told a humorous tale: "We crossed the dark corridor, piled with rubbish and damp with constantly dripping water, to the round landing with a dozen numbered doors. I opened mine. Apollinaire entered warily, as if he feared the entire building was about to collapse, dragging him into the ruins."

Chagall placed pieces of cloth on the walls and used them as canvases. "While in other Russians' studios the sobbing of an offended model could be heard, while the Italians were singing and playing guitars, and the Jews were deep in conversation, I sat alone in my studio, in front of my oil lamp. [...] I stayed up entire nights. Two, three o'clock in the morning? The sky is blue. Dawn breaks. A few streets away, cattle were being slaughtered; cows were mooing, and I was painting... I can still hear the sounds in the night when they cut off their heads, and an image of Russia would pop into my mind, a memory of my grandfather's butcher shop." He painted L'Âne et la Femme and À la Russie, Aux Ânes et Aux Autres in this period. Chagall also recalled a visit by Blaise Cendrars who had heard that, "some guy was painting cows and cut-off heads." "Cendrars burst into the room laughing, bubbling with youth. As I spoke bad French, he spoke to me in Russian. It looked like he was melting: his eyes, his face, his words. He wasn't looking at my paintings, he was drinking them in. A real love, a brotherly friendship was forged. At that time, when Cubism was on its way up, on the wings of Apollinaire's prose, my friendship with Cendrars was an encouragement to me [...] Another time, while in my studio, he wrote two poems about me, and declaimed them in front of the broken panes of my window. He became my Cicero, a secretary of sorts. One day, I'd be buying him lunch in a bistro, the next, he would be treating me. He'd be poor one minute, and then suddenly, an hour later, he'd be rich..."

Boucher in 1934 confirmed the community's decline. Between the two World Wars, only a few of the senior residents stayed on. They were joined by newcomers such as actor Alain Cuny.

After World War II, La Ruche was practically abandoned. Finally, in the 1960s, a new generation of artists, represented by Rebeyrolle, Biras, Simone Dat, and Sima, brought the low-rent studios back to life.

In 1965, Marc Chagall spearheaded a movement to defend the building from the wrecking ball. They won, and the property was listed on the historical register in 1972, two years after the fire that had ravaged the historic Bateau-Lavoir artist community in Montmartre.

The rotunda has now been completely restored and emptied. Today's artists are guaranteed the same comfortable working conditions in twenty-three well-lit and well-equipped studios.

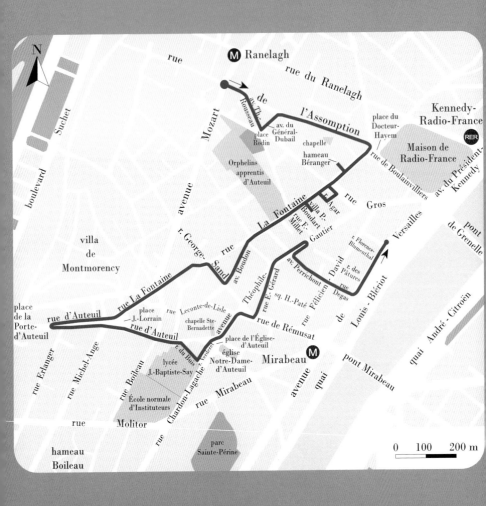

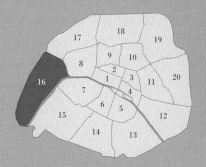

16th

Auteuil

- ▶ Start: Rue de l'Assomption, metro Ranelagh
- ▶ Finish: Avenue de Versailles, metro Mirabeau or RER Kennedy-Radio-France

There is a noticeable and pleasing contrast between the village-like Auteuil neighborhood and the rest of Paris. It seems to have resisted urbanization, preserving its old main street and many of its historic buildings. It can even boast the beautiful remnants of 18th-century aristocratic estates, which sat on large grounds. These *parcs*, to use the French term, were divided into lots in the 1830s. Some of the loveliest villas that sprang up in those years were in Auteuil. Hameau Boileau and Villa Montmorency are two fine examples.

Auteuil can also pride itself on being home to over half the buildings designed by the architect who spearheaded the Art Nouveau movement, Hector Guimard (1867-1942). Guimard had succeeded in forming ties with this area's rich industrialists and their families, many of whom were aware of the latest modernist trends and eager to implement them. Guimard received many commissions from clients in this arrondissement.

Rue de l'Assomption

Let's begin our neighborhood stroll by going down **Rue de l'Assomption** toward Place du Docteur-Hayem. Formerly called Rue des Tombereaux, it used to mark the boundary between the villages of Auteuil and Passy.

With its abundant clay soil, the area had attracted tile factories long ago. The first mention of a *tuilerie* dates to 1248. François I had a hunting lodge here. In 1782, the Marquis de La Tour du Pin-Gouvernet built a mansion so isolated and hidden by thick foliage that it was jokingly referred to as *le château invisible*. It stood at present-day **25** Rue de l'As-

somption. The 12-acre estate, stretching to today's Avenue Mozart, was sold in 1855 to the Augustinian Sisters of the Assumption. The nuns commissioned architect Aymar Verdier, a specialist in the restoration of medieval churches, to build a splendid neo-Gothic monastery beside the château. Completed in 1857, it included a boarding school for girls. The sisters were forced to give up their school in 1906, in the wake of the laws separating Church and State. The château and the monastery buildings were demolished in 1927, and most of the property was divided up with a network of streets radiating out from **Place Rodin**. In 1932, a famous statue by Auguste Rodin, *L'Âge d'Airain* [The Age of Bronze], was placed in the center of this traffic circle. The model for it was crafted in Brussels in 1876, and the piece was presented at the 1877 Salon. Because of its extraordinary realism, Rodin was accused of having cast a mold on a living model.

When the Sisters of the Assumption returned in 1953, nothing was left of their mother house except a magnificent garden and an annex building, now **17 Rue de l'Assomp-**

▲ *L'Âge d'Airain,* statue by Auguste Rodin, Place Rodin

▼ Mother house of the Sisters of the Assumption, 17 Rue de l'Assomption

tion. Over the years, much to the delight of greedy promoters, economic necessity has forced the sisters to sell off small lots of this garden. At least, the little that remains receives loving care. In 1961, the congregation hired architect Noël Lemaresquier to design a lovely chapel dedicated to Notre-Dame de l'Assomption. The stream-lined triangular shape suggests a tent, a ship, or a sail soaring towards the heavens. The interior is flooded by light streaming from large windows by Ingrand. A Christ by Stube adorns the altar.

▼ 18 Rue de l'Assomption

Across the street at **18**, a 1925 luxury building by Charles Lemaresquier (the father of the architect of the aforementioned Chapelle de l'Assomption) features a stunning, gigantic, bearded Bacchus.

Further down at **4 ter**, a picturesque brick chalet with ornate wooden gingerbread trim stands out

► 4 ter Rue de l'Assomption

of line with the rest of the buildings on this street. There is a pretty mosaic with a gold background around the door at **5**, designed by Pierre Gélis-Didot (1893).

Down Rue La Fontaine

Once we reach **Place du Docteur-Hayem**, we will turn right and take **Rue La Fontaine**.

According to certain sources, this street, named in 1865, does not commemorate the writer of fables who lived here. Instead, its namesake would be a spring, or fontaine of sweet-tasting water greatly appreciated by Louis XV. It was located on the present-day site of Place Jean-Lorrain, and flowed down the street. At that time, the first part of the street, located before Rue Gros, was called Rue de la Tuilerie.

The block on our left formed by Rue La Fontaine, Rue Gros, and Rue Boulainvilliers was initially occupied by municipal facilities such as the city art depot. After the depot was moved to the southeastern suburb of Ivry, the large parcel of land freed up offered developers the potential for a variety of infrastructures. In 1985, Roger Taillibert, architect of the Parc des Princes sports complex, was commissioned to design a park lined with low-income housing buildings and numerous facilities. The red and gray ceramic tiles make the façades bright and cheerful.

The most interesting creation, however, is the Francis-Poulenc conservatory at **11**. The building, with its concave façade, stands just opposite Castel Béranger (see below). The confrontation was challenging. In the end, Taillibert's design blends more harmoniously with the nearby Radio-France building than with its immediate surroundings.

Our next discovery is on the opposite sidewalk, at **14** Rue La Fontaine. Castel Béranger was designed by Guimard in the years 1895-1898, and won him instant fame. Budget limitations for the subsidized housing project precluded the lavish use of expensive materials like stone. Guimard ingeniously combined colors and a variety of building materials to create a harmonious and cheerful whole. Castel Béranger reads like a bestiary. Seahorses seem to latch on to the brick façade; the architect's caricature mask dances on the balcony railings. The courtyard fountain is disguised as a scorpion. Tile ornaments spell out the shapes of felines and birds. Painter Paul Signac (1863-1935) had a studio and an apartment on the seventh floor, from 1898 to 1912.

◄ Castel Béranger,
14 Rue La Fontaine

was called Rue Moderne, it was his largest project ever, coming relatively late in his career. The colors are more uniform. He had given up polychrome work, but continued to play with varying his building materials (nonetheless limited to stone, cream-colored brick, and black wrought iron trim).

Contrasting with Guimard's curvaceous style, the stern, flatly geometrical building at **39 Rue Gros**, designed by A. Guilbert in the 1930s, offers but one concession to ornamentation: a glittering mosaic of gold-speckled tiles by Gentil and Bourdet.

Villa Patrice-Bourdart is a private lane that opens at **25 Rue La Fontaine**.

Having feasted our eyes on the architectural spectacle, we can turn to the other side of the street, where another fine Guimard apartment complex was erected at **17-21**, at **43 Rue Gros**, and at **8 and 10 Rue Agar**. Dating from 1909-1911, when Rue Agar

▶ One of the buildings
in the Rue Agar complex
◄ 39 Rue Gros

▼ Trémois building, 11 Rue François-Millet

It was named for the architect who divided the plots and designed the residential buildings at **3 and 4,** in 1913. The development stands on the site of an old dairy farm, *La Grande Vacherie d'Auteuil*, which provided milk for much of Paris. As animal heat was thought to be beneficial to tuberculosis sufferers, rooms over the stables were rented out to patients.

On the other side of the street is **32 Rue La Fontaine**, by Deneu de Montbrun (1904), which is called Villa Jeanne-d'Arc. Further down, **Rue François-Millet** opens off the left side of our main street. Another Guimard building awaits us at **11**. In this luxurious building, erected in 1910 and contemporary with those on Rue Agar, stone is the main component, and the façade is an experiment in near-perfect symmetry.

The open iron gate at **40 Rue La Fontaine** beckons. Entering, we find a the grounds of the 19th-century orphanage L'Œuvre des Orphelins Apprentis d'Auteuil (see inset), now a park maintained by the City of Paris.

The Auteuil Orphan Apprentices

One evening in the winter of 1865, Father Louis Roussel took in a young tramp who was digging in a trash heap. A week later, there were six others in his room. In the spring of 1866, he moved his "children" to a dilapidated house at 40 Rue d'Auteuil. His goal was to feed them and give them basic religious training that might take them as far as their first communion. But the priest rapidly realized that he could not send the children back onto the streets without a trade. By 1871, he had begun to set up apprentice workshops for the Auteuil orphans. Thus began the Œuvre des Orphelins Apprentis d'Auteuil, to use its full name in French. In 1873, the print shop apprenticeship was launched. It was to become the institution's hallmark. To keep costs down for the construction of new workshops and a chapel, building materials from the 1878 Universal Exposition and other sources were recycled. The charity's most glorious years were in the 1920s and 1930s when an exceptional priest took over the leadership: Father Daniel Brottier (1876-1936), beatified in 1984. He taught his young charges to build radio sets! To keep them entertained on Sundays, he built a movie theatre with a seating capacity of fifteen hundred, and called it Auteuil Bon Cinéma. Older residents of the neighborhood still remember it. Its first showing was in 1927, and it kept doing business until 1978.

The prefabricated 1878 Exposition buildings were replaced by neo-Gothic buildings designed by architects Henri Chailleux & Fils. The chapel had to be "beautiful, spacious and attractive." It was built between 1924 and 1929, and

▲ Gardens of the Auteuil orphans' apprenticeship home, 40 Rue La Fontaine

the first church was dedicated to Saint Thérèse de Lisieux. The capitals celebrate vocations and the great French cathedrals. The stained-glass windows and the stations of the cross in mosaic are the work of the Mauméjean brothers. Auguste Maillard is to be credited for the statue of Saint Thérèse and the Monument de l'Adoption. Today, the institution has 4,100 students in 26 establishments.

Standing at number **60**, the townhouse of textile manufacturer Paul Mezzara was also designed by Art Nouveau wizard Hector Guimard, in the latter part of his career (1910-1911). Highly symmetrical, it is a symphony in beige. Inside, a two-story atrium lit by a skylight contains a staircase made of wrought and sheet iron, creating complicated, elegant shapes. Now the property of the national education ministry, used as a dorm for high school students, it can be visited by appointment (telephone: +33 (0) 155 746 920).

Coming to the fork in Rue La Fontaine, we will be heading left onto **Avenue Boudon**, which is a rather narrow street, despite its grand name. Bernard Reichen and Philippe Robert designed the luxury apartment building standing at **3** in 1979. They intended it "to reconnect with the spirit of Haussmannian architecture," without being a "gratuitous pastiche" of the style, despite the use of traditional materials. The façade features a vertically arranged stone cladding. As for the pattern of bay windows and the integration of climbing plants into the design, the aim was to compensate gracefully for variances with the street line.

At the end of Avenue Boudon, we will turn right and take **Rue George-Sand** back to **Rue La Fontaine**. Juliette Drouet's house stood at today's **57**. Claire, the daughter she had had with sculptor James Pradier, for whom she had modeled, died there before reaching the age of twenty. The girl's death inspired Victor Hugo to write these haunting lines:

Elle s'en est allée à l'aube qui se lève,
Lueur dans le matin, vertu dans
le ciel bleu.

(She departed just as dawn was breaking,
A glow in the morning, virtue
in the blue sky.)

96 was the site of a birth that changed literature, if not the world.. It was here, in her uncle's house, that Madame Adrien Proust had her first child, Marcel, on July 10, 1871, at the height of the Commune. Although Marcel lived with his parents in the 17th arrondissement, his great-uncle Louis Weil's house in Auteuil was a country home for him for twenty-five years. "The house that we lived in with my [great]uncle in Auteuil, in the middle of a large property that was cut in two by the creation of a new street (from Avenue Mozart), was utterly devoid of taste. Yet I can hardly describe the pleasure I felt when I would go up to my room after a walk along Rue La Fontaine in the sun, beneath the fragrant linden trees."

Across the way, contrasting with a rather gauche example of Belle-Époque style by Paul Furet at 61-63, we come to **65**, the Studio Building erected in 1927 by Henri Sauvage. This corner building (with equally interesting façades on 2-4 Rue du Général-Largeau and 21 to 35 Rue des Perchamps)is an impudent challenge to its more conventional neighbors.. The façade gleams with polychrome tile by ceramic artists Gentil and Bour-

◄ Hôtel Mezzara,
60 Rue La Fontaine

det. The duplex apartments have seven-meter-high ceilings (nearly 25 feet). Billed as "artists' studios," they were actually designed as luxury flats for wealthy buyers.

We will cross Avenue Mozart, staying on Rue La Fontaine.

At **85** we come to one of the rare buildings designed by Ernest Herscher. After the construction of this one, in 1907, and another, at 39 Rue Scheffer, in 1911, he dedicated his talents to illustration. While his work on this residence was not significantly original, it does excel in its splendid interplay of iron railings and balcony consoles along the upper levels and the roofline.

Rue d'Auteuil from Place Jean-Lorrain to Porte d'Auteuil

Until 1930, **Place Jean-Lorrain** was simply called Place de la Fontaine. We will cut across and enter **Rue d'Auteuil**, straight ahead.

By the 16th century, Rue d'Auteuil had become the village's main street. It has preserved its deliciously provincial ambience, at least in the portion between Place Jean-Lorrain and its church. Some of the fine mansions that made it famous still stand, although they have lost some of the splendor of yesteryear.

Let's begin by mentioning the ones that did not survive, on the part of the Rue d'Auteuil leading from Place Jean-Lorrain to the Porte d'Auteuil.

The Château de Boufflers once stood at **60** on our right.

Across the street, the buildings at **63-73** went up on the site of the

◄ Rue d'Auteuil.

▼ Studio Building, 65 Rue La Fontaine

old Château du Coq estate. We have no idea of what the mansion looked like when it was the home of Louis-XIV-era financier Samuel Bernard, prior to his move to the Château de Passy.

Louis XV bought it in 1761 to lay out a floral garden intended to supply plants to La Muette park and to satisfy his passion for botany. He would often come to this "little house" using the pseudonym Baron de Gonesse in order to escape the stifling etiquette in Versailles.

His thriftier successor, Louis XVI, sold the property, which then changed hands several times. In 1861, Baron Erlanger acquired it. He already owned the lands that the Thiers fortification walls had cut off from the Boulogne Woods. The following year, the château was demolished. The estate was chopped up by new streets – Michel-Ange, Erlanger, and Molitor – and was rapidly developed. The old idea of a royal garden still blooms, however. It is today's Jardin Fleuriste d'Auteuil - in other words, the city hothouses that supply plants to all the municipal parks. It is located on the other side of the city's outer boulevards.

Today, a copy of Michelangelo's *Moses* stands in the small garden of the 1965 residential building at **59**. This statue and a few trees are all that have survived of the lovely grounds that Madame Helvétius (nicknamed "Notre-Dame d'Auteuil") extolled in front of Bonaparte. "General," she said, "if people knew the immense joy a few acres of land can give, conquering the world would be far less attractive." It is true that while her garden was small, it enjoyed the shade of the trees from its neighboring Château du Coq. Claude-Adrien Helvétius, a for-

◄ Copy of Michelangelo's *Moses*, in the garden at 59 Rue d'Auteuil

mer Fermier Général tax collector who became a philosopher once he had amassed his fortune, died in 1771, leaving his wealth and pluckiness to his widow. In 1772, she bought this mansion, which had belonged to artist Maurice Quentin de La Tour since 1750. The members of her literary salon often joined her there. Among them were Diderot, d'Alembert, Malesherbes, Turgot, Condorcet, André Chénier, and even Benjamin Franklin, who, like Turgot, would have been delighted to marry her. While Madame Helvétius was spared by the Revolution, her friends were less fortunate. She died in 1800 at the age of 81. Her mansion was burned during the Commune in 1871.

Rue d'Auteuil from Place Jean-Lorrain to Place d'Auteuil

Let's move on to the section of Rue d'Auteuil running east to Place d'Auteuil to enjoy an enlightened look at some of the buildings and their colorful histories.

In 1905, Émile Jandelle designed the corner building, **1 Rue Michel-Ange**, now a florist's shop, as a gen-

▶ Hôtel Antier or de Verrières, 43-47 Rue d'Auteuil

▼ Sign at the Auberge du Mouton-Blanc, 40 Rue d'Auteuil

▼▼ Hôtel Véron (also called Hôtel Pérignon), 16 Rue d'Auteuil

eral store.

One of the old village's gems is **43-47 Rue d'Auteuil**. The classical ensemble, laid out around a courtyard-garden, was originally a gift to a lady. It was built in 1715 for an opera celebrity, the soprano Marie Antier. In 1726, she married a tax inspector and lived the merry life of the demi-mondaine, entertaining powerful men in the privacy of her boudoir. In 1744, courtiers and city officials attended the unforgettable gala she hosted, to celebrate Louis XV's recovery.

In 1752, the "folly" became the property of two sisters, Marie and Geneviève Rainteau, daughters of a Rue Greneta tavern-keeper. They were nicknamed "la Belle et la Bête" ("bête" meaning "dull-witted"), because the second sister was always mocked for

her stupidity. As actresses in army theater troupe, they caught the eye of Marshal of Saxe. After Marie became his mistress, she and her sister both added "de Verrières" to their family name to make it sound less common. She was as wild as she was unfaithful; each of her three children had a different father. However, her daughter Marie-Aurore, the grandmother of novelist George Sand, called Marshal of Saxe "papa." Marie Rainteau de Verrières was rumored to have had another daughter by the Marquis of Épinay, another prosperous Fermier Général. He thanked her for her favors with a townhouse on Chaussée-d'Antin, and the Hôtel Antier became their country retreat. The two sisters built a four-hundred-seat theater on the Auteuil estate, so that plays banned in the city could be performed. They were constantly holding receptions and parties; sometimes the villagers were invited. The property was sold in 1767 and changed hands several times. The grounds were divided up more than once, particularly to accommodate Rue Michel-Ange in 1862. The mansion itself was purchased in 1954 by the Compagnie Française des Pétroles (later Total oil company), which hemmed it in with office buildings. Aside from the park-side façade and a few decorative elements that include some wood paneling, none of the original structure has survived.

A restaurant at **40**, named Auberge du Mouton-Blanc, served the likes of Molière, Racine, La Fontaine, Boileau, and the composer Chapelle.

Along our way, we will see several lovely old houses from **27 to 15**. A solitary dormer window overlooking the façade of **19** is fitted with a pulley for hoisting furniture. It still looks serviceable!

Flanked by two pavilions, a pretty wrought-iron balustrade runs atop the gated entrance to the courtyard at **16**. This address is known by three names: Hôtel Véron, Hôtel Pérignon, and Hôtel Puscher. The property was listed in a register dated 1600 under the name "Clos du Buc," but by 1690, belonged to one Joseph de Puscher. Today's mansion was erected in 1756 by the son of a merchant, a certain Louis-Henry Véron. He then signed it over in 1800 to Pierre Pérignon, a lawyer and a future baron in Napoleon's empire. Pérignon had many children, but had the kindness of heart to adopt a young orphan girl. It was under his roof, at the age of 26, that she met the private tutor of the Choiseul-Praslin children, sixty-year-old Joseph Baudelaire, who would wed her and give her a son, Charles Baudelaire, born in 1821.

Pérignon had his mansion remodeled around 1806, giving it its present-day aspect. From 1852 to 1893, Hôtel Pérignon belonged to the Chardon-Lagache family. The following owner viewed it only as a source of revenue. He lopped off part of the grounds for the construction of Rue Leconte-de-Lisle and Rue Mignet. The mansion itself was rented out; part of it as a girls' boarding school, and part to an antiques dealer, who fortunately recognized it for its architectural value and had the interior restored. Since 1957, it has served as the parish center of Notre-Dame-d'Auteuil welcoming the lower grades from Saint-Jean-de-Passy school. A handsome staircase and some 18th-century wood paneling have survived the ravages of time, but the four panels

painted by Hubert Robert are in the collections of the Musée des Arts Décoratifs. The garden-side façade – one has to imagine the garden beneath the asphalt – is certainly attractive, with a pediment and four colossal pilasters, although it now stands higher than the original design intended despite having been raised. It is quite easily viewed from Rue des Perchamps.

The next notable building is the old Château Ternaux, at **11 bis**, on the other side of the little square. It is named for the prosperous shawl manufacturer who bought the building in 1804 for use as a dye-works. The land originally belonged to the monks of St. Genevieve, and was acquired by Galpin in 1714. He commissioned Nicolas Dulin to build him a mansion. The sprawling ten-hectare estate (25 acres) went all the way to present-day Rue Jouvenet. The textile maker, Nicolas Ternaux, found it ideal for grazing the sheep and Tibetan goats that provided cashmere wool for his factory. He changed the mansion's interior décor. In 1835, two years after his death, a large portion of the grounds along Rue Boileau was sold to real-estate developers, and the building

▲ Lycée Jean-Baptiste Say, formerly Château Ternaux, 11 bis Rue d'Auteuil

► Crest of the city of Paris on a outside wall of Notre-Dame-d'Auteuil

was sold to the Institut Notre-Dame-d'Auteuil. Purchased by the city of Paris in 1872, the facilities were shared by the École Normale d'Instituteurs, which trains teachers, and the Jean-Baptiste-Say high school. What remains of the original plan are the main courtyard and the center pavilion, now surrounded by classrooms constructed 1875-1897.

Around Place de l'Église-d'Auteuil

Let's take a right on **Rue du Buis**. On our left-hand side are **2, 4, and 6**, which date to the early 18th century and belonged to a mansion from that period that was remodeled. For the sake of economy, feminist writer Olympe de Gouges retired to number **4** before the Revolution. Though an advocate of revolutionary ideas, she was shocked by the horrors committed during the Reign of Terror, and thoroughly disgusted by the execution of the king. Ever outspoken, she wrote repeatedly to Robespierre, finally suggesting that he join her in jumping into the Seine. It was her final display of courage: she was sent to the guillotine.

At the end of Rue du Buis, let's turn left on **Rue Verderet**. All the buildings on the odd-numbered side were demolished to make room for Rue Chardon-Lagache. The corner building at **2**, clad in sandstone tile mosaic, was designed in 1936 by Paul de Rutté and Paul Sirvin, two architects known more for designing low-income housing projects, but who satisfied their well-to-do clientele with this apartment complex.

We now stand on **Place de l'Église-d'Auteuil**. The church's name is **Notre-Dame-d'Auteuil**.

Auteuil parish dates back to 1190. There are numerous surviving illustrations of the old church started in 1319. It stood on the site of today's church stands. Run-down and too small to accommodate a population that had swelled from one thousand in 1850 to ten thousand in 1875, it absolutely had to be rebuilt. Father Lamazou took his service as parish priest in 1874. Without his tenacity, and his own financial contribution, the new church might never have been built. He had to contend with the opposition of a left-wing city administration, as the engraved crest of the city of Paris on an outside wall of the church clearly indicates. Notice that there are stars instead of the traditional fleur-de-lys (symbol of French royalty), a gesture which appeased

▼ Rue du Buis

the city councilmen and a reminder of the fierce anticlerical sentiment which made the task all the more difficult for Auteuil's priest. Émile Vaudremer was commissioned as the architect. He had already designed Saint-Pierre-de-Montrouge. Construction started in 1877 and was completed in 1892.

What Father Lamazou wanted was, "a Romanesque church, crowned by a splendid bell tower rising high in the Paris sky." The steeple's tall, elongated dome is reminiscent of the pope's tiara, is also a reference to the work of Paul Abadie, the architect of the Sacré-Cœur. The tympanum over the entrance and the statue of the Virgin were executed by Henri-Charles Maniglier.

The interior, with its basilica floor plan, includes a raised choir above a crypt, modeled, like the furnishings, upon early Christian churches. Henri Compan painted a *Christ Pantokrator* on a gold background in the quarter-dome of the apse. Stepping to the right of the main entrance, we will see the tomb of Monsignor Lamazou and a Mater Dolorosa sculpted by Jean-Baptiste Carpeaux in 1870 and donated by his widow. The crypt is decorated with works of art from the old church.

The old town hall was located just left of the church, giving the square a real village feel. Established there in 1790, it was nevertheless transferred to Rue Boileau in 1844.

Construction of Sainte-Bernadette's chapel at **4 Rue d'Auteuil** began in 1936. Designed by Paul Hulot, it was intended as an annex for Notre-Dame-d'Auteuil. The archway brick façade aligned with the neighboring buildings is a 1953 creation by Raymond Busse.

An elegant obelisk in gray porphyry, on a marble pedestal, stands in the middle of Place de l'Église d'Auteuil, a memorial to Henri François d'Aguesseau, chancellor of France (1668-1751), and his wife. Construction was commissioned by Louis XV. Their tombs were desecrated in 1793 and the old cemetery was turned into a public space, but the monument was restored in 1802 on the orders of Napoleon, then First Consul.

From Avenue Théophile-Gautier to the Seine River

It is believed that the house where Molière slept during his stays in Auteuil between 1667 and 1672 was either at **2** Rue d'Auteuil or **62 Avenue Théophile-Gautier**. In 1786, the Duke of Choiseul-Praslin purchased a mansion near modern-day **57** (demolished in 1908 along with all its annexes) and had a temple to Thalia, the muse of comedy, erected at **62**, because he was convinced that this was where Molière had stayed.

Let's make our way down Avenue Théophile-Gautier. We will soon turn

right on **Rue de Rémusat** and then left onto **Rue François-Gérard**. In the basement of the modern building at **39** is the Sainte-Trinité Russian Catholic church. Just past this point is **Square Henry-Paté**, an ensemble designed by Pierre Patout and Camille Damman in 1930. The promoter of this development in 1933 was Alexandre Stavisky. When he was exposed as an embezzler and fled, development abruptly came to a halt. The south end was completed much later by a massive, high-rise apartment complex. A lovely courtyard-garden remains, however, laid out atop a garage and

◄ Square Henry-Paté

▼ 28-30 Avenue Théophile-Gautier

framed by beautiful buildings with recessed upper floors. The stone cladding on the façade is adorned with elegant, wrought-iron balconies.

Rue François-Gérard takes us back to **Avenue Théophile-Gautier**. Initially named Rue de la Municipalité, it became Rue du Point-du-Jour in 1879, before finally taking the writer's name in 1892.

The building numbered **28-30** was designed by Charles Blanche in 1905. This prolific architect was often commissioned in the 16th arrondissement, where his firm was located. While his rental buildings are of interest, they all share the same pattern: two contrasting colors for the brickwork and vertical white frames on the oriel windows. The ones here are mounted on metal brackets, but elsewhere he used stone and even wood.

24, built by Charles Lemaresquier around 1925, supports an impressive bas-relief including nude female figures and putti. Like 18 Rue de l'Assomption and many other examples of the work of "Lemar" – as he was nicknamed by fellow faculty members and students at the École des Beaux-Arts, whose academic tradition he defended fervently, the decorative elements are disproportionately large, betraying a poor sense of scale (e.g. the hefty consoles supporting simple balconies).

Architect Deneu de Montbrun and sculptor P. de Folleville collaborated on **21 and 23** in 1907 and 1908. (Montbrun also designed 6, 6 bis, and 8 in 1904). Like Charles Blanche, he too had his architectural "tics." The façades are posh, massive, featuring heavy stone consoles with pendant keys, similar to what we saw earlier in Villa Jeanne-d'Arc and at 32 Rue La

Fontaine (see page 231). Curiously, this building's simple Belle-Époque architecture is embellished by various Art Nouveau-style wrought-iron balconies.

Let's backtrack and take a left onto **Avenue Perrichont**. In 1911, Deneu de Montbrun completed another small building at **14** similar to the ones mentioned above. This time, however, Guimard designed the

wrought-iron decoration. Deneu de Montbrun seems to have made little effort to marry the stonework in his flat façade with the elegant, swirling lines favored by the high priest of the Art Nouveau movement.

In 1907, Joachim Richard designed **15**, his own rental building. He hired Gentil and Bourdet to create the flambé stoneware lintels patterned with chestnut-leaves, with Moorish windows giving it an exotic touch. This architect became interested in reinforced concrete early in his career. He was a student of Anatole de Baudot (one of the first to use the material). Richard's methods of using concrete allowed all sorts of new tricks. For example, there was no longer any structural requirement for the front door to be lined up with the floors above.

We will now cross **Rue Félicien-David**, formerly called Chemin des Pâtures, for it once led through com-

mon grazing lands. It was the first street to be flooded when the Seine burst its banks in January 1910, causing extensive damage throughout Paris. Here, the water stood three meters deep.

Along Avenue de Versailles

Let's continue walking down to the Seine on **Rue Degas**. To reach our next local landmark, at **3**, we will have to cross Avenue de Versailles. Designed in 1935 by A. Gille, it makes outstanding use of yellow tile mosaic on the façade.

Now we'll backtrack to **Avenue de Versailles** and turn right. Formerly named Route de Versailles, Route de la Reine, then Chaussée d'Auteuil, it makes up a small section of national highway 10, which runs from Paris all the way to Biarritz and the Spanish border.

42 Avenue de Versailles, where Rue des Pâtures comes in, is one of the most beautiful corner buildings in all of Paris. It was erected in 1933 by Jean Ginsberg, an associate of François Heep and Maurice Breton. It included a number of technological innovations, which, though daring in their time, are now quite common. The only one visible from the street is the use of glass balcony railings, then a first in architecture. The dirty gray concrete cladding can be overlooked. What is admirable, however, is the magnificent rounded angle, coupled with an asymmetrical effect, gracefully wedding the pattern of balconies on the Avenue de Versailles side with the plain façade on Rue des Pâtures.

Further down, we come to two more buildings designed by Charles

▸ 14 Avenue Perrichont
▾ Detail of a flambé stoneware lintel,
15 Avenue Perrichont

► 42 Avenue de
Versailles

▼ 25 Avenue de
Versailles

Blanche, located opposite Rue Florence-Blumenthal. The 1899 building at **33** uses the same pattern we described earlier; here, the window brackets are in stone. Far more original is **31**, dating from 1901. Its barely protruding oriel windows sit on stone consoles as well as a pair of slim wrought-iron posts rising from the balconies.

Next door, **29**, erected by P. Boëssé in 1929, is an elegant building in white concrete, designed for artists' studios. The pattern given to the windows is sober yet playful.

It would be a shame to give the remarkable but discreet building at **25** a mere superficial glance. Completed in 1931, it was the first building in Jean Ginsberg's career (earlier, we saw his work at 42). This architect of Polish extraction, a student of Rob Mallet-Stevens as well as of Le Corbusier and André Lurçat, was 26 years old when he asked his family to help finance construction on a narrow parcel of land. For this project only, he became partners with Berthold Lubetkin, an architect who was later successful in England. They set out to design small, luxury apartments. Space is suggested without ever being imposed. The rooftop terrace solarium used to be shared by all the tenants. There are only three pillars; the central pillar, visible here, has a narrow, horizontal band of windows. The detail work is of exceptional quality in this luxury building, where Jean Ginsberg set up his architectural firm.

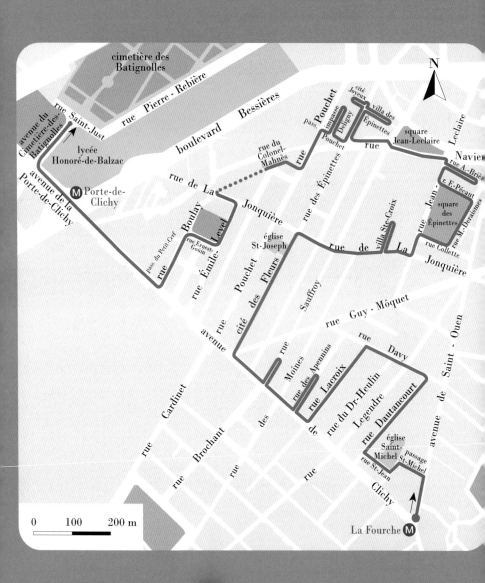

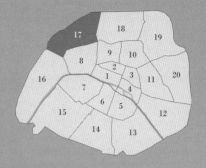

17th

From La Fourche to the Batignolles Cemetery

▶ Start: Avenue de Saint-Ouen, metro La Fourche

▶ Finish: Avenue du Cimetière-des-Batignolles, metro Porte-de-Clichy

A venue de Clichy, Avenue de Saint-Ouen, and Rue Guy-Môquet make a perfect triangle on the Paris map. The area invites exploration, despite recent transformations. If we extend this triangle northward, we reach the Paris city limits, right beside the Batignolles cemetery, a 19th-century necropolis slumbering as peacefully as possible beneath the city's noisy beltway, the périphérique.

This neighborhood's name comes from the Champ des Épinettes, which until the beginning of the 19th century was a vast stretch of farmland with a scattering of open-air quarry sites at the foot of Butte Montmartre. Small light industries began moving to the Épinettes area in the mid-19th century, and the old "Chemin des Bœufs" ("Ox Path," today's Rue de La Jonquière), gradually started to be lined with artisans' and factory workers' houses. On the other side of Avenue de Clichy, the Batignolles villages started to prosper and grow. For residents in Batignolles, the Épinettes represented a pleasure zone, ideal for rendezvousing in the thickets, and furtive embracing in ramshackle haylofts.

Construction of the Thiers fortification walls brought some normalization to the area. Sturdy, handsome buildings were being built about the La Fourche intersection and Place de Clichy, a popular place for revelers and entertainment-seekers. The petits bourgeois and factory personnel were giving "Les Épinettes" a working-class identity.

Around Saint-Michel-des-Batignolles

▲ Saint-Michel church

Our starting point, **La Fourche metro station**, was deep enough to be used as an air-raid shelter during World War II. Emerging, we take a right onto **Avenue de Saint-Ouen**. Let's move up to **5**, the "Bains-Douches de La Fourche" (the neighborhood bath house). In just a few more steps, we will come to **Passage Saint-Michel**.

Like soldiers at attention, nearly identical four-story houses line both sides of this cobblestoned passage, under the command of the dramatic red **campanile** of Saint-Michel-des-Batignolles standing tall and proud at the other end. For a moment, we might think we have been transported to a small, quiet street in a provincial town.

► Rue Saint-Jean

We soon reach the tiny square that serves as Saint-Michel's esplanade. In fact, this is oddly-shaped **Rue Saint-Jean** – in the form of a T. It will take us around the church. It is strangely calm here, a pocket of peacefulness between two noisy avenues. Notice that the old Saint-Michel church, located on Avenue Saint-Ouen, is still standing. The old church communicates with the newer church, as both have doors on Place Saint-Jean.

Saint-Michel, like many early 20th-century churches, has startling architecture, a mixture of austere Romanesque and Byzantine styles with futuristic construction techniques, which bring concrete all the way into the sanctuary. Let's go in and have a look at a few decorative elements. The church wardens' pew and the pulpit were designed by Haubold, the church architect. They are made of tigerwood from Africa and

precious Cuban, Cambodian, and Indian mahoganies.

The frescoes, by Malespinat, date from 1949. The Saint-Michel chapel is decorated with a *Weighing of Souls*. An *Annunciation* graces the Sainte-Vierge chapel. A Christ in Glory overlooks the choir. The stained glass window by Marcel Magne in Notre-Dame-de-Pitié chapel pays tribute to the victims of World War I. As for the organ, it was brought here in 1937 from the Hôtel Majestic in Paris. More astonishing, the church has two pieces by a little-known Brazilian artist named Maria Morgan-Snell. The first is entitled *La Présentation de la Vierge au Temple* (right aisle) and the second is *La Pentecôte* (left aisle). Monumental and impressive, the two paintings were a 1992 gift from La Trinité church in Paris. On the day they were unveiled in 1962, writer André Maurois exclaimed, "I was stupefied. They aren't just stunning, they are beautiful, sublime." .

The church attracts many West Indians. They have a particular attachment to St. Michael and frequently travel great distances to come pray here.

A Fallen Angel

Frémiet's gilded statue of the Archangel Michael, once perched high atop the tower, poised for flight like the Gothic Michael atop Mont Saint-Michel abbey in Normandy (albeit with a slightly reduced wingspan), had to be brought down in February 1989. It had begun to sway dangerously on its base, as if Saint Michael were trying to break loose and fly.

The parish priest alerted city firefighters, who, aided by the municipal architect, came to the conclusion that removing the statue was indeed urgent. The very next day, the contractors arrived, with their pulleys and ropes. Since then, the Archangel has sat in a Paris workshop, waiting to return to the top of the bell tower, to watch over the parish, wielding his mighty sword to fend off demons. In 2006, the Fondation du Patrimoine (a private foundation for the preservation of national heritage) sponsored a fund drive for the statue's restoration, at long last.

Rue Dautancourt, Rue Davy, and Rue Lacroix

As we exit short Rue Saint-Jean, we come out at **Rue Dautancourt**, created in the mid-19th century by a certain Mr. Lemarié. This street is remarkable for having preserved its 19th-century *petit bourgeois* ambience. The interesting façade at **3** seems to be an archetype for the homes in this neighborhood: a minimum of decorative elements, a plaster façade painted white. Fine freestone buildings were erected later. **8** was designed by Bocage in 1888, and **10** was designed by Lagrave in 1912.

Be sure to take a peek through the iron gates at **17** to admire the little garden with chestnut trees and the tiny shimmering pool between the paving stones. Between the street-side fence posts, topped by ornamental vases, a thorny yellow rosebush intertwines with barbed wire. A symbol of urban entanglement...

Further up, and on the other side of the street, is **40**, an Art Nouveau building that is particularly appealing. The wrought-iron window railings are the giveaway. The stoneware trim on the building doorway features such ornamental elements as plane tree leaves and scarabs.

We will soon reach **Rue Davy** and turn left. In 1864, this street (then Rue Sainte-Élisabeth) was renamed after the English chemist who invented the miner's lamp.

Let's cross Rue Legendre. Next, on our left, is Rue du Docteur-Heulin, formerly named Rue Trézel, opened on August 24, 1870 on lands belonging to the Deligny-Trézel family. It was

renamed in 1927 in honor of a much-loved neighborhood physician and philanthropist. We will stay on Rue Davy until we reach **Rue Lacroix**, in the next block. The garden behind the iron fence at **40** is calm and refreshing. It is not open to the public, but the gate on the street has two interesting medallions, one with a man's face and the other with a woman's face.

Dr. Georges Bouet made his home at **30**. Bouet was a physician, a well-known ornithologist, entomologist, and expert on the tsetse fly. He died here in 1957.

Next door, at **28**, now the headquarters of the Fédération Française de Sauvetage et de Secourisme (the French First Aid and Rescue Federation), was once the home of Montmartre artist Adolphe Willette. It was here that he drew throngs of angels with plump buttocks and young, smiling Pierrots.

The houses around **22** and **25** on both sides of the street are uncharacteristically low. These two- and three-story dwellings add to the charm of the street which was named for a certain Lacroix, a stonemason, whose only other claim to fame is that he owned several lots on this street.

At the end of the street, we return to bustling **Avenue de Clichy**. We will make a right here, and go past the old **Gloria Cinema**, now the Astros, a West Indian discotheque.

Going down Avenue de Clichy

Let's make a right onto **Rue des Apennins**. Property-owner Mabille created the street in 1845. It is lined with a long series of 19th-century façades of little interest. Their uniformity is

▲ Old hotel sign, Rue de La Jonquière

interrupted, however, by numbers **26 and 29**, built in the pre-World War II era by the same architects, Bertin and Kandjian. We should also have a look at **12**, a small building erected around 1860. Its plaster façade with its conspicuous pilasters and moldings is a veritable catalogue of architectural ornamentation.

Let's head back out to Avenue de Clichy. One block after Rue de Moines, we will take a right onto **Rue Sauffroy**, which is an alteration of the name of a local landlord, Soffroy. Around 1884, a mineral spring at **11** that had been tapped since 1852 ran dry. The output had long been three liters per minute of a sulfurous, iron-bearing water. It was recommended for treating respiratory diseases. Auguste Libert referred to it in an article published in 1909 in *L'Intermédiaire des Chercheurs et des Curieux*, "I recall that in my youth, before the war, I would often go draw water at this enclosed spring, in the middle of a garden. It was on private property. Its medicinal virtues were greatly appreciated in this remote neighborhood. It had high iron and sulfur content. In many ways, it was comparable to the waters from Enghien, so universally known. Large rental properties now stand on the garden where it used to flow."

The only building of any interest on this street is at **18**. Seven stories high, it was erected in 1902 by architect Lamoureux. The decorative elements are of Art Nouveau inspiration, using the theme of chestnut leaves and thistles. The sixth-floor occupant went so far as to plant a chestnut tree on the balcony, a lively echo to the motifs on the façade.

Now we'll backtrack to **Avenue de Clichy**. After crossing Rue Guy-Môquet, we will reach the iron gate opening onto **Cité des Fleurs**.

Cité des Fleurs

This magical, delightful world is set between Rue Guy-Môquet and Rue de La Jonquière. The visitor is enchanted by the climbing rose bushes, ivy, acacia and cherry trees, which are such a rare sight in Paris. They give it a distinct charm, an other-worldly atmosphere.

▶ Cité des Fleurs

To our right, a sign nailed to the wall of the manager's house informs us that her duty is to enforce the regulations. The regulations are posted in plain view. If you feel the urge to read them, go ahead, and take heed!

The author of a 1910 guide to Paris ventured the remark that the quiet, coquettish street nearly resembles a sea resort town. It is true that this short, bumpy street, lined by fence posts topped by wrought-iron ornamental vases, exudes a very special ambience. It was undoubtedly the effect developers Lhenry and Bacqueville were hoping to achieve when, in 1846, they evenly divided the parcel into lots. They originally named the development in honor of Pope Pius IX. They imposed building-height codes for all constructors, required that at least three trees be planted in each front yard, selected which type of ornamental vase would be allowed on fence posts, and - attentive to every detail - which species of flowers could be planted in them! Very strict regulations published by the neighborhood homeowners' committee in 1864 indicated that public traffic on their street was merely tolerated and could be prohibited at any

▲ 29 Cité des Fleurs

moment and for as long as it was deemed in the interest of the community.

Today, time and the destructive hand of man have inflicted much damage on this calm and tranquil private street. Some of the homeowners have given up a segment of fencing for the sacrosanct driveway and garage. Others have chopped down trees, which, granted, can be terrible nuisances in an urban setting...

Fortunately, however, many other owners have carefully and respectfully restored their historic homes.

At **8 and 10**, two opulent, freestone buildings provide clear proof that errors in taste are not restricted to our contemporaries.

A double-helix staircase embellishes the 1852 townhouse at **17**. A sober, freestone façade at **21**, dating from the late 19th century, incorporates a monogram of the letters CS in an oak-leaf décor. **25** is a small two-story building signed "A. Lx." Its spiral columns are repeated on a façade further down the street.

The most typical building in the Cité is undoubtedly **29**, with its freestone, neo-Renaissance façade. Grotesque masks crown the trim on the front door. . The second story is ornamented with black and white marble inlays. One of the windows on the left is decorated with a small bas-relief elephant, which is barely visible. The property is so charming, it is a shame that the fence and gate are so out of harmony with the original.

The modern buildings at **30** belong to the Foyer des Jeunes Travailleurs de la Cité des Fleurs, a residence for young workers, as well as a parish building, both of which are run by the Communauté Aveyronnaise de Paris (an association of workers from the Aveyron, in south central France).

All in pink and white, an upper portion of the façade at **31** is decorated with two medallions. The one on the left is a lady, and the one on the right seems to be her mustachioed companion.

33 is similar in style to 25; the spiral columns on the façade create a picturesque effect. **40** is from the same period. It is particularly pleasing, with its highly original windows and niches. **47, 48, and 50** also date from the mid-19th century, when the first dwellings went up here.

A Red Cross building at **54** has a mosaic frieze from the 1930s that reads "Crèche Marie-Ernest May" (a daycare center still in operation). The ground floor bas-relief at **56** was inspired by 18th-century tastes. Upstairs, there are artists' studios.

At **59**, there is a rear entrance to Saint-Joseph-des-Épinettes church located at 40 Rue Pouchet, which is undoubtedly the only building of interest on that street. Built in 1909 by an architect named Thomas, it is composed entirely of reinforced concrete clad in brick. This modest church was consecrated on May 24, 1910. Inside, we can admire a truly exceptional 18th century organ, which was restored by an association.

Rue de La Jonquière

As we exit the north end of bucolic Cité des Fleurs, we will turn right onto **Rue de La Jonquière**, heading toward the Guy-Môquet metro station. Jacques de Taffanel, the Marquis de La Jonquière, was a naval officer and

▲ 44 Rue de La Jonquière

◄ 42 Rue de La Jonquière

governor-general of French possessions in Canada. The street was named after him in 1890. Prior to that, it was Rue Marcadet, a cattle path etched on 18th-century maps and probably dating much further back in history. The initial path is on a thalweg (a natural path through a valley) along the gentle slope of the Butte Montmartre.

Today, it is a fairly busy street, where some local shops are located. Certain passageways still bear the mark of the neighborhood's industrial past. **44** is a prime example. Behind the industrial entrance that was typical in this quarter up to the end of the 19th century, there is a narrow, melancholy alleyway paved in stones. At nearby **42**, the plaque under glass over the doorway informs us the building housed a print shop, a glazier, and a painting contractor. The courtyard is worth the visit.

A little further on, still on the left-hand side, we will walk beneath the portico of a modern building in order to reach **Villa Sainte-Croix**. In fact, **Square Sainte-Croix**, located between a colorful school and a contemporary building, is a good exam-

ple of a park that is well-integrated into a dense urban fabric.

We will continue strolling down **Rue de la Jonquière** one more block to **Rue Jean-Leclaire**, on our left. It will take us up to **Square des Épinettes**.

Square des Épinettes

It's a shortcut for many heading to the market on Avenue Saint-Ouen, yet it is also a convivial and pleasant place with all the amenities associated with your typical Parisian square: a kiosk, the park guard's office, and above all, splendid flowerbeds neatly bordered by paving stones. A century-old copper beech tree (*Fagus*

Épinettes and Batignolles: Country Names for Two New City Quarters

Many historians have tried to find plausible explanations for the etymology of the quaint name Épinettes. But none of the hypotheses devised thus far have been entirely satisfactory. The mystery remains: why should this part of Paris be associated with either spinets or chicken coops (two meanings of the word *épinette*)?

Épinettes was the name of one of the fields on the *Chemin des Bœufs* (today's Rue de La Jonquière). The name simply stuck. It even survived all the 19th-century urban development phases. For all we know, the original Épinettes might have been a mere briar patch (*épine* = thorn) beside the field, which would have been a natural landmark for local farmers.

Until the end of the 18th century, the fields between the *Chemin de Saint-Ouen* and the *Chemin de Clichy* (today's avenues) were referred to as belonging to *les batignolles*. By 1790, the name was being used more for the new hamlet at the Barrière de Clichy (the Clichy tollhouse), now Place de Clichy. In 1830, it referred to the new village officially named Les Batignolles. As for the origin of Batignolles, every imaginable theory has been suggested, some a little wilder than others, but none very convincing.

sylvatica purperea) shades the guard's shack. Rising fifteen meters and having a girth of over three meters, this tree is impressive.

Dalou's statue of Jean Leclaire stands with its back to visitors. It was destroyed by the Nazis in 1943, but was recast by the Sosson firm and put back on its pedestal in 1971. Jean Leclaire (1801-1872) is still famous for discovering that zinc oxide could replace white lead. Lead was destroying the health of building painters. In 1842, he created a profit-sharing scheme for workers. The Société de Prévoyance et de Secours Mutuels (a mutual insurance company) erected this monument in his honor in 1896. He received further homage when a company town, thousands of miles away in Illinois, was named after this modest benefactor to humanity.

Standing tall, proud, and brave, the statue of Maria Deraismes faces visitors entering the square via Rue Collette. This bronze, too, was destroyed in 1943. Fortunately, it was recast and returned to its original position a few years ago by the city of Paris. In the original, the subject's left hand rested on the back of a chair. It now floats in midair because no plaster of the chair could be found at the art depot. As a woman of letters, president of the association for women's rights, Maria Deraismes (1828-1894) is remembered as a courageous pioneer in the feminist movement. She lived at 72 Rue Cardinet, across the street form the Lycée Carnot.

The square is lined with numerous rental buildings, many of Art Déco inspiration with bay windows, colorful stained glass, and wrought-iron balcony railings. **17 Rue Collette** is a remarkable eight-story, late-19th-century building with stained-glass bay windows.

At the north end of the square, the austere façade of the **old Félix-Pécaut school** frames the street of the same name. In 1989, it was turned into an annex of the École Nationale de Commerce on Boulevard Bessières. This 1898 brick-and-stone structure is typical of its period. The pediment on the left and the pediment on the right still tell us one side was the boys' school and the other was the girls' school. It was a time when school administrators frowned on co-educational classes.

◄ Old school buildings on Rue Félix-Pécaut

► Statue of Maria Deraismes, Square des Épinettes

◄ Old train station, Rue Navier

Around Rue Navier and Rue Pouchet

Leaving tree-lined Rue Félix-Pécaut, we come to **Rue Jean-Leclaire** and make a right. Note the 1930s building at **23-25**, across the street. The façade is covered in a mosaic of red tile and innumerable pieces of broken yellow tile, typical of this era. Continuing down the right-hand side of the street, we will take a stroll up **Rue Arthur-Brière**. Formerly named Passage Lagille, it was widened on the odd-numbered side when the schools were erected. On our left, we will walk past **8**, a quaint little three-story building with old-fashioned charm. Number **10**, a red-white-and-blue building, houses a school cafeteria. Opposite, at **3**, the school wall still bears an impressive crest of the city of Paris, carved in stone.

Let's go back to **Rue Jean-Leclaire** and enter **Rue Navier**, named for an engineer who died in 1836. Sometimes called *Chemin des Épinettes* or *Chemin des Fruits*, the paved street was laid out at the same time as the city's Ceinture (beltway) railroad, as it ran beside the sunken tracks. In 1963, passenger service having been halted for nearly three decades, the railway trench was covered by an esplanade with trees and a modest-sized lawn bowling area. In the distance, if you look a bit to the right, you will be able to pick out the **old train station**. After having been a cinema, it became a supermarket, and was next converted to a home-appliance store.

◄ 8 Rue Arthur-Brière

► Entrance to Cité Joyeux at 53 Rue des Épinettes

◄ Passage Pouchet

Continuing along Rue Navier, we pass small **Square Jean-Leclaire**. We then turn right on **Rue des Épinettes**. Although Cité Joyeux at **53** is secretive and mysterious, locked up behind its metal gates, stone-paved **Villa des Épinettes**, just across the street, invites us for a stroll. Take a look at the experimental home "Film House," built in 1998 by architect Christophe Lab. The elegant concrete and alu-

minum structure is designed as a box allowing light to shine through it. "It's a five-meter-wide strip that is thirty meters long," he explained. "I designed this house like a big camera, with light entering through the viewfinder."

Once back on **Rue des Épinettes**, we will backtrack a little so that we can take **Passage Pouchet** off to our right at the end of the block. It has new paving stones, new street-lamps, and is astutely hidden from hurried passersby. To our right is the very charming **Impasse Deligny**. Vir-

ginia creeper and wisteria cover the iron bars on some ground-floor windows, to discourage even prying gazes, no doubt.

As Passage Pouchet dead-ends in a tree-shaded alcove, our path leads us left onto **Rue Pouchet**, over the old Petite Ceinture railway tracks. Note the subsidized housing project on our right at **75**, handsome brick garden apartments with a semicircular façade, decorated with green brick medallions.

After the railroad bridge, we will take a little street called **Rue du Colonel-Manhès**, which veers right

▼ 75 Rue Pouchet

◄ Green walkway beside the old Ceinture railroad tracks

and leads to a pleasant **green walkway** newly planted beside the long-disused tracks. The benches here and there beside the shrubs are inviting, a good place to sit down and give our feet a rest.

Our neighborhood walk leads us next to the **Bernard-Lafay swimming**

pool, a brick building renovated in the 1980s. Turning onto **Rue de La Jonquière** takes us around the sports complex to **Rue Émile-Level**, where we turn right. This was formerly named Passage Dhier, lined on its right side by the (now demolished) Goüin iron and locomotive works (see inset). Émile Level, for whom the street was named, was an engineer, a city council member, and the mayor of the 17th arrondissement. Starting from **36**, the little lodgings bordering this street were designed to house factory workers. The ironworks was moved to Nantes prior to World War II.

Rue Ernest-Goüin takes us around the square to **Rue Boulay**,

◄ The Bernard-Lafay swimming pool complex

The Goüin Factory

The Goüin industrial site used to occupy the entire area between Avenue de Clichy, Rue Boulay, Rue Émile-Level, and Rue de La Jonquière. The enormous company employed many residents in the Épinettes-Batignolles quarters.

Ernest Goüin, the founder of the factory, was born in 1815, at the height of the Industrial Revolution, a promising time for a young man with a passion for mechanics. His first job involved him in the construction of the Paris-Saint-Germain railroad. In 1846, with financial backing from the Duke de Noailles, the Rothschilds, and Mr. Rodriguès-Henriquès, he founded his own factory on land he had only recently acquired in the Batignolles. In the space of a few months, the property had walls around its forges and boiler works, fitting and assembly shops, warehouse, and residence: all the infrastructure needed to build locomotives.

The factory produced numerous models of locomotives for the rail networks being set up around the country by the regional companies (Ouest, Orléans, Nord, and Etat). This enterprise's immense output included pieces for metal construction projects such as the bridges in Asnières and Langon.

The Goüin factory exported its savoir-faire to Russia and Italy. During World War I, the factory focused essentially on manufacturing weaponry. In 1920, Goüin produced over two hundred locomotives. The ironworks was then moved to Nantes. There, a new neighborhood was founded and named Les Batignolles in honor of the company's stunning Parisian adventure.

named for a local land owner. This rather ordinary street intersects midway with **Passage du Petit-Cerf**. Two modern buildings are embellished with corner caryatids, allegorically referring to the name of this passage. On the right, a female figure supports the second-floor balcony; on the left, another figure, half-man, half-stag, defends himself from a dog.

Let's stay on **Rue Boulay** until we reach **Avenue de Clichy**. There, we will take a right and head up to **Porte de Clichy**.

Crossing Boulevard Bessières, we will walk past the facilities of the **Lycée Honoré-de-Balzac** (an international high school). On the right, **Avenue du Cimetière-des-Batignolles** will take us straight to **Rue Saint-Just**. The entrance to the **cemetery** is directly in front of us.

◀ Rue Émile-Level
▶ Allegorical caryatid, Passage du Petit-Cerf

Cimetière des Batignolles

If you are familiar with the Père-Lachaise cemetery, do not expect to find any of its luxuriant vegetation at the Cimetière des Batignolles. Although a nice row of trees was planted, giving much needed relief to this concrete jungle, the foliage cannot absorb the din of the traffic on the nearby périphérique (the Paris beltway). When public concerns take precedence, respect (especially respect for the dead) flies out the window. City officials did not hesitate a minute to build the freeway over the final resting place of our ancestors, turning a haven of eternal rest into a field of noise. Fortunately, this only applies to the oldest part of the

cemetery, which has a total area of ten hectares, laid out in thirty-two divisions.

The land on the Clichy plain was requisitioned in 1833 to provide the young Batignolles-Monceaux community with a decent burial site. By August 22 that year, the first graves

►▲◄ Cimetière des Batignolles

A Few Celebrity Graves

(Cemetery maps available at the caretaker's office)
- 7th division: Blaise Cendrars, writer († 1961)
- 15th division: Gaston Calmette, director of Le Figaro († 1914)
- 16th division: Léon Dierx, poet († 1912)
- 21st division: Hector Formica, inventor († 1967)
- 24th division: Édouard Vuillard, painter († 1940)
- 31st division: André Breton, poet († 1966) and, a few graves further down, Benjamin Péret († 1959), another famous Surrealist.

This stroll will also lead us to the graves of Alfred Bruneau (a composer and illegitimate son of Émile Zola), the tomb of the Puteaux-Droux family (promoters and elected officials in Les Batignolles), the Lathuille family's grave (cabaret owners on Avenue de Clichy).

had been dug. It started out as a small graveyard. The entrance was then on Route de la Révolte (now Boulevard Victor-Hugo in Clichy). It was expanded in 1847. Between the date it was created and the year 1860, 17,688 bodies were interred here. As it had to take in all of Paris's temporary burials, more expansion was soon required. In 1883, the city of Paris endowed it with nearly seven more hectares and built the entrance we see today.

Some celebrities who were buried in the Cimetière des Batignolles were transferred elsewhere for various reasons. The Soviet Union demanded the return of the remains of famed opera singer Feodor Chaliapin. Blaise Cendrars' remains were transferred from the 5th division to his hometown in Switzerland, La Chaux-de-Fonds.

Poet Paul Verlaine's case is rather unusual. He was initially buried beside his parents in the oldest part of the cemetery (20th division). His grave was covered in dust from the freeway overhead. On May 30, 1989, it was moved to a place of honor beside the central roundabout.

The oldest part of the cemetery is actually on the other side of the périphérique. The freeway pollution constantly casts a grayish veil over the graves, making them look all the grimmer. Interestingly, numerous tombstones indicate 18th-century birthdates and the place of death as Batignolles-Monceaux. Due to a lack of upkeep, some tombs have had to be destroyed out of concern for public safety, resulting in voids. Families seek quiet, clean resting places for their loved ones. The périphérique has damaged cemetery real-estate values!

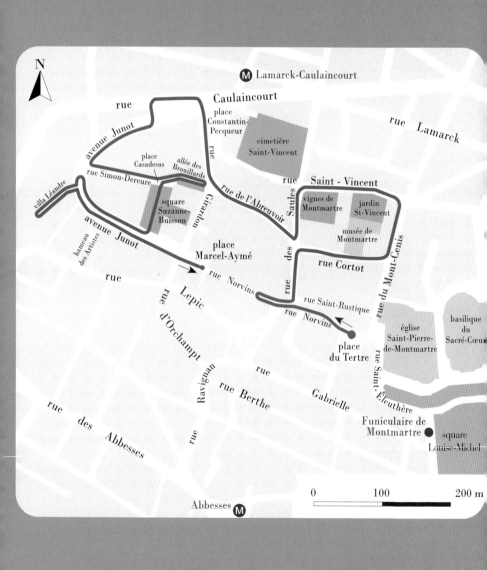

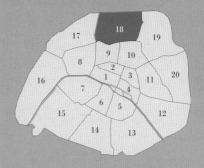

18th

From Place du Tertre to Avenue Junot

▶ Start: Place du Tertre,
  metro Abbesses
  or Funiculaire de Montmartre,
  upper station
▶ Finish: Place Marcel-Aymé,
  metro Abbesses
  or Lamarck-Caulaincourt

Place du Tertre is the ultimate tourist destination and a marketplace for artists. The local art trade is a tradition that was created and anchored on the slopes of Montmartre between 1890 and 1940 by world-famous painters: Modigliani, Utrillo, Valadon, Picasso, Braque, Gen Paul, etc. Each year, city officials grant one hundred and forty licenses for a one-square-meter stall to be shared by two artists on alternating schedules.

Place du Tertre

This mound appears in records as "le Tertre" as early as 1336. It has long been called **Place du Tertre**. This stroll takes us into the heart of the centuries-old village of Montmartre, winding through the streets on its plateau. Our starting point was repaved in 1992. It is framed by three- and four-story 18th-century buildings.

The village of Montmartre was officially founded in 1790, and its first town hall opened at **3 Place du Tertre**. Félix Desportes de Blinval (1763-1849) was the community's first mayor. He served until 1793, a time when Revolutionary Montmartre was often referred to as "Mont-Marat." In 1795, the new municipality had a population of somewhere between 800 and 1,300.

The portrait of sculptor Maurice Drouard (1886-1915) is embedded in the façade of the house at **7**. Roland Dorgelès penned the epitaph which translates, "Born in Montmartre, lived in this house and left it on August 3, 1914 to go with the 236th Infantry Regiment from the Butte to defend its old church and its windmills. He was killed in Tahure while bandaging the wounded."

A plaque on the tourist bureau's façade at **21** informs us that the first automobile to reach Place du Tertre arrived on Christmas Eve 1898 with Louis Renault behind the wheel, "thus marking the dawn of the French automobile industry." The same car, the first designed with a transmission, gave Renault his victory in the first Paris-Trouville automobile race on August 27, 1899. He was clocked at 35 kilometers per hour.

▲ 7 Place du Tertre
◄ Rue Norvins

Rue Norvins and Rue des Saules

Let's take **Rue Norvins**, at the north end of Place du Tertre. It was named for Jacques Marquet, Baron de Montbreton de Norvins (1769-1854), an ardent defender of the Emperor who wrote an *Histoire de Napoléon*. This street was referred to in the 11th century as the *chemin de charroy qui va de Montmartre à Paris* (the cart road that goes from Montmartre to Paris).

The Mère Catherine restaurant at **6**, founded by Catherine Lamotte in 1793, replaced a 15th-century presbytery.

We will stay on Rue Norvins, the old village's main street. The **even side** is lined with townhouses made up of

▲ Restaurant Mère Catherine, 6 Rue Norvins

▶ 24 Rue Norvins

Pinel, the physician who abolished the use of chains to restrain psychiatric patients. In 1805, Prost opened a clinic for the mentally ill in the large mansion, "providing care in a climate of gentle benevolence." Prost expanded the building shortly before selling it in 1820 to Dr. Esprit-Silvestre Blanche. For a quarter of a century, the new owner took in people with little or no resources, as well as writers and artists such as Gérard de Nerval, who was hospitalized here from March 21 to November 21, 1841 after a fit of madness (see inset on page 184).

This address has been property

two or three bays, with wooden shutters, wrought-iron window railings, and dormers. On the odd side, the two- and three-story houses from **1 to 1 ter** continue to give this street its authentic village atmosphere.

At today's address **22-22 bis**, a certain Mr. Sandrin had a country home built. An inventory drawn up in 1795 listed the main three-story hall as having a tile roof, a southern exposure with twenty-seven windows, a ground floor with a large drawing room, a boudoir, a billiards room, a kitchen, and a pantry. This quiet, sprawling, one-hectare property just outside the capital greatly pleased Dr. Pierre-Antoine Prost, a disciple of

of the city of Paris since 1972. Municipal funds were allocated to renovate the mansion and to build some thirty artists' studios next door at **24**. The ensemble is now an annex of the Cité Internationale des Arts (located on Rue de l'Hôtel-de-Ville). The grounds on the steep northern slope have been taken over by Mother Nature.

Let's backtrack now and turn left onto **Rue des Saules**. In the 15th century, the *Chemin de la Saussaie*, as it was then called, traversed swampy lands where willow trees (saules) grew. This street, which plunges down the north side of the hill, is hemmed in by a buttressed wall on one side, and a retaining wall taken over by sycamore maples on the other.

▶ 22-22 bis Rue Norvins

Rue Cortot

The next intersection is with **Rue Cortot**, to our right. It was named for sculptor Jean-Pierre Cortot (1787-1843).

The villas at **22 to 18** have tiny, fenced-in front yards. Aristide Bruant rented a house at **16**. "He had a vegetable patch, a chicken coop, and even something he called a bicycle track. It was merely a circular walk, but he would ride his bike on it, not so much for exercise as to entertain his dogs. He had nailed a sign on his door that read: Aristide Bruant, popular cabaret singer. His own title, his own coat of arms, his own crown. He was proud of it." (Roland Dorgelès, *Bouquet de Bohème*, 1947).

At **12**, we will cross the threshold and step back in history as we discover the Musée de Montmartre (see insert). It was founded in 1961 in the "La Maison de Rosimond." In ruins when the city of Paris purchased it in 1922, it

12 Rue Cortot: A Hothouse for Artists

The main hall is flanked by two wings that were set up for use as artists' studios in the 19th century. Renoir rented a studio and stables in the left wing in 1876 to store Le Moulin de la Galette, the extra-large painting that he was working on. In 1896, Suzanne Valadon moved into the second floor with her husband Paul Moussis and her son Maurice Utrillo. Marie-Clémentine Valadon, who usually went by Suzanne (1867-1938), received encouragement to paint and

draw from Degas. Until she moved to Rue Cortot, she had done nothing but pencil sketches. It was there that she took up painting.

In the right wing, Raoul Dufy came in 1901 and shared the second-floor studio occupied by his childhood friend Othon Friesz. His paintings generated little interest. He was making a living by designing fabrics for Bianchini and Poiret. In 1911, he married Eugénie Brisson at the 18th arrondissement hall, and rented a studio at 5 Impasse

Guelma. The next tenant was Surrealist poet Pierre Reverdy (1889-1960), a native of Narbonne, who occupied the studio from 1913 to 1926. A spiral staircase used to lead to his front door. Reverdy and his wife called it "our private turret."

Émile Bernard (1868-1941) lived on the third floor from 1906 to 1912. He had rejected all the innovative ideas of his youth and had gone back to Renaissance principles. He hung his motto on his front door, "Que celui qui ne croit

was restored by Claude Charpentier. This long, low, white, 17th-century building stretches out between a cobblestone courtyard and a very large garden extending to 17 Rue Saint-Vincent. In 1680, one of the king's actors, Claude La Roze, Sir Rosimond (1640-1686), made this his country home. He came here to write comedies and take a break from the stage, where he had been immensely popular in Molière's play *Le Malade Imaginaire*. The museum was created thanks to the efforts of the Société d'Histoire et d'Archéologie du Vieux Montmartre, founded on August 26, 1886, Charles Sellier, president. This association's purpose was the preservation of historical objects from old Montmartre such as the pewter counter from a bistro that used to be at 14 Rue de l'Abreuvoir, composer Gustave Charpentier's desk, and the zinc shadow puppets from the Chat Noir Cabaret.

A set of steps lined with espalier trees leads up to the front door at **6,**

home to composer Erik Satie (1866-1925) from 1890 to 1898. When he moved in, he took an upstairs room "well above any creditors," but in 1896, he had to forsake it for a tiny room that he called le placard (the closet). To make ends meet, the composer was the band leader at the Chat-Noir and the piano player at the Auberge du Clou. His interest in Rosi-

◄ 18 Rue Cortot
► 6 Rue Cortot

▲ The Montmartre museum,
12 Rue Cortot

pas en Dieu, en Raphaël et en Titien n'entre pas ici." ("Anyone who doesn't believe in God, Raphaël or Titian, keep out.") His studio was taken over by Valadon and her new partner, painter André Utter, after she divorced Moussis in 1909. In the roomy, skylit third-floor studio with a view of the garden, Valadon created large compositions, portraits of her mother and her son, nudes, landscapes, and still lifes, with strong pencil lines and bright colors. Her son Maurice Utrillo (1883-1955) worked in a little room overlooking Rue Cortot.

Raised by his grandmother Madeleine, he had a difficult, lonely childhood. At 16, he was already an alcoholic. In 1903, he had begun painting scenes of Montmartre such as Le Passage Cottin (now part of the collection in the Centre Pompidou Musée National d'Art Moderne in Paris) and the nearby suburbs. From 1906 to 1914, he was in his prime, executing powerful, evocative pieces. After being hospitalized several times for detoxification, he was locked up on Rue Cortot from 1921 to 1926.

ralist scenes, landscapes, seascapes, and bas-reliefs applied over the doors. **22** used to be the address of a low house that Hector Berlioz and his actress wife Harriet Smithson rented from 1834 to 1836. It was demolished in 1926.

We will take a left now, onto **Rue Saint-Vincent**. At **15**, the Saint-Vincent wild garden deserves a look. In 1985, the city of Paris decided to leave this abandoned plot of land undisturbed and let it return to Nature. Poppies, foxglove, and water mint grow here. Insects, birds, and small mammals have made it their home. The pond is alive with freshwater shrimp, fish, and amphibians. Admission is free, but it is only open on Saturdays from April to September (10 AM to 12:30 PM and 1:30 PM to 6:30 PM) and in October (until 6:00 PM). Guided visits are available upon request (tel.: +33 (0)143-284-763).

◄ Water tower at the start of Rue Cortot

► A villa on Rue Saint-Vincent

crucianism earned him the nickname "Ésotérik Satie." His limpid, crystalline, elliptical music may be technically simple, but his performance of it remains inimitable. Satie's hovel was eliminated when the house underwent renovation.

Around 1930, J. Boucher and G. Chevillard erected a large building at **1-3**. Subjects of the bas-reliefs on the pale façade include spiders, bats, eagles, hens, butterflies, and a fox.

Rue Cortot begins just opposite the **water tower**. It holds 660 cubic meters of drinking water and 200 cubic meters of non-potable water, and has been supplying the neighborhood since 1927.

Rue du Mont-Cenis and Rue Saint-Vincent

We will turn left on **Rue du Mont-Cenis**. From house numbers **23 to 31** on the odd side and from **18 to 22** on the even side, the street metamorphoses, becoming flights of stairs overlooked by more Boucher & Chevillard buildings from the 1930s. The embellishments are limited to natu-

The street has a provincial feel. Villas with small front yards extend from **18 to 30**, to the end of the block.

The famous cabaret **Le Lapin Agile** (see inset) stands on the corner of Rue Saint-Vincent and Rue des Saules.

Le Lapin Agile

This village-style house was successively named: "Au Rendez-Vous de Voleurs" ("Thieves' Hangout"), "Le Cabaret des Assassins" ("Murderers' Cabaret") and "À Ma Campagne" ("To my Countryside"). Then, in 1886, the establishment was taken over by Adèle Decerf. Adèle's specialty was sautéed rabbit. immortalized by illustrator André Gill as a rabbit cheerfully hopping about in Adèle's skillet. The sign he painted now hangs in the Musée de Montmartre. For his sake, the restaurant became "Le Lapin Agile," a pun on le lapin à Gill ("Gill's rabbit") and agile (both pronounced the same in French). . In the early 20th century, Aristide Bruant bought the cabaret and had it

managed by Frédéric Gérard (a.k.a. le Père Frédé). This is how Mac Orlan described Gérard, "On his head, he wore a red scarf, like fishermen in the south, knotted behind his neck. Shod in boots, he had a taciturn walk: hunched over, head low, ready to attack or defend." The Lapin Agile was the center of the Bohemian life on Montmartre. Dorgelès, Carco, Renoir, Courteline, Forain, Picasso, Fargue, Utrillo, Couté, Manolo, Van Gogh, Clemenceau, Dullin, and many others joined the evening performances that "Père Frédé" hosted. Picasso liked sitting out on the terrace beneath the big acacia with his dog Frika. The cabaret inspired its regulars. Mac Orlan used it as a setting in Quai des Brumes, although Marcel Carné

▲ Le Lapin Agile, 22 Rue des Saules

transplanted the restaurant to Le Havre when he adapted Mac Orlan's novel for the silver screen in 1939. Today, under the management of Yves Mathieu, the establishment has preserved its original low-ceilinged dining room and warm ambience.

The **Montmartre vineyard** is right across the street. Planted in 1933 to prevent any new construction on the grounds of an abandoned open-air dance hall called Le Parc de la Belle Gabrielle. Although this tiny vineyard of 1,556 square meters (about a third of an acre) with a northern exposure gets a meager amount of sunshine, it perpetuates the memory and tradition of the Montmartre vineyards that used to cover these slopes. 75% of this vineyard is gamay; 20% is pinot noir. The yearly harvest is generally in early October. The crop is hauled to the cellars of the 18th arrondissement hall. The 800-odd bottles of wine are sold at auction the following year, during the popular harvest festival.

▼ The Montmartre vineyard

15 Rue de l'Abreuvoir

From Rue de l'Abreuvoir to Avenue Junot

We will climb **Rue des Saules**, then turn right onto **Rue de l'Abreuvoir**, which appears in a 1325 record as *Ruelle du Buc*. Neighborhood residents followed it to fetch water for themselves and to lead horses and cattle to the watering trough (*abreuvoir* in French).

At **2**, the little pink house painted by Maurice Utrillo is now legendary. When the canvas drew a high price at the Octave Mirbeau estate sale, Utrillo's fame was assured. later

The imperial eagle hanging outside **4** is a mystery until we read the

plaque informing us that this was the home of Henry Lachouque (1883-1971), a historian of the Napoleonic wars. The stone building, enhanced with exposed beams and a balcony, is decorated with a statuette of the Virgin and a sundial with a rooster, complete with the comical inscription that would have the rooster telling the sundial *Quand tu sonneras, je chanteray* (I'll crow when you sound the hour).

While Camille Pissarro and his family were staying in the Oise, north of Paris, he rented a pied-à-terre at **12** between 1888 and 1892 so that he could entertain friends and maintain contact with art dealers. Nevertheless, he still felt isolated. When Eugène Manet invited him to Mallarmé's lecture on Villiers de L'Isle-Adam, he declined, "I am sorry, but cannot accept [...] as my eyesight prevents me from making the trip so late in the evening. We live at opposite ends of the earth. My perch is on the heights of Montmartre [...]" (letter dated February 25, 1890).

▲ Old sign, Rue des Saules

▶ 2 Rue de l'Abreuvoir

▲ Monument to Eugène Carrière, Avenue Junot

A 19th-century house at **15** is the site of the village's old watering trough, mentioned by Nerval in his *Promenades et Souvenirs*, "One then reaches the vicinity of the watering trough, quite busy in the evenings, with horses and dogs being washed down, and a fountain built in antique taste, where washerwomen would chat and sing like in the first chapters of *Werther*." This intersection with Rue Girardon was named **Place Dalida** in 1996. A bust by sculptor Alain Aslan pays tribute to the greatly loved pop singer, whose real name was Yolanda Gigliotti, and who lived at 11 bis Rue d'Orchampt from 1962 until her death in 1987.

The stairs on **Rue Girardon** will lead us to **Place Constantin-Pecquer**. This was where the But (or Buc) fountain used to flow, until it was eliminated by the construction of Avenue Junot. Paul Vannier's **stone statue** of a man kissing a woman stands on the square. It is an interpretation in stone of one of Théophile Alexandre Steinlen's famous, endearing illustrations. The Swiss Steinlen (1859-1923) lived at 73 Rue Caulaincourt from 1890 until his death. A veritable street chronicler, he drew for such newspapers as *Le Chat Noir* and *Le Gil Blas Illustré*, and made paintings and posters.

We will take a left onto **Avenue Junot**. Opposite **40 and 42**, on the median strip, Jean-René Carrière and Henri Sauvage erected a monument to Eugène Carrière (1849-1906). The artist is caught in a familiar stance, dressed in a painter's smock. Carrière devoted his energy to tender evocations of friendship, childhood, and maternal love – themes that inspired the four bronze bas-reliefs on the pedestal. They are captioned with compelling aphorisms; for example, *L'amour sincère pour les autres hommes nous donne une force invincible qui triomphe de tout.* (The sincere love for other men gives us invincible strength that triumphs over everything.)

Avenue Junot was named for General Andoche Junot (1771-1813), who had been a comrade-in-arms of Bonaparte since the siege of Toulon in 1793. The avenue was laid out in 1905, skirting the entire northwest side of the butte. It was supposed to end on the Sacré-Cœur esplanade, but that would have required the demolition of Rue Norvins and Saint-Pierre church.

Let's head up the beautiful avenue lined with linden trees. The eight- and nine-story buildings at **40** and **42**, erected in 1910 by the Griès brothers, are followed by Adolphe Thiers' 1930 development for artists at **36, 36 bis, 36 ter**. The sober façade features geometric windows to light the studios. The same talented hand designed the private mansion at **28**. Rectangular windows, an oculus, a bay window, and a mashrabiya (a window shaded by a carved latticework screen) give relief to the sober pinkish-ochre façade.

▼ 28 Avenue Junot

Around the Château des Brouillards

Let's make a left onto **Rue Simon-Dereure**. The street was named after the deputy mayor during Georges Clemenceau's term as mayor of the 18th arrondissement from 1870-1871. A bas-relief at **22**, over the front door of the Hôtel Lejeune, praises the art of sculpting stone. Rue Simon-Dereure will take us to **Place Casadesus**, named for a family which spawned five generations of artists. Marius Casadesus (1892-1981), the youngest of the first generation, was an excellent violinist, composer (notably of the *Adelaïde Concerto*, initially thought to be a lost work by Mozart), and luthier. In 1928, he bought **5**, known as the "Château des Brouillards" (literally: Fog Castle). Sitting on a 7,000-square-meter lot (1.8 acres), the three-story white house with a triangular pediment can be admired from Allée des Brouillards and is a vestige of the old Moulin des Brouillards, purchased in 1772 by Legrand-Ducampjean, a lawyer in the Parliament of Paris. He tore down the dilapidated windmill and replaced it with several buildings which he then sold, just prior to the Revolution. In

▲ Place Casadesus
▶ 22 Rue Simon-Dereure

1850, the outbuildings of the chateau were torn down to make room for individual houses separated by mere hedges, now on a little street with the poetic name of Allée des Brouillards. Around 1890, several poor artists – Steinlen, Poulbot, Duchamp-Villon, Van Dongen, to name names – took up quarters in the abandoned chateau. Other "marginals" moved in, creating makeshift dwellings for themselves on this property, nicknamed "le maquis" (the bush). Modigliani found a roof for himself there in 1906. Jeanne Modigliani, in her 1990 biography of her father, reports that he asked masons working on nearby new buildings for stones to carve. The dust from all the stone cutting was a

constant irritant to his throat and lungs, forcing him to take short breaks from his sculpture. In 1920, Victor Perrot, a notary and the president of the Société du Vieux Montmartre, bought the decrepit chateau, then threatened by the planned extension of Rue Simon-Dereure, and convinced officials to preserve it. Let's go up the **stairs** on the left side of the square and explore **Allée des Brouillards**, laid out between the chateau and the private homes in their verdant settings. Pierre-Auguste Renoir and his family lived at **8** from 1890 to 1897. His son Jean, the director of numerous films, including *French Cancan*, was born here in 1894.

We will return to **Place Casadesus** and enter **Square Suzanne-Buisson**,

named in honor of the national secretary of the Committee of Socialist Women part of the SFIO, the Section Française de l'Internationale Ouvrière), also a heroine of the Résistance, put to death by the Nazis for both her Jewish origins and her political activities. The square was originally a children's park opened in the late 1930s on the property of Alexandre Godefroy-Lebeuf, who grew trop-

ical plants like coffee, rubber, and pepper trees in hothouses) and exported them around the world, at the turn of the century. We shall walk round the Art Déco millstone **rotunda** to reach a **mall** shaded by plane trees. A **statue of Saint Denis** by Fernand Guignier (1941) overlooks the fountain. Legend has it that after his martyrdom (circa 275), the saint washed his decapitated head in the spring that flowed here until the early 19th century.

Back to Avenue Junot

We will take a right on **Avenue Junot**, where several interesting villas in a variety of styles await us. The entrance to the Hameau des Artistes is at **11**. Maurice Utrillo lived here from 1926 to 1937. The recluse painted tirelessly from postcards. Pétridès, an art dealer, sold the canvases.

In 1925, Francisque Poulbot (1879-1946) commissioned Pierre Boudriot to build a house at **13**. The millstone grit and concrete house has a running frieze of children taken from Poulbot's works featuring Paris street urchins, now commonly called "poul-

◄ Statue of Saint Denis in Square Suzanne-Buisson

► Frieze by Francisque Poulbot, 13 Avenue Junot

bots." This eminent Montmartre figure is still famous for his artistic talent and his generosity. He founded a health clinic at 42 Rue Lepic and poured all his energy into it.

The Tzara house at **15** is undoubtedly the most architecturally audacious. Tristan Tzara (1896-1963), a French writer of Romanian extraction, founded the Dada movement in Zurich. He arrived in Paris in 1919, and immediately struck up a friendship with Breton, Aragon, and Soupault. In 1926, his Viennese friend Adolf Loos (1870-1933) built a house for him to match his ideal in aesthetics: a 100% modern, functional structure, devoid of ornamentation. The result is a smooth, white cube atop a rough, brown millstone. The volumes, the windows and doors, and the position of the rain gutters are all handled with great rigor and symmetry, respecting the golden section.

A rather special staircase at **23** allows us a glimpse of the Rocher de la Sorcière (Witch's Rock). Until 1982, a shack stood beside it, home to clowns Footit and Chocolat.

Beside **23 bis** is Villa Léandre, created in 1926, and named Villa Junot for its first ten years of existence. The quiet lane is lined with colorful white and pink brick houses, covered with climbing plants, and with little front yards. There is a bronze of humorist Charles Léandre, also known for his paintings and lithographs. Léandre died at 87 Rue Caulaincourt in 1934. His caricatures of politicians and his thirty theater show posters brought him fame.

Let's go back up **Avenue Junot**. Outside **3**, we will notice the Moulin Blute-Fin, built in 1622. It was incorporated in the dance hall *Bal du Moulin de la Galette* in the 1870s. As its name indicates, galettes, or cakes, were served to the hungry revelers. Renoir, Toulouse-Lautrec, and Picasso all immortalized the entertainment in their paintings. Of the thirteen mills which once stood on the Butte Montmartre, only this one and the Radet, at the corner of Rue Girardon and Rue Lepic, survive.

The creation of Avenue Junot caused the soil to sink six meters, and resulted in the demolition of the Moulin à Poivre and the south end of Impasse Girardon.

Two houses from 2 and 4 **Impasse Girardon** survive at **2 Avenue Junot**. In October 1911, sculptor Henri Laurens and his wife decided to make their home on Impasse Girardon. They

▲ Villa Léandre, a lane starting at 23 bis Avenue Junot

◄ Rocher de la Sorcière, visible from 23 Avenue Junot

▼ Bronze portrait of humorist Charles Léandre, 23 bis Avenue Junot

lived at **4 bis** from 1913 to 1927, never sure where their next paycheck would come from. Laurens created constructions - figures, guitars, and bottles, as well as collages, influenced by his friend and neighbor Georges Braque.

Expressionist painter Gen Paul (1895-1975) lived at **2**. Paul painted portraits of friends, art dealers, musicians, clowns. He enjoyed having his friends from the Butte over on Sunday mornings: Céline, his neighbor, musician Jean Nocetti, Daragnès, actors Le Vigan and Arletty, playwright René Fauchois, artist Ralph Soupault. Dutch artist Kees Van Dongen (1877-

1968), his wife Guus, and their daughter Dolly, stayed on Impasse Girardon, from 1900 to 1905. The artist was then illustrating satirical newspapers and sketching scenes of life in Montmartre.

Place Marcel-Aymé

We now reach **Place Marcel-Aymé**. This ledge formed by the junction of the uncompleted Avenue Junot and Rue Norvins is stunning at cherry-blossom time. Inghelbrecht and Aymé lived at **2** late in their life. It is a posh place built by Charles Adda. Désiré Émile Inghelbrecht (1880-1965) was the conductor of several orchestras before founding the French National Radio Orchestra in 1931, when the medium was young. His symphonic

pieces were influenced by Debussy and Ravel. At the far end of Place Marcel-Aymé, the garden wall of the **Cité Internationale des Arts** at 24 Rue Norvins offers a surprise. A man in **bronze**, larger than life-sized, is breaking through the wall. Created by Jean Marais in 1989, *Passe-Muraille* personifies a short story written by Marcel Aymé in 1943. "An excellent man named Dutilleul had the extraordinary gift of being able to walk through walls without any trouble." It was an homage to the writer, who lived at 9 ter Rue Paul-Féval for forty years.

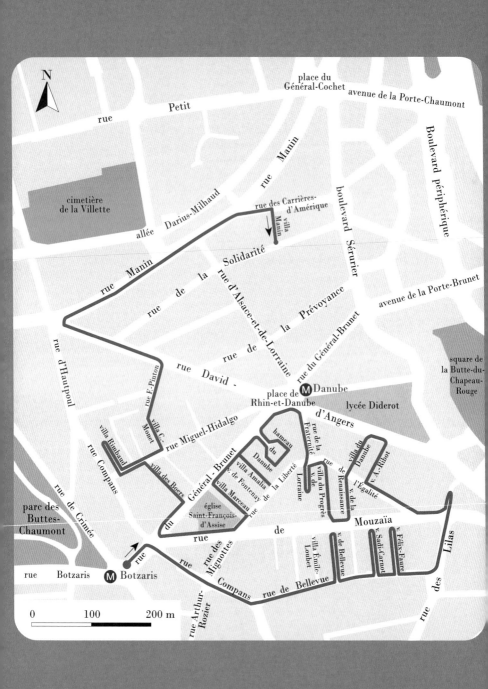

N

place du
Général-Cochet

avenue de la Porte-Chaumont

rue   Petit

Boulevard   périphérique

rue   Manin

cimetière
de la Villette

rue des Carrières-
d'Amérique

boulevard Sérurier

allée   Darius-Milbaud

villa Manin

rue   Manin

Solidarité

rue   de   la

rue d'Alsace-et-de-Lorraine

la   Prévoyance

avenue de la Porte-Brunet

rue   de

rue du Général-Brunet

rue   David -

rue d'Haurpoul

rue   E-Pinton

villa C.

villa Monet

place de
Rhin-et-Danube

M Danube

lycée Diderot

square de
la Butte-du-
Chapeau-
Rouge

rue Miguel-Hidalgo

d'Angers

villa Rimbaud

rue   Compans

villa des Boers

Général - Brunet

hameau
du

rue de la
Fraternité

rue de la
Liberté

villa du
Danube

v. A.-Ribot

villa Amalia

Danube

v. de Fontenay

villa Marceau

église
Saint-François-
d'Assise

parc des
Buttes-
Chaumont

rue   de   Crimée

du

rue

rue des Mignottes

v. de la Lorraine

rue de la

v. de la Renaissance

villa du Progrès

v. de l'Égalité

villa du
Danube

Mouzaïa

de

villa Émile-
Loubet

v. de Bellevue

v. Sadi-Carnot

v. Félix-Faure

rue   Botzaris

M Botzaris

rue

rue

rue Arthur-
Rozier

Compans

rue de Bellevue

rue   des   Lilas

0   100   200 m

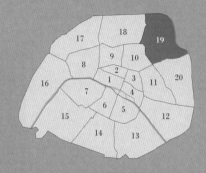

19th

Butte de Beauregard

▶ Start: **Rue du Général-Brunet, metro Botzaris**
▶ Finish: **Rue de la Solidarité, metro Danube**

The name of the Butte de Beauregard, one of five tall hills in the 19th arrondissement's Combat and Amérique quarters, reflects the reality of the lovely views to be had from its heights. In the 18th century, it was surrounded by several paths that have since become streets: Rue des Carrières-d'Amérique (most of which is today's Rue Manin) Rue Compans, Rue Bellevue, Rue des Lilas. Numerous windmills once stood atop the hill on Rue de Bellevue, adding to the quaint and bucolic atmosphere. Naturally, each had a name: Moulin Vieux, Moulin Neuf, Moulin de la Motte, Moulin Basset, Petit Moulin, and Moulin du Costre.

This quarter, generally called the Mouzaïa neighborhood, after a local street, is greatly appreciated by artists.

We start our stroll near the **Botzaris metro station**, taking **Rue du Général-Brunet**, to **Rue Compans**, where we turn right.

Until 1855, Rue Compans was called Rue Basse-Saint-Denis. In 1864, it was named after Jean Dominique de Compans, a division general who

◄ 74-76 Rue Compans

defended Belleville in 1814. At the corner of Rue Arthur-Rozier there is a **large mural** painted by Casadesus in 1993. It is composed of hundreds of white marbles, a bit smudged now, and one enormous black bubble. We continue climbing up steep Rue Compans. At **74-76**, behind the gate to a private lane, a double row of houses peeks out of thriving gardens. An artist's studio overlooks the street. We reach **Rue de Bellevue**, which got its name in 1812. The towering apartment buildings on the right are the Place des Fêtes high-rises.

A Succession of Tiny Lanes Called Villas

On the left side, adorable dollhouse-like dwellings line the lanes that connect to Rue de Mouzaïa. These are perhaps some of the oldest structures in the area. They were constructed according to a strict code regulating building atop quarry tunnels. Built on sloping lots, none are

◄ Casadesus mural at the corner of Rue Compans and Rue Arthur-Rozier

French presidents. Take for example: Villa Émile-Loubet, Villa Sadi-Carnot, and Villa Félix-Faure. The area deserves to be viewed from all sides, from Rue de Bellevue where we now stand and from Rue de Mouzaïa. From the top of the hill, these houses appear to be clinging to each other, whereas from the bottom of the hill, they seem to stand shoulder to shoulder, as if they were digging in to prevent each other from sliding.

Villa Bellevue has wide paving stones and the houses on this lane form a single, uniform row.

over two stories high. They used to be located on closed, private lanes. Today, these lanes are open, paved, and lit by quaint streetlamps with a characteristic intertwining sprig of ivy. The townhouses huddle one against the other, all with fenced-in front yards.

Despite their narrowness and relative insignificance, several of these small lanes, or villas, to use the French term, were named for former

Villa Sadi-Carnot is astoundingly peaceful. Even the cats seem to be on good terms with the blackbirds fluttering from tree to tree. The wisteria spills over into the lane and runs along the walls.

Villa Félix-Faure plays on color, with its red half-timbers at **5** and its blue shutters at **7**. Then, at **10**, behind the big lilac bush, is a house painted entirely blue.

Strolling through the Mouzaïa quarter requires no particular itinerary. Wherever we go, it's certain to be pleasant and rewarding.

We will return to **Rue de Bellevue** and head to **Rue des Lilas** somewhat off the group of lanes we have just visited. It crosses Rue de Mouzaïa and finishes with a few wide steps at Rue David-d'Angers, a street that was named in 1877 for the sculptor Jean David, a native of Angers (1788-1856) and the creator of the bas-relief on the pediment of the Pantheon. The homes built here are more recent, particularly the large white house at **43**. A path at **45** leads to other houses set back and invisible from the street.

Let's backtrack and return to **Rue de Mouzaïa**. It, too, took its name in 1877. It was named after a gorge in Algeria, the scene of battles in 1839 and 1840 between the French army and the "emir of believers," Abdelkader. He violated the Treaty of Tafna that he had signed with General Thomas Bugeaud in 1837, and proclaimed holy war to establish his power.

▲ Villa Alexandre-Ribot
▼ 43 Rue des Lilas
▶ Rue de l'Égalité

Let's walk along Rue de Mouzaïa to the right until we reach **Rue de l'Égalité**, forming a Y with Rue de la Liberté and Rue de la Fraternité. These three streets have honored values of the Republic for over a century. They were laid out in 1889 as part of celebrations of the French Revolution's centenary.

None of the *villas* that we are about to explore are dead ends. Rue de l'Égalité is fairly wide and has but four such lanes. Two of them run rather steeply down to Rue David-d'Angers. **Villa Alexandre-Ribot**, created in 1923, was named for the minister of finances and foreign affairs, a friend of sugar magnate Lebaudey. Between 1878 and 1917, the two of them were the main leaders of the

▲ Villa de la Renaissance
◀ Rue de la Liberté
▶ 3 Rue de la Fraternité

moderate Republican party. **Villa du Danube** is a reminder of the first name given to nearby Place Rhin-et-Danube. The corner houses here are quite spacious. The ones in the lanes are nearly all the same, more modest size.

Across the way, **Villa de la Renaissance**, then further down, **Villa du Progrès**, are lined with much more modern homes, in tune with the names of their streets.

Let's continue onto **Rue de la Liberté**, up to the dead end on the left, named **Villa de Lorraine**, as charming as its neighbors.

From here, let's go straight ahead into **Rue de la Fraternité**. At **3**, a large chalet in Normand style is the surprising neighbor of the much humbler **5**. This is the Bouchée de Pain charity. Its name is lettered in green on a background of white tile in the pediment. In this warehouse-like dining room, meals are served daily to some two hundred and fifty destitute people.

Around Place de Rhin-et-Danube

Place du Danube was renamed in 1951 in honor of the First French Army, which fought along the Rhine

and the Danube in World War II. The web of streets in this particular neighborhood was laid out in 1875 shortly after one of the old quarry galleries had been closed and filled in.

Between 1868 and 1878, two major, tri-weekly markets were held on Place de Rhin-et-Danube. The horse market took up the triangular space David d'Angers-Brunet-Hautpoul, and the hay market, requiring far less space, stood on the edge of the first two streets and Boulevard Sérurier. These markets were almost exclusively for the capital's horse-drawn public transit companies.

A **statue** (1933) by Léon Deschamps stands on the square, graced by flowerbeds. Entitled *La Moissonneuse*, it features a robust, energetic girl harvesting wheat, with a freshly cut bundle tucked under one arm. Her head is turned to one side in a serious, preoccupied attitude. Her apron, tied about her hips, is typical of this period's attention to detail and realism.

To our right, the **Lycée Diderot** replaced the old Hôpital Hérold, now absorbed by the nearby Hôpital Robert-Debré. Hérold had a long history. In 1792, during a cholera epidemic, the administration isolated patients in wooden shacks on a plot of land on Place du Danube. After the epidemic, the barracks were kept to take up eventual overflow from any other Paris hospitals. A real hospital was erected in 1904. Lebrun, the architect, designed it on the principle of separate buildings for containment of diseases. The hospital was named for a prefect of the Seine department. Just three years after it opened, a severe epidemic of scarlet fever required an entirely new unit to treat the disease. Finally, in 1936, the hos-

pital was endowed with a disease prevention center. The smallest of children's hospitals, with only twenty-four beds, it nevertheless remained the neighborhood children's hospital until 1988.

The Lycée Diderot was moved here in the 1990s from Boulevard de la Villette, although some of the high school classes were left behind in the old establishment. The new building, designed by Jean-François Laurent, occupies an impressive two-hundred-meter stretch along Rue David-d'Angers. An ultra-modern take on the 1930s ocean-liner style in architecture, it is the only recent building in the quarter, and, as such, definitely stands out.

Around Saint-François-d'Assise Church

Stepping away from Place de Rhin-et-Danube, with the high school now behind us, we will take **Rue du Général-Brunet**. The gates at **46-48** mark the entrance to **Hameau du**

◄ *La Moissonneuse* (Harvest Girl), a statue by Léon Deschamps, Place de Rhin-et-Danube

▲▼ Hameau du Danube

▲ Saint-François d'Assise church

◄ Villa Marceau

entrance is framed by two symmetrical buildings, each with a curious, semi-circular balcony, equipped with a central pillar. Getting past the gates guarding this private street sometimes requires a bit of luck. The eighty houses on the looping street are all perfectly symmetrical. There is great architectural harmony in form and materials. They all have millstone-grit basements and stucco façades offset by a play of red brick here and there.

Further down on **Rue du Général-Brunet**, we come to **Villa Amalia** (formerly called Villa Acacia). It is such a charming lane, it would be a pity to miss it. Next is **Villa de Fontenay**; then we come to **Villa Marceau**, which will take us back to **Rue de la Liberté**, then onwards to **Rue de Mouzaïa**.

To our right, at **7**, is the Saint-François-d'Assise church, begun in 1913 by the Courcoux brothers. A forty-one-meter-deep excavation was required for the concrete foundations of the bell tower. World War I brought the construction to a halt, and it resumed in 1920. The Saint Landry crypt, built to house "a 1768 relief showing the martyrdom of an unidentified saint," was consecrated in 1921. "The church opened for its first Mass in 1926. The architecture is perfectly in line with municipal public housing projects of the same period. The same construction techniques were used: brick-clad reinforced concrete, simplicity of volumes, a nave composed of three rows, side aisles, exposed roof beams, and a choir ending into a flattened apse" (Roger-Henri Guerrand, *Cahiers de l'Iforep*, No. 51).

At the intersection, we turn right on **Rue du Général-Brunet**. Note the inviting terrace visible from beside

Danube, the only lane in the quarter making a loop. The lots were purchased in 1922 and the houses erected in 1923-1924. This lane is also the only one with its own guardhouse, complete with flowerbeds, standing watch over the gated entrance. The

◄◄ Rue Miguel-Hidalgo
◄ Villa des Boers

◄◄ Villa Paul-Verlaine
◄ Villa Claude-Monet

the bank standing on the corner. Continuing down the street to 19, we reach the entrance to **Villa des Boers**. The first house on the lane boasts a roof terrace with a pretty wrought-iron grapevine railing. The other end of the lane opens onto **Rue Miguel-Hidalgo**, laid out in 1889 and providing access to a series of small streets named after famous painters and poets. **Villa Rimbaud** is a quaint dead-end alley that we should explore. **Villa Claude-Monet**, with its gardens and empty lots, is airier than as its neigh-

bors. The sparser construction provides relief from overcrowding. At its far end, the steps lined with houses give a romantic ambience that visitors who steal a kiss here will cherish for a long time. The street at the bottom of the stairs here will take us back to **Rue David-d'Angers**. At the corner, is the **Georges-Hermant public swimming pool**, which, two decades ago, replaced the old Grimaud playing-cards factory. The single-family dwellings give way to large housing projects.

Rue Manin and Villa Manin

Rue David-d'Angers leads to **Rue Manin**, where we will take a right and walk along the frontage that replaced the old tracks of the circular rail line. Rue Manin carries a lot of automobile traffic to Porte de Pantin via Boulevard Sérurier. The Fondation Louise-Koppe at **38 bis** occupies a building erected in 1904 by architects Jandelle & Hommet. This foundation still takes in struggling mothers and their children aged three to sixteen, offering free shelter for one year. At **40**, we come to an impressive school complex built in 1900-1901. Its footprint covers the entire block framed by Rue Manin, Rue Alsace-Lorraine, and Rue de la Solidarité. The buildings' exposed metal skeleton interplays with the two-tone brick façade. Each floor on the Rue Manin side has twenty-three windows, and three doors with decorated lintels announce

▶ 40 Rue Manin
▼ 38 bis Rue Manin

which entrance is for the old girls' school, the boys' school, and the nursery school.

Past the intersection with Rue d'Hautpoul, this portion of Rue Manin used to be called Chemin des Carrières-d'Amérique (a quarry road). Today, only one segment of this old road still reminds us of this quarter's main activity in the old days. The rock that was extracted from the quarries here was baked in ovens to produce plaster that was reportedly sent to America, hence the name. While the story is disputed, it is one explanation for the name given to the quarter. Let's take a right onto **Rue des Carrières-d'Amérique** to reach **Villa Manin**. It is all the more remarkable as it is a veritable island, surrounded by recent buildings and older housing projects. It takes us to **Rue de la Solidarité**, where numerous apartment complexes have now replaced the old 3M printers' ink factory.

We will extend our neighborhood walk by crossing Rue Manin and going down the steps leading to Allée Darius-Milhaud. Visitors interested in 1920s architecture will want to cross Boulevard Sérurier to explore streets named after cities of France and its former colonies, lined with interesting housing projects that go as far as Place du Général-Cochet.

◀ Villa Manin

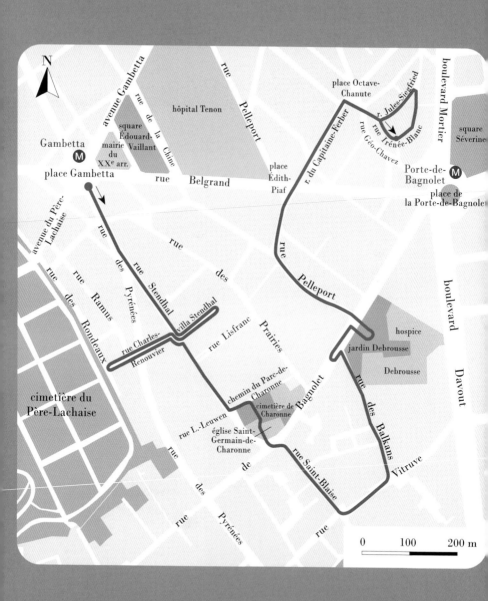

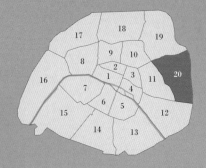

20th

Charonne:
The Country
in Paris

▶ Start: **Rue des Pyrénées,
metro Gambetta**

▶ Finish: **Rue Irénée-Blanc,
metro Porte-de-Bagnolet**

Charonne seems still to be a village huddled around its church. Chalk up the successful illusion to an expertly planned and well-funded urban rehabilitation program, which even preserved the old layout of the streets. Perhaps there's something artificial about it, for the old-fashioned atmosphere is hard to find. And yet, in a few places, Charonne has preserved its rural feel.

Setting out from the **Gambetta metro station**, let's start our stroll on **Rue des Pyrénées** and go up to **Rue Stendhal**, where we will come to several posh buildings on a lane named **Villa Stendhal**. It was the first incursion of Parisian wealth into the Charonne area, and breaks with the scale of its surroundings. Across the street, **Rue Charles-Renouvier** spans Rue des Pyrénées with a bridge bordered by stone balustrades which looks almost like a stage set. To the southwest, this street ends at **Rue des Rondeaux**, which runs along the back wall of Père-Lachaise Cemetery. With its low houses, this street is wonderfully peaceful.

▲ Rue Charles-Renouvier

◀ Charonne Cemetery

Saint-Germain-de-Charonne and its Cemetery

We shall continue along **Rue Stendhal**, walking beside the lawns covering the Charonne reservoir, until we reach **Chemin du Parc-de-Charonne**. A small door to the right is the gateway into the **Cimetière de Charonne**, beside Saint-Germain church. Two of André Malraux's sons are buried in this cemetery, as is Robert Brasillach, who wrote in 1936 how pleasant this area was, "a refuge, from which one sees only trees and a bucolic bell tower. The huge city's tall buildings are invisible." Three hundred uniformed bodies of Commune soldiers were discovered here and transferred to Père-Lachaise.

Seated on a wooden bench, lulled by the church bells calmly tolling the hours, the visitor is transported to another world.

A flight of steps beside the church leads to **Rue de Bagnolet**, which once

▼ Saint-Germain-de-Charonne church

marked Charonne's village limits. Two *guinguettes* (dance halls which were tax-exempt because they were located outside Paris city limits) used to stand here. This point offers a delightful view of the **church**. Enlarged several times over the centuries, the core of the building dates from the 15th century, although we know that the first church on this site was erected in the 9th century. Saint-Germain-de-Charonne and Saint-Pierre-de-Montmartre are Paris's only surviving churches with adjoining cemeteries.

▲ Rue Saint-Blaise

The Saint-Blaise Quarter

Let's take **Rue Saint-Blaise**. Now a pedestrian street, it was long the backbone of the old Charonne village. The houses have been either carefully restored or... demolished. With nothing in transition, the street is almost uncannily quaint, especially the small square shaded by magnolias.

2 was once the site of a home designed by Jean-François Blondel (1683-1756), the uncle of the famous architectural theorist Jacques-François Blondel. City historian Jacques Hillairet notes that the house "stood at the end of a circular court-yard lined with outbuildings. The gardens were composed of diamond-shaped flowerbeds ending at a horse-shoe-shaped fountain with both jets and sheets of water." The property was divided up in 1820, and nothing remains of it today. Architecture buffs will find the plans for the estate in Blondel's *L'Architecture Française*, which described it as a model of elegance, refined taste, and ingenious design. "A basement made up for the difference in level between the court-yard and the garden. The balcony was narrow, so as not to interrupt the upwards movement. The double-run staircase to the garden matched the angle of the inclined figures in the pediment."

Camus de Mézières's mansion at **5**, erected in the mid-18th century, was demolished in 1929. In its place, there is a chapel dedicated to Saints Cyril and Methodius. This property belonged to the family of Nicolas Camus de Mézières, a neo-classical architect who lived in Charonne for half a century. According to Lucien Lambeau, in 1771, a certain doctor Le Camus set up a hospital at **28**. He wanted to experiment on neighborhood residents to see if his smallpox invention worked. Fortunately, he was barred from practicing medicine.

The other portion of the street, with its housing projects, offers regrettable and grim examples of 1970s "totalitarian" architecture. The architects of the period occasionally deigned to make a few concessions to Nature, with a tiny garden here and an opening for oxygen there, all lost in the magma of concrete. The only advantage was that the neighborhood gained in greatly needed infrastructures such as schools.

Wandering onto **Rue Vitruve** on our left, we finally get another whiff of yesteryear. Many houses and workshops here have been nicely restored. To the right of Place des Grès, from **39 to 47**, a middle school with a tiled façade was designed by Jacques Bardet in 1982. The architect aimed for a design that would be integrated by its environment, respecting heights and proportions of nearby buildings, and bringing light into the classrooms. Across the street at **62** is a nursery school designed by Bernard Agopian in 1984.

Taking **Rue des Balkans**, we return to **Rue de Bagnolet**. Across the street at **135 and 137**, two village-style houses have been preserved.

One of them has a niche, which is empty today. At the corner is a **café** established in 1914. Fortunately, its tiles and wood paneling are still intact.

On the left-hand side of the street, numbers **134 and 136** feature elegant staircases leading up to their front doors, high above the street level. The reason for this is that the houses were built before Rue de Bagnolet was re-graded and the slope of was reduced, to put less of a strain on horses drawing heavily-laden carts uphill. This explains how first floors wound up becoming second floors!

▲ 134-136 Rue de Bagnolet

▼ Place des Grès

▲ Mascaron, Rue Vitruve

We'll backtrack a little now on Rue de Bagnolet. The impressive 18th-century building behind the gates of the old Hospice Debrousse is the **Pavillon de l'Ermitage**. Today, it stands in the middle of a park. Erected in 1734, it is the last vestige of the Château de Bagnolet, an estate which covered no less than 80 hectares (197 acres, about twice the present-

▼ Pavillon de l'Ermitage

◀ 137 Rue de Bagnolet

day size of Père-Lachaise cemetery) in the early 18th century. Divided into lots, the property was built up and gradually absorbed by the city in the 19th century.

The Pavillon de l'Ermitage has gone down in history as the headquarters of the royalists who tried unsuccessfully to orchestrate the escape of Louis XVI and Marie-Antoinette, before they were sentenced to death. The "Charonne conspirators," as they were called, were also arrested and sent to the guillotine.

La Campagne à Paris

As we exit the square, let's head north on **Rue Pelleport**, straight ahead of us. After crossing Rue Belgrand, we will walk along **Rue du Capitaine-Ferber** until we reach **Place Octave-Chanute**. A set of steps will then take

▼ The Campagne à Paris quarter

us up to that most coveted of Paris neighborhoods, **La Campagne à Paris**. "The Countryside in Paris" is indeed a rare occurrence. Streets like **Rue Irénée-Blanc** and **Rue Jules-Siegfried** are so picture-perfect, they could practically be operetta sets. Millstone grit, brand new paving stones, gardens planted with lilac bushes – a delightful place in spring –, this is an early-20th century residential dream come true.

The Roussel gypsum quarry off Rue des Montibœufs was an open pit when the village of Charonne was annexed by Paris in the 1860s. The simplest way to fill it was to pour in the rubble from all the demolitions carried out by Haussmann for the construction of Avenue de la République and Avenue Gambetta. A hillock was quickly raised, and was held in place the best possible by quickly planted woods. The manmade butte was purchased in 1908 by a coop for low-cost housing that called itself "La Campagne à Paris." It undertook the construction of ninety-two homes amid luxuriant vegetation, each with its front yard. They were erected between 1907 and 1928 by a variety of architects. The financing plan was exemplary. Each homebuyer took out a loan that was paid off by monthly installments. This allowed low-level civil servants and bank clerks with modest but steady incomes to acquire property. The homes were well-built and luxuriously detailed. The pleasure of living in the quiet development encouraged the homeowners to keep up their properties. All the factors were there for decades of successful neighborhood living. The area has remained intact – a resounding success.

Édition : Clara Mackenzie
Direction artistique : Isabelle Chemin
Cartographie : Bénédicte Loisel

Avec la collaboration d'Anita Conrade, Lilith Cowan
et Sandrine Calas

Achevé d'imprimer en France en septembre 2012
sur les presses de l'imprimerie Gibert-Clarey Imprimeurs à Chambray-lès-Tours.

ISBN : 978-2-84096-559-6
Dépôt légal : janvier 2009